Why the French Love Jerry Lewis

Why the French Love Jerry Lewis

FROM CABARET TO EARLY CINEMA

Rae Beth Gordon

STANFORD UNIVERSITY PRESS
STANFORD, CALIFORNIA
2001

Stanford University Press
Stanford, California

Printed in the United States of America
on acid-free, archival-quality paper

Library of Congress Cataloging-in-Publication Data

Gordon, Rae Beth
Why the French love Jerry Lewis : from cabaret to early cinema / Rae Beth Gordon.
p. cm.
Includes bibliographical references and index.
ISBN 0-8047-3893-9 (alk. paper) —
ISBN 0-8047-3894-7 (paper : alk. paper)
1. Music-halls (Variety theaters, cabarets, etc.)—France—Paris—History—19th century. 2. Hysteria. 3. Hysteria in motion pictures. 4. Lewis, Jerry, 1926—Criticism and interpretation. I. Title.
PN1969.C34 G67 2001
792.7'09443'6109034—dc21 00-052649

Original Printing 2001

Last figure below indicates year of this printing:
10 09 08 07 06 05 04 03 02 01

Designed by Janet Wood
Typeset by James P. Brommer in 10/14 Janson
and Franklin Gothic display

This book is dedicated to all those who can't resist trying out a few tapdance steps upon leaving a Fred Astaire and Ginger Rogers movie, and to all my friends in Paris.

A psychiatrist threatened that our generation would end up in the pile of disarticulated beings; he was probably leaving a café-concert when he made that dire prophesy. A good half of the hit songs of the period belong to the home for the agitated jigglers (*le trémoussoir*) of the late Dr. Charcot. They tremble and stamp (*elles trépident*). They have gesticulatory hysteria.

—GEORGES MONTORGUEIL, *Les Demi-Cabots, 1896*

Film is nothing but a relay between the source of nervous energy and the auditorium. . . . Chaplin has created the overwrought hero. A bell or an automobile horn makes him jump, forces him to stand anxiously . . . a synopsis of his photogenic neurasthenia.

—JEAN EPSTEIN, "Magnification," *1921*

His whole body, all the features of his face are in a state of agitation: he rolls back and forth on armchairs and sofas; a strident racket emanates from his chest. . . . The attack has to cease of itself, for his will . . . is powerless to stop it. . . . [This man] is a curious spectacle. . . . [He suffocates] and nearly falls into convulsions.

—Description of a man overcome by spasms of laughter in Alfred Michiels, *Le Monde du comique et du rire, 1886*

ACKNOWLEDGMENTS

When, in 1984, I first came across the existence of the *chanteuse* and the *comique épileptique* in François Caradec and Alain Weill's book, *Le Café-concert*, I had already embarked on what would turn into a ten-year period of reading case observations and theories of hysteria for another project. The descriptions of the café-concert performers jumped off the page. And the fact that this extremely popular phenomenon in the café-concert took place in the final thirty years of the nineteenth century, when interest in hysteria was so intense in France, could not help but suggest the analogy that I proposed in a colloquium the following year, and which is further explored here. It is, moreover, perfectly logical that this link would not have occurred to twentieth-century specialists of the cabaret . . . and just as logical that it *should* to contemporaries of the nineteenth-century spectacle whom I cite here. The majority of people over sixty in France today can sing Ouvrard's "Je ne suis pas bien portant" (I'm Not in Good Health / I'm Sick), but they are not aware of how very typical the theme of illness was.

Of the many people I have to thank for the encouragement they offered, I would first name the writer and documentarian Pierre Philippe, who was archivist at the Gaumont Cinémathèque when I first began working on early cinema for this project in 1992. His extraordinary knowledge of early cinema, as well as of cabaret, music-hall, and popular song in general, combined with his excitement about my project bolstered me in moments when I feared that learning enough about a new area (early film) so as to able to write about it was unfeasible in a five-year period of time. Along with Pierre Philippe, who did me the honor of mentioning my work and illustrating it with film clips in his documentary film for ARTE, *Le Roman du Music-Hall*, shown on French and German television, the team at Gaumont was exceptionally kind, helpful, and generous. Béatrice Valbin, the film editor and restorer of such early films as Feuillade's *Judex*, pulled *phono-scènes* of Dranem and other café-concert performers out of the archives, as well as the two films made at the Salpêtrière. Manuela Padoan was wonderfully patient with my requests for photographs, and I thank her most sincerely for extending to me Gaumont Cinémathèque's generosity in granting the rights to these images, without which this book would be so much poorer. Thanks to Roger Descamps and Bruno Polsinelli for placing the threads and rewinding innumerable times. Madeleine Malthête-Méliès was extraordinarily generous in screening over sixty films at her home, cranking the films herself! and discussing the world of the cabaret and the turn of the century. Her rendition of Xanrof's "Le Fiacre" at the Cerisy Colloquium is also unforgettable. I offer my thanks to her for granting me the permission to publish the photogrammes of Méliès's films in my book. Other film archives were crucial for viewing the films, and I give my thanks to Alain Marchand at the Cinémathèque Française and to Eric Leroy at the CNC (along with Laure Bouyssou at St. Cyr and David Courbet at Bois d'Arcy). Thanks, too, to Charles Silver at MoMA for screening the Lubitsch films in the early 1980s, and, finally, many thanks to Madeline Matz at the Library of Congress. I want to thank Pierre Courtet-Cohl for his unflagging interest in this book, for opening the Cohl family archives to me and granting me permission to publish two of Cohl's drawings here, and for his help in organizing the evening of Emile Cohl films that I presented at the Harvard Film Archive in December 1997. His friendship and that of Anne-Marie Quévrain, Méliès's great-granddaughter, with whom I have greatly enjoyed discussing film comedy, hypnotism, and epileptic singers, are much appreciated. A stimulating dialogue and camaraderie with François Jost has also been one of the rewards of embarking on this work in early film. Friends in and out of academia know who they are, but I particularly want to thank Lucienne Frappier-Mazur for her support and for her enthusiasm regarding the project, which she first heard when we were on the same colloquium panel in 1985. In tracking down photographs, Jocelyne Van de Putte at the Musée Carnavalet, Noëlle Giret at the Bibliothèque de l'Arsenal, and Anne-Marie Sauvage, curator of the poster collection at the Bibliothèque de France, Richelieu, were wonderfully patient and efficient. Thanks go to the Photothèque de la Ville de Paris for its very rapid response in summer 1999. Over the years, the curators at the Bibliothèque Nationale de France and at Sainte-Geneviève have been very helpful. Special thanks go to Jack Eckhardt in the rare books collection of the Countway Medical Libary at Harvard.

I would like to thank the University of Connecticut Research Foundation for the support I've received over the past several summers. In lieu of any external funding that would have made it possible for me to focus on it for an extended period, they have made it easier for this book to come into existence. The help of a graduate assistant, Annette Ackley, facilitated the compiling of photos, rights, and checking new revisions in summer 1999. The fine work in creating the index is due to another graduate assistant, Margaret Colvin.

Santhosh Daniel at Stanford University Press has shown concern for this manuscript from the beginning of the publication process, and Kate Warne, Stanford's in-house editor in charge of production, has been extremely competent and efficient in speeding the manuscript along. They have been wonderful *compagnons de route*. Finally, I extend warm thanks to Helen Tartar for her continuing interest in my work. It is a pleasure to work with an editor whose passion, humanity, intelligence, and enthusiasm are truly exemplary.

Portions of this book have appeared previously in the following journal articles or book chapters: "Le Caf'conc' et l'hystérie," *Romantisme* 64 (1989); "Pathologiès de la vue et du mouvement dans les films de Georges Méliès," in *Georges Méliès: Illusioniste fin-de-siècle?* ed. Jacques Malthête and Michel Marie; "Laughing Hysterically," in *Moving Forward, Holding Fast*, ed. Barbara Cooper and Mary Donaldson-Evans; and "Epileptic Singers on the Parisian Stage," in *Women Seeking Expression, 1789–1914*, ed. Rosemary Lloyd and Brian Nelson (Monash Romance Studies, 2000).

CONTENTS

ILLUSTRATIONS

PREFACE

This book answers the perplexing question, "Why do the French love Jerry Lewis?" by presenting a theory of comic performance between 1870 and 1910 as it intersected with psychiatric and physiological theories of the psychological automatism and of unconscious imitation. In doing so, it casts new light on the tradition of physical comedy in the French cabaret and café-concert, and, finally, in early French film comedy. This tradition of performance style nearly exactly duplicates the same movements, gestures, tics, grimaces, fantasies, hallucinations, and speech anomalies found in nineteenth-century hysteria.

Performance style in the Parisian cabaret and café-concert, as my work between 1985 and 1989 has demonstrated,[1] was greatly indebted to the body language of hysteria. Early French film carried on this tradition of frenetic gait, not surprisingly, since the great majority of performers up until 1910 came from these entertainments and from the circus. The genre that dominated French cinema until 1914 was comedy, as Laurent Le Forestier reminds us, noting that no one has explored the reasons for this dominance (14). Certainly, comedy has been linked to a mass public for film;[2] this study elucidates this link from a new point of view and proposes a broadly generalized phenomenon as the explanation for the dominance of the comic genre in France between 1896 and 1914. Comic performance style drew from and contributed to a larger realm of cultural expression known between 1870 and 1910 as hysteria, epilepsy, double consciousness, and, especially in the last decade of the period, neurasthenia. All of these nervous disorders fell under the rubric of psychological automatisms, and all evoked the fear of unconscious imitation.

The absolute fascination that hysteria and surrounding phenomena like hypnotism and magnetism held for the general public in France from the 1880s to the beginning of the twentieth century is evident from the hundreds of contemporary newspaper and magazine articles that deal with those subjects. Hysterics were conscious of being marvelous performers, and there was no shortage of audiences for their extraordinarily "theatrical" displays. Case observations often cite aspirations to write plays, sing, or dance, and inmates sometimes became street performers after their release from the hospital. At the same time, artists like Sarah Bernhardt and the Chat Noir poet and singer Maurice Rollinat attended Charcot's lessons and visited the hospital wards, incorporating the gestures and poses they saw there into their work.

In the seventeen years that have elapsed since Jacqueline Carroy (formerly Carroy-Thirard) published her seminal essay, "Hystérie, théâtre, littérature au dix-neuvième siècle" there has been an explosion of interest in the history of hysteria in nineteenth-century France, and an impressive number of important studies have been published, most of which are inflected in terms of gender and/or framed in a sociopolitical context. Studies centered on cultural and artistic manifestations of hysteria have been long in coming. In a recent exploration of hysteria as a cultural phenomenon, Janet Beizer accords a central place to the dialogue between literature and medicine. Carroy's and Beizer's work are, to my mind, landmarks in the growing number of studies that analyze hysteria in relation to cultural/artistic production.[3] It is not my aim here to reiterate or to reconstruct the evolution of medical diagnosis, observations, and theorization of hysteria in the second half of the nineteenth century in France. This history and discourse has been admirably recovered and interpreted by other scholars, including Jan Goldstein and Mark Micale. My aim is to foreground two threads that run through so much of the writing on hysteria in the 1880s and 1890s in France: (1) the notion of the self divided between the higher and lower faculties, and (2) theories of unconscious imitation in psychophysiology, psychophysics, and psychiatry. This book looks at the reciprocal influences of medicine and popular culture in light of contemporary theories of the psychological automatism and unconscious imitation emanating from the lower faculties.

The growing body of work on spectatorship and entertainments in nineteenth-century France includes studies like Charles Rearick's panoramic

Pleasures of the Belle Epoque (1985), which situates a great number of entertainments in their sociopolitical context, and the detailed analysis in Leo Charney and Vanessa Schwartz's *Cinema and the Invention of Modern Life* (edited by Leo Charney and Vanessa Schwartz), written a decade later, which encompasses a variety of forms of spectacle and approaches. While the relationship between theater and hysteria has long been accepted (see Racamier), studies of specific performance styles have only recently begun to appear. Building on my previous work on hysteria[4] and the cabaret, and bringing together previously unconnected strands in popular culture and medicine, *Why the French Love Jerry Lewis* contributes to a new theory of spectatorship that is at work in the performances of magnetizers and in cabaret and early cinema.

The French love Jerry Lewis because he, more than any other comic and filmmaker of the second half of the twentieth century, incarnates this tradition of performance style.

Why the French Love Jerry Lewis

CHAPTER ONE

From Charcot to Charlot: The Corporeal Unconscious

Experimental psychology, clinical observations, and psychiatric theory in late-nineteenth-century France furnished the Parisian cabaret and early film comedy with a new repertory of movements, grimaces, and gestures. At the same time, scientific experiments in physiological stimulus/response lent themselves to new ways of looking at how spectators reacted to certain performance styles. It is these lost components in the history of the two forms of mass culture that I want to reconstruct here. Notions and, especially, *images* from medical science must be included alongside images from the wax museum, puppet shows, pantomime, and pre-cinematic devices in the cultural series that contributed to the genesis of performance styles in the Parisian cabaret and in early film comedy.

This book proposes and examines a previously unnoticed relationship between a significant cultural and aesthetic style and the extraordinary upsurge of concern with and diagnosis of hysteria in late-nineteenth-century medical practice and theory. It also makes more understandable the famous Surrealist pronouncement that hysteria was the "greatest poetic discovery of the nineteenth century" and "a supreme means of expression" (Aragon and Breton 20, 22).

Is there a relationship between ways that movement was staged in early cinema and corporeal pathologies related to hysteria and epilepsy—for example, tics, grimaces, contractures, catalepsy, and convulsive movement? I believe that hysterical gesture and gait are an important inspiration and basis for the style of frenetic, anarchic movement that is so present in early French film comedy, and that many spectators recognized this source. One needs only to go back in time to the twenty-year period that preceded 1895 to find many cultural observers using the medical vocabulary of hysteria to describe cabaret singers and comics. Pathologies of the body, along with pathologies of perception, furnished the cabaret and early cinema with images that an avid public couldn't seem to get enough of. This book uncovers and explores the pathologized body in cabaret and film, examining the dynamics of laughter and fear in relation to this body. I will also argue, in Chapter 2, that there are correlations to be made between movement in these popular entertainments and induced gesture in the public exhibitions of magnetizers in the 1890s.

The expectations that spectators brought with them to film screenings, knowledge about science that was common currency, and the inevitable associations in the minds of spectators around 1900 with other forms of entertainment (in this case, magnetizers' shows, cabaret performance, and Grand Guignol theater, but also the stereoscope, other fairground attractions, or wax museums)—all of these factors are crucial if we want to try to get back to what audiences in the period 1895–1910 experienced.[1] The Grand Guignol staged plays based on mental pathology and set in hospitals, written (in collaboration with André de Lorde) by one of France's most important experimental psychologists, Alfred Binet. Notions about hysteria, magnetism, hypnosis, and physiology, popularized in the press, were at work in the Imaginary of the period.

Popular knowledge of hysteria predates the period that this book takes as its frame. For example, readers were informed by Nestor Roqueplan in the 12 November 1837 issue of the newspaper *La Charte de 1830* that hysteria, hypochondria, convulsions, tetanus, St. Vitus's Dance, and catalepsy could produce a cessation of vital functions and create the temporary appearance of death. The writer was concerned that these attacks were occurring on the streets of Paris: thus the article appears under the rubric "Hygiène publique." Still, there can be no comparison to the way that hysteria made news and found its way into a wide variety of media from around 1880 to the turn of the century. From the "Causerie du Docteur" column that appeared in so many newspapers of the time to the more worldly pages of the *Nouvelle Revue* or of *Figaro*'s literary supplement, French readers were inundated by articles on hypnosis, hysteria, and the Salpêtrière school, written by vulgarizers such as Louis Figuier and by well-known doctors. As Mark Micale points out, "Around 1878, the name of the Salpêtrière invaded even the popular magazines and newspapers" (*Approaching Hysteria* 198). As we will see in Chapter 3, it was also between 1875 and 1878 that epileptic singers became a major draw in the café-concert and that the English mime troupe the Hanlon-Lees perfected their unique blend of gymnastics and pantomime. The Salpêtrière/School of Nancy controversy about the role of hypnotism was followed closely by educated lay readers as well as physicians. In the journal he founded and published with the collaboration of Henri Beaunis and Théodule Ribot, *L'Année psychologique*, Alfred Binet devotes a two-page review to Dr. de Fleury's 1897 book, *Introduction à la médecine de l'esprit* (Paris: Alcan). The review gives one an insight into the "crossover" quality of books like these: "This book is one of series of [similar] writings that have been published recently and which . . . [are] works of popularization, but which also [contain original research]." One analogy commonly drawn in the contemporary press was that between the amphitheater of the Salpêtrière and the theater proper (Micale, *Approaching Hysteria* 199). The medical notion that physical states could be transferred from one person to another from a distance, in the same way that thought and cures for disease could be transmitted, corresponded to popular superstition and the practice of magnetizers in France. The medical confirmation or "stamp of approval" for such practices was, of course, readily accepted among the general public. Popular belief, charlatanism, and medicine were intertwined in complicated ways in late-nineteenth-century France, and it is not the aim of this book to untangle this complex web. I want simply to make the reader aware of the variety of conduits for medical themes and explorations in the period. The spate of novels in the 1880s and 1890s featuring hysterical heroes and heroines—some set in the Salpêtrière Hospital itself—further promoted detailed knowledge of the illness. While the writing style of Joris-Karl Huysmans discouraged a larger readership for his work among the general public, other Decadent writers (for example, Rachilde) who took hysteria as a major theme were commercially successful. Many novels, such as Léon Daudet's *Les Morticoles* (1894) and Armand Dubarry's *Hystérique* (1897), became bestsellers and went through as many as twenty editions.[2] In a lecture delivered at the Salpêtrière Hospital, Dr. Jacques Roubinovitch, who was a medical associate there (as well as Head of Clinic at the Faculté de Médecine), stated that "Even the public who reads a great deal and thinks that they are up to date on all new scientific discoveries possess many erroneous notions on mental illness" ("La Pathologie" 4). The "less cultivated public" informs itself "about the pathology of mental illness by way of melodrama and tear-jerker novels (*romans pathétiques*)" (5).

Why this preoccupation? The sensationalist aspects of the illness perfectly met the anticipations of a late-nineteenth-century public who has thrived on sensationalist accounts of crime, passion, and alcoholism in the popular press, in the wax museum, and, earlier in the century, in melodrama. This public would soon be attending the bloody extravagances of the Theater of Grand Guignol (see Chapter 3 for a discussion of the genre of "Medical Theater" initiated there by André de Lorde). Indeed, in the 1880s and 1890s sociologists and psychologists immersed in degeneration theory associated hysteria with criminality (from kleptomania to murder), with sexual pathologies such as syphilis, and with alcoholism. Degeneration was supposedly a product of alcoholism, heredity, and mental insufficiencies such as imbecility and idiocy, which were an indication of the failure to genetically ascend the evolutionary ladder. The number of degenerates in France was, in fact, a clear indication that evolution had already reached its pinnacle and that there was no direction to go but downward. Psychiatrists stated with assurance that it was commonplace to see hysteria develop where there was a background of degeneration. Finally, these symptoms strangely duplicated certain traits observed in "savages," that is to say, the unwilling prospective recipients, in the colonies, of lessons in civilized French manners. The language of mental pathology was present in all of these areas, as Robert Nye has stressed, noting at the same time the reciprocal influences "running between the lay public and the [medical] community" (172).

In 1881 Dr. Paul-Max Simon could state simply: "Hysteria is everywhere around us" (L'hystérie court la rue). In fact, according to Legrand du Saulle, there were approximately 50,000 hysterics in Paris, including 10,000 who also suffered from hysterical convulsions.

Between 1890 and 1910, four histories of hysteria were published in France, two of them medical dissertations.[3] (Other dissertations, such as that of Jacques Roubinovitch on male hysteria, consist of case observations.) These histories concur in attributing to Charcot the scientization of hysteria in the 1860s. For Charcot and his disciples, following Briquet,[4] hysteria was a manifestation of neurological disturbance caused by functional lesions of the central nervous system. The extraordinary array of hysterical symptoms (the illness was called a "wastebasket of symptoms") included double consciousness; somnambulism; motor disturbances; hallucinations; digestive problems; fugue states; intellectual, language, and visual disturbances; yawning; laughing; and hiccups. The present study concerns itself with only the first three and yawning (see, in particular, Chapter 3 for case observations). Charcot's view of the disease enabled him to superimpose an order on the proliferation of diverse symptoms, and his rather rigid classification of hysteria (*grande hystérie*, or *hystéro-epilepsie*) with its four progressive stages of the major hysterical attack, is the conception and imagery that was transmitted to a remarkably wide range of the general public. Hysteria, as Sander Gilman has emphasized, became Charcot's visualization of it. Paul Richer and Charcot collaborated on works that reproduced prototypes of hysterics in art (such as those that appeared in *Les Démoniaques dans l'art*). Richer's most important work on the subject, however, was his *Etudes Cliniques et thérapeutiques sur la Grande hystérie ou hystéro-épilepsie* (1881). Richer cofounded the *Nouvelle Iconographie de la Salpêtrière* with Gilles de la Tourette. In 1882, Richer became head of the Clinic of Nervous Diseases Laboratory at the hospital. And despite the fact that epilepsy and hysteria were later differentiated by Charcot and the classification of *hystéro-epilepsy* rejected, the epileptiform stage of the attack remained a compelling feature attraction at the Salpêtrière, where epileptics and hysterics were confined to the same ward. In 1884 Gilbert Ballet (responsible for some of the most important work on male hysteria) published an article in *Les Archives de Neurologie*, in which he classified the different forms of epilepsy that manifested themselves in hysterical attacks: partial epilepsy, Jacksonian epilepsy, and epilepsy due to cerebral lesion. Those hysterical attacks were indistinguishable from epileptic fits, except for the absence of hypothermia. Jacques Roubinovitch's 1899 doctoral thesis on male hysteria demonstrates that the term "*hystéro-epilepsy*" remained in use medically up to the end of the century: "Such is the attack of major hysteria or of *hystéro-epilepsy*, as one still says today in order to recall the epileptiform phenomena that occur in the course of this attack" (24). A profound confusion between hysteria and epilepsy did, in fact, exist until the early twentieth century.[5] Both *The Photographic Iconography of the Salpêtrière* (1876–1880) and the *New Iconography of the Salpêtrière* (1888–1918) were widely publicized and circulated. As has often been noted, the peak of public interest in the *New Iconography* coincided with the emergence and invention of cinema. The images of contractures, grimaces, and convulsions were soon conflated with those of hypnotic trances induced by psychiatrists (not only those in the Nancy school of psychological medicine, but also in the experiments of Alfred Binet and Charles Féré in Paris), or brought on by auto-suggestion, or with a variety of other curious treatment techniques to which patients were subjected, such as the use of magnets to transfer hysterical zones from one part of the body to another or the homeopathic *fauteuil à trepidation* (agitating armchair).

Jacques-Joseph Moreau de Tours, Alexandre-Jacques-François Brierre de Boismont, Hector Landouzy, and Pierre Briquet had also reported some pretty spectacular phenomena in their hysterical patients in the first sixty years of the century. Moreau de Tours's somnambulist patients led a double existence, one of them even waking up several years later to find himself in a Russian prison. Brierre de Boismont listed supernatural phenomena such as succuba in his diagnosis of the disease, and Briquet had already studied abnormalities of movement and sensation in detail before Charcot set about studying ambulatory automatisms. And these phenomena were already appearing in the fantastic tales of Théophile Gautier in the 1830s and 1840s. What explains, then, the increased fascination that the disease commanded in the last quarter of the century? This can perhaps be ascribed to the extraordinary rise in the number of cases of hysteria in the 1870s (see Goldstein), to the emphasis placed on the spectacular epileptiform fit in the attack (one-third of Briquet's 430 cases did not experience convulsive symptoms), and to the framing of hysteria with evolution theory, degeneration theory, and crowd theory. The beginning of the rise in the hysteria diagnosis, moreover, coincided with the Paris Commune, while the height of popular fascination with the illness in the 1890s coincided with anarchist acts. This framework for a disease that was apparently communicated by suggestion and unconscious imitation (and where a condition as utterly commonplace as congestion was deemed to be a symptom) considerably dramatized it and provoked fears that seemed well founded, given the possibilities for contagion. The sociologist Gabriel de Tarde induced the *Laws of Imitation* from theories surrounding nervous reflex and hypnosis, proclaiming his debt to Hippolyte Bernheim, in particular. Unconscious imitation, as I've stated, is the focus of the present study. As Mark Micale has noted, "The use of the language of nervous and mental pathology . . . became a common feature of French social, cultural, and political commentary between 1870 and 1914. . . . For the first time, the reading of medical books by lay people became a pastime [including] a large and largely alarmist literature on the nervous disorders" (*Approaching Hysteria* 201).

The context for the infiltration of hysterical gesture and movement into cabaret and early film comedy between 1870 and 1910, therefore, is to be found in medicine, literature, ethnology, and sociology. It is perhaps no coincidence that the 1880s were both the golden age of hysteria in Paris hospitals and the golden age of Parisian cabaret and café-concert. Although by 1900 the heyday of French hysteria had drawn to a close on the European (medical) scene, the concepts and images from observations of hysteria between 1870 and 1900—particularly those involving hypnosis, ambulatory pathologies, and automatisms—coupled with observations of hysteria's offshoot, neurasthenia,[6] remained a part of popular entertainment in France, perpetuated in early film comedy.

Spectatorship and Physiological Aesthetics

Interest in spectatorship is not of recent vintage. At the beginning of the twentieth century, tests were conducted by screening films and monitoring subjective response at dramatic or comic moments, so as to measure the exact intensity of sensations (which were then interpreted as emotions) in the spectator. According to late-nineteenth-century theories of physiology, successive stages of intensity in aesthetic emotion corresponded to changes in the body (Féré, *Sensation*). Walter Benjamin's insights into film as "perception in the form of shocks" evolved at a time when the theories in physiology and psychiatry that I describe here were still being discussed in France. In fact, the relationship of shock and nerves to modern life had already been noted by the 1860s, and was a recurrent theme in newspapers, scientific journals, and fiction from the 1880s on. As Ben Singer so justly notes, "Benjamin [and Kracauer] were tapping into an already widespread discourse about the shock of modernity" (Singer 73–74), an experience that Singer aptly calls neurological modernity (72).[7] In an often cited passage, Walter Benjamin writes that "there came a day when a new and urgent need for stimuli was met by the film. In a film, perception in the form of shocks was established as a formal principle" (175). He goes on to say that the "distracting element of [film] (the sudden and constant changes of focus that "assail" the spectator) is primarily tactile," and he compares it to Dada, which "hit the spectator like a bullet . . . promot[ing] a demand for the film" (238). In the same passage, Benjamin refers to Georges Duhamel's anxiety about moving images replacing thought. It is this aspect of shock—the singularly physical experience of perception in watching a film that forces one to abandon conscious mental processes—that I want to analyze. Film is experienced in the body, and if, in the nineteenth century, the body is understood to be distinct from the (conscious) mind, that is because the body is believed to be the site of the unconscious. Benjamin continues: "Tactile appropriation is accomplished . . . by habit" and "reception in a state of distraction . . . finds in the film its true means of exercise" (240). What is habit, according to late-nineteenth-century physiologists and philosophers? Habit is equivalent to the automatic responses exemplified by nervous reflex and by unconscious mental processes. Benjamin's notion of the "rhythm of reception" in the film experience, as well as its tactile quality, can thus be best understood in the context of nineteenth-century physiology, and specifically, in the importance of physiological response in the production of affect in aesthetic experience. Clearly, not only *visual* shocks are involved in film spectatorship. To begin with, perception and mental images do not take place in the mind or eye alone; they are linked to their motor component. Further, psychophysiologists of the 1880s and 1890s proposed that the dynamic infrastructure of perception had to include not only a motor component but one that was governed by the forces of instinct.[8]

Physiological aesthetics tried to measure and analyze the impact of form, movement, and color not only on the eye but also on the body. Research in psychophysiology ascribed specific emotions to certain gestures and forms, a mechanics of emotion that could then be used by painters, actors, and, later, filmmakers.[9] Charles Henry, director of the Sorbonne laboratory of physiology, applying Gustav Fechner's psychophysical formulae of stimulus-response, "established" that directional movements are either inhibitory or dynamogeneous. For example, discontinuous lines and downward movement retard movement in the body; they are inhibitory. Continuous lines and upward movement stimulate it: they are dynamogeneous. Correspondingly, perception of the former causes sad and anxious emotions, whereas perception of the latter causes calm and happy emotions. Henry's theories were tested at the Salpêtrière Hospital: "The dynamometric experiments of Dr. Féré, and the expressions [on the faces] of hypnotized subjects that characterize all the states of pleasure and pain in response to the different directions of the arm of the experimenter, establish the validity of the relation between the direction of line and emotion."[10] His research informed the work of neo-Impressionist painters like Georges Seurat and Paul Signac as well as that of poets Gustave Kahn and Jules Laforgue. Pursuing the application of psychophysics to aesthetics (specifically in the context of pain and pleasure), the American Henry Rutgers Marshall wrote that it was "probable that, in the future, one will tend to limit the use of the word *emotion* to the description of those states determinable by the content of their muscular sensations" (in Ribot, Review of *Mind* 110). From the work of Théodule Ribot[11] and Pierre Janet in France to that of Marshall and to the James-Lange theory in America, scientific psychology was busy looking for the somatic basis of emotions.

Moreover, at the same time as we *perceive* an object, our "internal machinery" *recreates* it. Charles Henry writes that thanks to eye movements, and to phenomena in our vascular and muscular systems and in our breathing, "there is no idea without virtual, then real, movement. . . . One can consider the sensation and the idea as virtual exercises of our mécanique naturelle" (the mechanics of our body) (2). This notion comes to Henry from Richet, who concisely stated: "There is no perception without movement" (*L'Homme* 520).

In addition, when a movement is directed to a particular organ or member of the body, the latter *remembers* and tends to later repeat this movement. When Nietzsche wrote in 1881 that "all nerves, for example in the leg, remember their past experiences. . . . What the nerves have assimilated continues to live in them" (in Gauchet 208), he was drawing on Théodule Ribot (*Les Maladies*) and Henry Maudsley, as Marcel Gauchet has pointed out. For Ribot, the personality is formed by the sensations received from the organs, the tissue, from movements—all the bodily states represented in the *sensorium*. Thus, the personality varies with them. Pathologies like doubling (*le dédoublement de la personnalité*) are directly tied to changes in bodily sensations "and are but an extreme example of the phenomenon" described by Ribot ("Conditions organiques" 627). I want to look at a contemporary concern about the sensations that *film viewers* received, which were also stored in the memory of the nerves and active in the construction of the personality.

In his 1877 *Sensation et mouvement*, Charles Féré showed that all sensation was accompanied by an augmentation of muscular force, measurable on the dynamometer. Consciousness, however, does not even perceive this augmentation. The acuteness of joy, pain, desire, or shame results from the automatic movements that these feelings engender. Virtual movement, set in motion from the outside (stimuli and sensation) *and* from the inside (ideas and internal sensations), if it can be gauged by the dynamometer and other instruments, makes possible a scientific aesthetics.[12] To summarize: psychophysical experiments originating with Gustav Fechner in 1860 that purported to measure sensation led to experiments for gauging aesthetic emotion (first in Germany in the 1870s, then in France in the 1880s, and later in America in the 1890s); these correlations were aligned with Henry's theory that perceiving the aesthetic object not only produces specific sensations but also corporeal reactions that retrace the form and movement of that object. It is to Henry's work that Henri Bergson refers when he writes that we may not be able to "consciously comprehend an emotion that an artist tries to express, but we can be made to *feel* it; artists set down those outer manifestations of their emotion *that our body will mechanically imitate, however lightly*, so as to place us in the undefinable psychological state that caused them" (*Essai* 13). The barriers between the artist's consciousness and our own disappear thanks to unconscious imitation.

Henry had noted that when the "hypnotizable subject" perceives the movements of another Subject, s/he first recreates them virtually as ideas, then as acts. We know that hysterics are eminently hypnotizable, thus their bodies will always be solicited by this form of internal mimicry. But many normal people are hypnotizable—*all people*, according to Hippolyte Bernheim and the Nancy school of psychology—, so the reverbations of what everyone sees are mirrored in and by the body. The mimetic tendency so marked in hysterics, due to corporeal automatisms, is inherent to aesthetic experience. The instinct to imitate "seems to come . . . from the unconscious parts of the nervous system" (Simon, *Hygiène* 37). Epilepsy is one of the afflictions in which the influence of imitation is most to be feared, according to Dr. Simon. In fact, imitation was believed to be a frequent cause of epilepsy, and impressionable people were warned against witnessing epileptic attacks. Hysteria was also viewed as contagious through imitation. In *L'Esthétique du mouvement* (1889), Paul Souriau remarked that convulsive movements in dance or in design can, "by a kind of contagion, provoke in the viewer similar symptoms," as I noted in 1992.[13] From the most general point of view, according to Ribot (in *Les Maladies*), if one looks at the number of acts that are due to automatisms (automatic reactions), habit, passion, and especially imitation, the number of purely voluntary acts is quite small (in Grellety, *Névrosés* 16).

In the mid-1880s, as I've aleady mentioned, Gabriel Tarde was situating the problem and theme of imitation and contagion in a broader context. This research was collected and published in 1890 under the title *Les Lois de l'imitation*. Suggestion and its corollary, unconscious imitation, is a *universal phenomenon*, according to Tarde. Hippolyte Bernheim and other psychiatrists furnished convincing support for this thesis, and by 1890, "There [was] no more commonplace knowledge than this point of view" (Tarde 82). If imitative behavior in response to unconscious suggestion is a universal phenomenon, then the paradigmatic figure of the individual in society is the somnambulist. This is exactly what Tarde says: "Society is imitation, and imitation is a form of hypnosis" (93); the somnambulistic state *epitomizes* social behavior.

Applying the "scientific aesthetics" to cinema, Drs. Edouard Toulouse and Raoul Mourgue[14] wrote that "since it is scientifically proven that the perception of movement gives birth to the beginnings (*l'ébauche*) of the corresponding movement, a phenomenon would take place on the screen akin to hypnotic suggestion being practiced on a subject placed in a given pose" (in Moussinac 174).[15] In 1923 Sergei Eisenstein was certain that he had found the perfect vehicle for measuring the emotional effects of art. "The attraction (in our diagnosis of the theater) is every aggressive moment in it, i.e., every element of it that brings to light in the spectator those senses or that psychic action that influence his experience—every element that can be *verified by means of experiment and mathematically calculated to produce certain emotional shocks* in a proper order within the totality" (*Film Sense* 230–31; italics mine; translation slightly modified). Eisenstein's concept of the "montage of attractions," worked out in 1922–1923 in the theater before being applied to such films as *October* and *Battleship Potemkin*, and published in an article in *Lef* (vol. 3 [1923]), is yet another example of the impact of psychophysics on aesthetics. Indeed, he later said that had he had a greater familiarity with Pavlov's theories, his system might well have been named "the theory of aesthetic excitements" (in Barna 63). Eisenstein's ideas for his Acrobatic Theater emerged from Vsevolod Meyerhold's theory of bio-mechanics (whose biological component was based on Pavlov's work on conditioned nervous reflexes). In Meyerhold's theater, as in that of Artaud, every movement of the body corresponds to and expresses an emotion. Eisenstein stressed the power of circus performers, music-hall performers, and mimes to produce physical and emotional reactions in the spectator, "bridg[ing] the chasm separating the actor and spectator" and "uniting them in such a way that the spectator would identify with the action" (*Notes* 134). Eisenstein offers an example of the attraction in film: it is communicated "by the specific mechanics of [Chaplin's] movement" (*Film Sense* 231). (Two years earlier, the filmmaker Jean Epstein identified Chaplin's "photogenic neurasthenia": his "entire performance consists of the reflex actions of a nervous, tired person" ["Magnification" 238].[16]) It was Donald Crafton who, in a colloquium discussion, originally suggested that Eisenstein's conception of the attraction should be applied to the study of early cinema. The suggestion was, of course, brilliantly taken up by Tom Gunning and André Gaudreault. Continuing his work on the concept and description of the cinema of attractions, Tom Gunning has considered Benjamin's "perception in the form of shocks" in the context of an aesthetics of astonishment. The cinema of attractions foregrounds "the role of the spectator, [addressing him or her] in a specific manner" ("Now You See It" 32). It is a "series of visual shocks" that exerted an "uncanny and agitating power . . . on audiences" (Gunning, "Aesthetic of Astonishment" 66; see also Gunning in L. Williams, *Viewing Positions* 116). To understand this power, I believe that we must see it in the context of contemporary notions about the body and the unconscious. Considering not only the visual but the corporeal shocks, recourse to physiology and psychiatry explains *why* the shocks, jolts, in the viewer occurred and how they are linked to the unconscious, instinct, hysteria or—in the shorthand of the period—the "lower orders."

An idea that preoccupies philosophers, psychologists, psychiatrists, and physiologists alike from midcentury on is the radical division between the higher and lower faculties: reason, judgment, choice, and will as opposed to sensation, motor response, automatisms, and instinct. Lodged in the opposition between High and Low was the specter of insanity and hysteria: hysterics were precisely those people in whom the lower faculties dominated the higher faculties to the point where the latter were totally subservient to the former. In his 1889 *L'Automatisme psychologique: essai de psychologie expérimentale sur les formes inférieures de l'activité humaine*, Dr. Pierre Janet developed this notion more fully than anyone had up until then. In addition, from around 1870 in France, a capital new way of envisaging High and Low was introduced which quickly became the intellectual event of the last decades of the century: I am referring to Darwin's theory of evolution. The kind of performance style described in this book quite deliberately appeals to the lower faculties. And, while the predominance of the lower over the higher faculties was seen to lead to hysteria, hallucination, and split personalities, it also generated an absolutely new aesthetic, an aesthetic that was, above all, *magnetic*, a word used by innumerable observers to describe it. The concept of "high" and "low" culture takes on new meaning in light of nineteenth-century psychiatric and physiological theory.

What exactly were bodies doing in the music-hall, sideshows, circus, exhibitions of magnetizers, and cabaret acts? Because of the spectator's purported incorporation of what s/he sees (whether one takes this dynamic to be a function of biomechanics, psychophysics, or unconscious imitation), it is important to reflect on the *kinds* of movement reproduced. The spectator's physical experience is exciting and stimulating, yet anxiety-producing; the experience of the body involuntarily imitating convulsive movements, cataleptic poses, and facial contortions could not help but remind the viewer of the all-too-common attacks of epilepsy and hysteria which found their way into the popular press. "Epileptic performers" cause anxiety and hilarity, and the latter is in response to the former. This is why deformity, dismemberment, contortions, grimaces, tics, and epileptic convulsions are so funny to so many spectators.[17]

And since the majority of performers in film came from the cabaret—one of the forms of spectacle that inspired the concept of the montage of attractions and, later, the "cinema of attractions"—I analyze many of these problems in the cabaret chapter of the present volume and in the chapter on magnetism, before going on to look at film. There is a continuous line and directing force running from the cabaret and café-concert performances of the last quarter of the nineteenth century, through the films of Méliès, to the silent film comedies of Ernst Lubitsch, and, finally, to the films of Jerry Lewis. It is hysterical gesture and gait.

What's so Funny about Pathology?

> As a patient looks into the microscope in the doctor's office, the images of the germs in his body fill the frame. Simply by virtue of having seen these bizarre images of pathology, the patient becomes a "raving lunatic."
>
> —Scenario from Emile Cohl's *Les Joyeux Microbes*

The world's best-known essay on laughter was written in France during the very period when Parisian cabaret was at its apogée and Méliès was making his first films. Henri Bergson's *Le Rire* (1899) owes a debt to psychiatric theory, as well as to Charles Baudelaire's "De l'Essence du rire," published a half-century earlier.[18] In addition, I feel certain that Bergson would never have made mechanical rigidity and automatic movement the centerpiece of his theory had it not been omnipresent in cabaret, mime, circus, and early cinema.

First, consider the reflections on laughter of the infallible critic of aesthetics, Baudelaire. It is well known that those who are wise don't laugh; Baudelaire inverts this dictum and declares that "laughter is the privileged domain of madmen" (245). He then writes that laughter is "satanic" and comes from a belief in one's own superiority. And where can one find the greatest number of people convinced of their superiority? In madhouses. "Laughter is one of the most frequent . . . expressions of madness" (248). Laughter is a symptom of weakness, like the inability to restrain tears: "What sign of debility is more marked than a nervous convulsion, an involuntary spasm?" (ibid.). What makes us laugh is often a physical infirmity or the result of a fall which makes one's face contort like a "toy on springs" (ibid.). So, weakness and infirmity make us laugh, and although our laughter is prompted by a feeling of superiority, it reduces us to a similar state of weakness and debility. E. T. A. Hoffmann's creations and the "terrible and irresistible drunkenness of laughter" (258) caused by an English pantomime troupe that Baudelaire saw in the 1840s illustrate his idea of *le comique absolu.* The distinctive sign of the mimes' comic genius was violence combined with the grotesque (Baudelaire describes Pierrot's decapitation and the bloody, severed head center-stage, as well as the headless torso that continues to act on its own—an illustration of the corporeal unconscious that we will be examining shortly.) As for Hoffmann's grotesque "visions of drunkenness, . . . we are dealing with *a physiologist or an alienist* of the most profound cast . . . who [clothes] this profound science with poetical forms" (261, italics mine).

Bergson too draws analogies between psychiatry and the comic. We laugh when a living being becomes a "puppet or marionnette" (*Le Rire* 83) just as we laugh at "grimaces or tics" (18). When a human being is transformed into a thing, it illustrates Bergson's law of the comic: *du mécanique plaqué sur du vivant* (the mechanical superimposed onto the living). "Some of the subtlest results of psychological science" can be inferred from our reaction of laughter when we see this happen. Circus clowns not only offer a "precise verification" of the law, but their transformation "into" big rubber balls or wooden dummies is experienced by us in the same way as a Subject under hypnosis is made to see an unreal object. "Often the magnetizer . . . will start with objects that are really perceived . . . and he'll try to render the perception more and more confused: then, . . . he will make . . . the precise form of the hallucination he wants to produce emerge" (46). Hypnotic suggestion is only one of many parallels drawn between comedy and hypnosis or psychiatry. The very principle of Bergson's theory, *l'automatisme*, is a psychiatric term used by Pierre Janet, Eugène Azam, Charles Richet, and others in the 1880s to describe the involuntary—that is, the unconscious—words and acts of hysterics. Nowhere in this essay does Bergson refer to the psychiatric definition of the term, yet he uses it to mean unconscious and involuntary acts as well as to underline the automaton-like character of mechanical gesture. He didn't *need* to define the term: by 1899 it was common knowledge. "It is a sort of automatism that makes us laugh. He is comic to the exact degree that he is *unconscious* of being as he is. The comical is unconscious" (12–13). Bergson writes that internal states manifest themselves through gesture (including discourse) with "no end in view, solely by dint of a sort of inner 'itch' (*démangeaison*). . . . Gesture escapes from one, it is automatic. . . . In it an isolated part of the person is expressed, despite or separated from the total personality" (109–10). This notion is in line with the psychiatric theory of the corporeal unconscious that is studied in the next section of this chapter. What makes us laugh is the outward expression of the person's unconscious being emanating from the motor centers. These movements and gestures must necessarily have put people in mind of epileptics, hysterics, and somnambulists—those who were "most subject to this activity." "*Unconscious phenomena bearing on sensation and on movement* are easily observed in hysterics" (Binet and Féré, "Recherches" 332; italics mine). *Explicit* representations of hysteria and epilepsy *unfailingly* provoke laughter, but in fact these conditions (in embryo) are implicit in nearly everything comical in cabaret, café-concert, and early film comedy.

As for the phenomenon of imitation or contagion that is the focus of *Why the French Love Jerry Lewis*, Bergson, like Baudelaire, makes it central to his theory: laughter "needs an echo," and there is complicity with others, real or imagined" (*Le Rire* 4–5). Because infirmities and illnesses, including "mental debility and all varieties of madness" (14), are represented by the lack of elasticity or mechanical rigidity, society is "in the presence of something that makes it uncomfortable . . . as a symptom, with only a hint of menace" (15).

Laughter is our response and attempt to "correct" these defects. This, I suggest, is why images of hysteria formed the very basis for comic effect in the cabaret and in early cinema. But to what degree is mental aberration placed under control? If nineteenth-century audiences laughed in an attempt to "correct" troubling resemblances of their own bodies to those of hysterics or somnambulists/automatons, was there only "a hint" of menace present? Let's not forget Baudelaire's reminder that laughing is itself a "nervous convulsion, an involuntary spasm." If the perception of clowns and of characters in films transforming themselves into objects was tantamount to an hallucination produced by a magnetizer or a psychiatrist, was there only a hint of menace present? Bergson ends by rejecting the notion that there is a parallel between the comical and madness because he has initially stated that laughter is incompatible with emotion and madness elicits pity. Yet he does admit a parallel with dreams, and "dreams imitate madness" (142), as Moreau de Tours, moreover, had masterfully shown in his 1855 *De l'Identité du rêve et de la folie*. Now what variety of madness typically found in dreams does Bergson say is most pertinent to the spirit of the comic? The alienation of a part of oneself into an Other, and the viewing of oneself and one's "double" from the outside. The images that make us laugh are mirrors: "For a very short instant we put ourselves in the place [of the performer], we adopt his/her gestures, words, acts" (148). In the forms of comedy I examine in this book, spectators become the doubles of figures whose involuntary gestures belie nervous pathologies, pathologies which, according to nineteenth-century physiologists, our bodies unconsciously imitate.

In his essay on "The Uncanny," Freud writes that the most frequent manifestation of the uncanny, the involuntary recurrence of the same thing, can "call forth the comic." Among the examples given are epilepsy and automatons, two figures of the pathologized body that we will encounter again and again in popular entertainment between 1865 and 1912. I discuss this essay in the section on the Double in Chapter 5; here, I simply want to underline the relationship of the uncanny body and laughter: the alienated part of oneself is invariably a representation of the corporeal unconscious with its automatisms, always so visible in the hysteric. This is our double, and laughter is the attempt to exorcise that double.

A study of laughter at the turn of the century cites the following sonnet:

"The mouth / Makes a black hole, gaping, savage and full of drool. . . . The convulsed stomach expands. . . . And the lungs spit out the spasms . . . in hard, strident cries. / But what is this illness, this case of epilepsy / Where one rattles foaming at the mouth, the brain thickened, / The senses lost, the nerves gone haywire. . . . It is Laughter" (Dugas 122). Unlike the other reflections on laughter considered here, this study was written by a psychologist, Dr. Ludovic Dugas. His *Psychologie du rire* is dedicated to the physiologist Théodule Ribot. (It may already be clear to the reader that Ribot's work forms an important basis for the present study.)

Although Dugas's study synthesizes and discusses several theories of laughter, it is the physiological and the pessimist theory of laughter that are pertinent to the present study. Conversant with contemporary theories of psychophysics and psychophysiology, Dugas posits that laughter is not an emotion, "but an emotive tone, which expresses—not its determining states —but rather the *dynamogenic action* of those states, not surprise . . . but what surprise contains that is tonic and awakens us" (81). (The reader has recognized the allusion to Charles Henry's scientific aesthetics.) It can not be explained solely by physiology, as Herbert Spencer would have it, but partakes of consciousness as well. Dugas condenses Lamennais's, Hobbes's and Bain's pessimist theories of laughter in the following exposition: "Our laughter always expresses foremost the feeling of superiority over others [we compare our being to their infirmity or to our previous weaknesses]. But surprise is always mixed in with this sentiment; and a superior sense of pride that is astonished at its triumph can only be relative" (83–84). Why is this theory "pessimistic"? One laughs not only from a feeling of superiority: there is a "purely malignant laughter directly caused by the view of suffering, . . . the misfortune of others . . . physical difformities, . . . stupidity" (93, 94). This laughter is found especially in "children and savages" (ibid.). It is also present in many others, but, according to Aristotle, "the ridiculous face which is ugly or difformed must not show traces of suffering" (94). Yet the laugher is insensitive and detached, feeling no sympathy with the objects of his/her mockery. Their misfortune is "*conceived by us* as tolerable and light" (97). The more unrefined the person, the more cruel and brutal his or her laughter: "These people will even laugh at the twisted walk of someone with a clubfoot, at the ugliness of a hunchback, at the repulsive hideousness of an idiot"

(98). The three objects of mockery chosen by Dugas each happen to correspond to a very popular café-concert attraction (see Chapter 3). There (with the exception of the hunchbacked performer), the infirmities were merely mimed, a form of granting permission to laugh at what some might otherwise hesitate to deride. At the same time, there were many spectators lacking in "refinement" at the café-concert. Some people would (and did) compare them to "savages." Ribot, cited here, perceives two sorts of laughter, corresponding to two phases of evolution: the brutal and ferocious laughter of the barbarian (*le sauvage*) and the intellectual laughter of civilized people. As Henry Jenkins's book *What Made Pistachio Nuts?* analyzes so well, this Spencerian view of comedy, reflected in James Sully's study of laughter, for example, was very influential in England and America. Here, I would underline that the diversity of the crowd at the French venues for popular entertainment, combined with the contagion of laughter, is crucial to the spread of this form of hilarity. Contagion is emphasized in the physiological theory of laughter (as it was in Bergson's theory, but from the point of view of sociability). "Laughter is contagious . . . it is propagated like yawning, by reflex action" (36). "Hysterical laughter" (*le fou rire*) is "involuntary, . . . irresistible, and inextinguishable" (24). Darwin writes that it resembles "falling into convulsions" (in Dugas 25). Herbert Spencer demonstrates that the explanation of nervous laughter and "*le fou rire*" holds true for intellectual laughter as well. Intellectual laughter is caused by the sight of discordances; the nervous system is in a state of tension before one bursts into laughter, and the contrasting event "causes a discharge that runs through the motor nerves . . . and produces the convulsive movements that we call laughter" (in Dugas 27). Not convinced by Spencer that all laughter is physiological, Ribot asks: "Is there a purely nervous and physical laugh that must be classed among the 'reflexes,' like the laughter caused by tickling, cold, the ingestion of certain substances, the laughter of hysterics, etc.?" (in Dugas 3).

Dugas concludes that the laughter that is poorest in psychic elements is the one that is the most violent, the spasmodic or convulsive laugh. "It is but an unleashing of animal life" (122). He believes in progress: "The spirit grows finer and malignity diminishes. One learns to distinguish the infirmities that one can laugh at and the infirm being one must feel sorry for" (100). Notwithstanding this optimistic view of humanity, one has to observe that the shock stimulus provided by most physical comedy in the cabaret, as well as the prominence of physical infirmities in that comic tradition from the 1870s to the 1910s clearly appealed to and drew forth the low forms of laughter described in Dugas's study. A plethora of examples will be found in Chapters 3 and 6 below.

In a recent book where Jerry Lewis is very much present, Steven Shaviro writes, "I am invested by what I see: perception becomes a kind of physical affliction, an intensification and disarticulation of bodily sensation. . . . Much work remains to be done on the psychophysiology of cinematic experience, the ways in which film renders vision tactile, short-circuits reflection and directly stimulates the nervous system" (52–53).[19] This is precisely the focus of the present book, informed by research in the fields of psychophysiology and psychiatry on the nervous system, hysteria, hypnosis, and imitation. As we look at parallel forms of body language in pre-cinematic mass spectacle and in early cinema, we cannot help but be struck by the offstage presence of scientific observations and notions in the construction of performance style. The story that leads from Charcot to Charlot will enable us to fully appreciate why Jean Epstein characterized Charlie Chaplin's extraordinary appeal in France as "photogenic neurasthenia" and why physical comedy was associated with devolution. Our story begins with the corporeal unconscious.

The Corporeal Unconscious

French psychiatry's notion of the unconscious (worked out in the 1880s and early 1890s by Janet, Charcot, Binet, and Féré, before Freud and Breuer's 1895 *Studien über Hysterie*) is based on research in nervous reflex and on observations of somnambulists, hysterics, and hypnotized subjects which date back to the mid-nineteenth century.[20] It is a *corporeal* unconscious—it is the body's automatisms that remember what the conscious mind ignores. Automatic movements and speech were the key to understanding somnambulism and hysteria. In hypnosis, the conscious awareness of sensation is abolished; "the sensation, although unconscious, is registered in the nervous centers of the patient, and it is this physiological registering that allows him or her to reproduce the movement without being conscious of it [suggested or induced by the psychiatrist]" (Binet and Féré, "Recherches" 348–49). The first characteristic of suggestion is to *suppose or to create* this dissociative operation (Binet, *La Suggestibilité* 10). Binet first defined his notion of the unconscious as a result of his research with Charcot's well-known student, Charles Féré, in Charcot's laboratory at the Salpêtrière.

> The Subject has lost consciousness of the passive movements [that is, suggested or imposed by the psychiatrist] in his anesthetic member, but this loss of consciousness is not absolute. . . . Another personality, so to speak, exists in him and it is conscious of these movements; *it* receives the suggestion and executes it. . . . This is an episode of major hypnotism that one can encounter in the waking state in certain predisposed individuals. (Binet and Féré, "Recherches" 332)

What constitutes this "other personality"? Pure sensation and nerves. The sensation may be erased from consciousness, but it remains present in the patient's nervous centers. Poses suggested by the psychiatrist could be held by the hypnotized subject for up to one hour and twenty minutes, a fact that led the doctors to reflect that "it seems as though the [anesthetized] member doesn't belong to the subject" (326).[21] The anesthetic member might be compared to a form of *corps morcelé* or dismemberment. This phantasy also mirrors the mental phenomenon of *désagregation*, the dismemberment of the personality that, according to psychiatrists in the last half of the nineteenth century, characterized hysteria; thus Lacan was able to remark in the *Séminaire III*, that "anatomical dismemberment, as a phantasy, is hysterical" (201). I believe that the multitude of images of dismemberment in fin-de-siècle mass spectacle like the magic theater, the Grand Guignol theater, and early cinema owe something to the sense of wonder surrounding the sensation or phantasy of hysterical anesthesia. The members and the cataleptic plasticity of the somnambulist's body present the "flexibility of wax" and "waxlike catalepsy" (Binet and Féré, "Recherches" 325; *Nouvelle Iconographie* 3:124). The waxwork figures in the Musée Grévin, with their arrested postures, may well have evoked images of the cataleptic poses of hysterics and somnambulists in the minds of visitors. It also seems likely that somnambulism and hysteria were summoned to mind by the frozen poses in the very widespread parlor entertainment of tableaux vivants. What *is* certain is that grotesque dislocations of the body, weird exaggerations of motor capability ("an essentially pathological phenomenon," according to Binet and Féré ["Recherches" 331]), and the specific gestures and gaits observed in hysteria and in somnambulism were a major part of the repertoire of mimes, clowns, acrobats, contortionists, and singers. Gestural exaggeration is an hysterical trait because the *expression* of desire is an absolute need for hysterics. At the same time, it earned them the label of "theatrical." Corporeal anomalies, along with automatic, repeated gestures, tics, grimaces, and contractures, characterize the pathologized body at the center of performance style in cabaret and early film comedy.

Thus it was—through the automatic gestures and speech of the hysteric and through the repeated gestures and the extraordinary muscular capabilities of the anesthetized side of the body in somnambulism[22]—that Binet made the capital discovery in 1887 that "doubling of the personality exists in the waking state and isn't successive but simultaneous . . . the second personality is coexistent with the conscious personality" (352).[23] Up until then, the second personality was perceived as alternating with the normal, conscious personality. Not a Dr. Jekyll and Mr. Hyde, then (Stevenson's novel dates from 1886, the previous year), but two very different selves always present.

Doubling of the personality, or double consciousness, is one of the most dramatic symptoms of hysteria and had been studied from the 1840s on, the second personality equated at that time with the somnambulistic state. The theme of the Double in Romantic literature, enveloped in the aura of the supernatural, gained considerably by drawing on these psychiatric observations and theories. The fantastic tale, in particular, exploited the supernatural and psychiatry in equal parts, inextricably fusing mystery and the unknowable with scientific "truth" (see Ponnau; Banquart; and R. B. Gordon, "Le Merveilleux scientifique"). Thanks to the strangeness of the double personality and its link with somnambulism, it quickly found a place in the popular imagination.

At the end of the nineteenth and at the beginning of the twentieth centuries, doubling is everywhere. "One becomes a stranger to oneself, witnessing as a mere spectator what one says and does" (Bergson, *L'Enérgie spirituelle* 110). The philosopher is not describing the alienation of madness, but a phenomenon that nearly everyone has experienced: déjà vu. Bergson conceives of memory in general as a "doubling [of] our real existence and its virtual image," for if one becomes conscious of the simultaneity of present perception and perception doubled by its memory, "the second makes us feel as though we're repeating a learned role, converts us into automatons, and transports us into a world of theater or of dream" (*L'Enérgie spirituelle* 136, 139). Memory, in fact, is always an instance of déjà vu, which we normally don't witness because it is "hidden" in the unconscious, but when it does surge up, it immobilizes the present into a tableau vivant (the popular nineteenth-century parlor entertainment to which I've already referred). Now look at the way a psychiatrist analyzes the same phenomenon: it is a "clearly pathological state" due to the character of self-alienation at the moment of déjà vu and due to its automatic nature (Janet, *Les Obsessions* 287). An extremely common, benign, and fleeting experience is swept into the maelstrom of pathological symptoms surrounding the Double that obsess the late-nineteenth-century French imagination. It is important to note that common conditions such as digestive problems, head congestion, and color blindness were all considered to be symptoms of hysteria by Salpêtrière doctors. The blurring of the border between normal and pathological conditions in the 1880s and 1890s made for a population that was (understandably) anxious about falling victim to the nervous disorders that they read about.[24] In the 1880s the experience of déjà vu was thought to emanate from two simultaneous perceptions in the cerebral centers, what Alfred Fouillée called a kind of "double vision" or "morbid echo and internal repetition." Théodule Ribot accounted for these simultaneous images by proposing that one was an hallucination, more intense than the initial perception, which was thereby pushed into the background with the effaced quality of a memory (in Bergson, *L'Enérgie spirituelle* 117).

Double consciousness is a trait that was considered common to all cases of hysteria in the nineteenth century. From midcentury on, there was a proliferation of cases of double consciousness. Dr. Alfred Binet stated simply: "The hysterical subject is doubled; he possesses two distinct consciousnesses; and one of these consciousnesses accurately perceives all the excitations that have been impressed upon the anesthetized region" ("Hysterical Eye" 36). At the end of the century, Pierre Janet observed "a more or less pronounced feeling of doubling in nearly all of [his] patients and could present a hundred examples" in his book on obsessions and psychasthenia (*Les Obsessions* 312). The two "lives" of Dr. Eugène Azam's hysterical patient Félida, the paradigmatic case study in double consciousness, are separated by a brief swoon or loss of consciousness: when she wakes in the new "existence" she "has become another person. Her disposition is changed" and her intelligence and feelings are different from those in her primary state. During the twenty-nine-year course of this illness, Félida often experienced periods while in the somnambulistic state that were similar to insanity. She is "really two moral persons" having "two egos" and "two alternating mental lives" (Binet, *Altérations* 20–21). "The old mesmerists were quite right when they described [this new mode of mental existence] as a second personality" (80). The second personality in these patients was always dramatically different from their "everyday" existence, and events that occurred in the second state of consciousness were not remembered. Gilles de la Tourette observed a patient whose personality and memory alternated according to modifications in his sensory-motor apparatus (due to stimuli by the doctors). In somnambulism, modifications of the personality, character, and emotional tone most frequently have their source "in unconscious sensations" (Binet, *Altérations* 80). Visual and auditory disturbances are common symptoms of hysteria, as are, oftentimes, anomalies in taste and smell; the different characteristics of these sensations, combined with unusual internal sensations, contain "all the elements of a new ego. . . . 'I have lost the consciousness of my being; I am no more myself.' Such is the formula that is repeated in the majority of the observations. Others go even further, and at times, fancy themselves double. . . . 'I seem to possess one ego which thinks and another which acts'" (Ribot, *Diseases of Personality* 97). The 22 February 1886 *Bulletin de la Société de Psychologie physiologique* published an observation of handwriting changes in an hysterical patient with induced somnambulism who was first told she was Napoleon, and then told she was a twelve–year-old child. Two very different graphological styles resulted, in harmony with the changes that took place in her physiognomy and attitude (in Binet, *Altérations* 79). Double consciousness, as I've said, was equated with the somnambulistic state, whether "natural somnambulism," somnambulism occurring in the course of an hysterical attack, or induced (hypnotic) somnambulism. (Spontaneous hysterical attacks, according to Charcot, are produced by *autosuggestion*, where an idea is split off from the rest of the self.) In 1891 Alfred Binet was still forced to admit that, although the psychological phenomena concerning somnambulism and double personality were fairly well known, the *nature* of the physiological phenomena that occur during those modifications "is quite unknown," and that "these phenomena of consciousness that we describe are often vague [and] indefinite" (*Altérations* 79):

> In reality, the unconscious being obeys . . . a purely mechanical activity, born of the violent dissociation between the higher centers of perception (which have been annihilated) and the secondary or motor centers. It is the *automatism*, the unconscious activity, . . . that escapes all directive action. The principle groups subject to this "impulsive" activity are epileptics, hysterics, and some somnambulists. (Ernest Mesnet, in Azam 123–24)

As Théodule Ribot noted, "The hypnotized subject is an automaton" (*Les Maladies* 140). Mental automatisms observed in epileptics by Hughlings Jackson "come from an excess of activity in the lower nervous centers which substitute themselves for the higher centers or directing centers. This is but a specific instance of the generally observed physiological rule that the power of motor excitation in centers of nervous reflex augments when their connection to the higher centers is broken" (in Ribot, "Conditions organiques" 59–60). As I stated earlier, this radical division between the higher and the lower faculties (reason, judgment, and will as opposed to sensation, motor response, instinct, and automatisms) preoccupied philosophers, psychologists, and physiologists alike from midcentury on. The higher faculties are altogether abandoned as the lower faculties take over the hypnotized or hysterical person. In *L'Automatisme psychologique*, Pierre Janet, following up on Binet's 1887 discovery, clearly saw that whether one looked at somnambulism, anesthesias, hallucinations, or automatic writing, one was forced to admit the existence of a "second consciousness that persists under normal thought" (in Chertok and Saussure 4). Janet enumerated the essential aspects of the self given over to automatisms: distraction, instinct, habit, and passion (*L'Automatisme psychologique* 432). Like the cabaret and café-concert performance style that will be analyzed in Chapters 3 and 4, the shows of magnetizers (inducing a state of "complete suggestibility," which gives free rein to the automatisms of the unconscious), to be considered in Chapter 2, deliberately appealed to the lower faculties. These were "popular" entertainments, "low" as opposed to "high" culture, and that has less to do with the proportion of proletariats in the public than it does with their direct appeal to the body, and with the attendant implications that the direct appeal to the body carried in psychiatric theories of the new physiological psychology. Somnambulism and doubling, theatrical subjects well before 1800, would become familiar behavior to nineteenth-century audiences. They would provide scenarios and visions for the "legitimate" theater, for pantomime ("Pierrot magnétiseur"), for the magic theater (Méliès's "Catalepsie et gendarmerie"), for the Grand Guignol (*Obsession*), the cabaret, and cinema well into the twentieth century. Moreover, Darwinian and Spencerian theories of biological and social evolution were joined to these psychiatric views in nineteenth-century France to create a vast phantasmatic realm in the popular imagination as well as in intellectual circles. The double would therefore be the animalistic, instinctual self, the beast in man; this darker half would characterize the discourse and symptomatology of degeneracy. Alongside Evolution's backward course into Degeneration, Anne Harrington poses a similar discourse in Broca's "polarized brain," stigmatizing the right hemisphere with these ills: remaining in an uneducated, animalistic state, it "was responsible for various dark psycho-physiological processes out of human conscious control: sensibility, emotion (hysteria, passion, criminal impulsiveness), and trophic, instinctual life" (Harrington 102).[25] As I have indicated, my study takes as its model one of the other two European neurological concepts of duality: the hierarchical model of the nervous system, with its higher and lower faculties. It is the model referred to by the medical researchers and clinicians who are most important to this book: Pierre Janet, Charles Féré, and Alfred Binet, as well as being the model that passed into familiar parlance in the period (see Chapter 3). It was thought that since, for centuries in the development of species only the lower forms of mental activity had existed, with the higher forms being recent additions, the latter were the first to disintegrate in the nervous system when the human organism was attacked by epilepsy or hysteria. Hughlings Jackson wrote in 1873 that the nervous system is in fact "a hierarchical integration of levels of evolution" (in Delay 86). Ontogeny recapitulates phylogeny; thus, automatisms signal evolutionary regression and degeneration. In an age when the sexual and purely physical aspects of the human being are repressed and feared,[26] hypnotism, exhibiting the division between reason and will on the one hand, and base animal instincts or sensations on the other, very logically becomes a subject of curiosity and fascination. Moreover, as the advances of technology elevate the idea of progress through the machine, the purely physical or animalistic side of human beings becomes more and more a subject to be explored in science and in literature. The paradoxical exchange or confusion between the two, though, was not ignored by writers and filmmakers: two wonderful and well-known examples of the oscillation between the animal and the machine in the human body and psyche are found in Zola's *La Bête humaine* and Lang's *Metropolis*. The importance for mass spectacle of this strange mechanical beast that nineteenth-century psychiatry called the corporeal unconscious will become clearer when we look at gestural language in magnetizers' shows in the next chapter, and subsequently at gesture in the cabaret.

CHAPTER TWO

Imitation and Contagion: Magnetism as Popular Entertainment

"Society is imitation, and imitation is a species of somnambulism."

— GABRIEL DE TARDE, *The Laws of Imitation*

Reading descriptions and looking at photographs of somnambulists in magnetizers' shows and of hysterics in the *Iconographie photographique de la Salpêtrière*, one can't help but be struck by the resemblances. This in itself is not surprising: many poses that psychiatrists suggested to their patients were typical of those that magnetizers commanded their somnambulists to take—for example, that of the rigid body stretched between two chairs, held up only at the neck and heels (other reasons for these similarities will later become clear). Even without the aid of a psychiatrist, the hysteric in the period of "passionate poses" in the major attack "is, in reality, a spontaneous somnambulist" (Regnard 243). What is arresting is the precise resemblance between the gestures and poses of hysterics and somnambulists and the gestures and poses of performers in the cabaret, in the theater, and in early cinema. The well-known "theatricality" of the hysteric has a specific as well as a general sense; not only is the hysteric always "dramatic," the poses s/he strikes are the same as those seen on contemporary stages. As mentioned in the preface, Sarah Bernhardt visited the Salpêtrière wards: this visit took place in 1884 as la Divine Sarah prepared for the mad scene in *Adrienne Lecouvreur*. What is more, the Salpêtrière Hospital literally put on shows for the crowds of fashionable Parisians who flocked to the lessons of Dr. Charcot. It is for these reasons that it is important to examine spectatorship in the period in light of the dynamics of somnambulism and hysteria orchestrated by magnetizers in their shows. As the celebrated comic monologuist Ernest Coquelin recalled, at the circus the spectator "is grabbed by the eyes, by the huge breath of physical pleasure that circulates, by muscular life in all of its radiating power . . . doesn't all that magnetize the crowds in a healthy way?" (*La Vie humoristique* 73–74). As I will argue here, the *suggestive* and magnetic power of gesture and movement takes on a previously unsuspected dimension in popular entertainment. Clearly, in a medium like early cinema where the *only* currency is that of gesture (as Pascal Bonitzer put it), it is essential that we understand its impact on the spectator. As I mentioned in the previous chapter, animal instinct and the mechanical are joined in the body's automatisms ("animal" because of the nature of the instincts, "mechanical" because they surge up in an unconscious, automatic manner). Nowhere is this fusion seen more clearly than in somnambulism and hysterical gesture. In order to explore the dynamics at work in magnetism, somnambulism, and hysteria, one must be familiar with nineteenth-century theories of imitation. In the course of this familiarization, the reader will have a chance to see that these unusual, unconscious workings of the body have interesting implications for late-nineteenth- and early-twentieth-century spectacle and spectatorship.

The enthusiasm for hypnotism[1] in French medical circles dates from around 1882, and by 1885 theories surrounding hypnotism had begun to circulate widely among the general public. It was Dr. Eugène Azam who brought back hypnotism and used it as a treatment technique for hysterics (see Charcot, preface to *Hypnotisme*). After an initial enthusiasm among French doctors for Mesmer's animal magnetism (when Mesmer was forced out of Austria and experienced his well-known success in Paris salons), animal magnetism was discredited by the French medical academy in the 1830s. One of its proponents, Dr. Alexandre Bertrand, was nonetheless convinced that "the problems of magnetism . . . belong properly to psychology" (116).

Its resurgence as treatment, experimental, and diagnostic tool in the 1880s at the Salpêtrière and in the School of Nancy coincides in time with the period studied here.[2] In 1888 Azam, in the forefront of research on split personality disorders, or double consciousness, wrote: "Induced somnambulism is the form [of marvelous phenomena] that most fascinates and impassions [the public]" (347). Bergson wrote in *Le Rire* that "[even] uneducated minds can instinctively dimly sense" that some comedy has to do with "psychological science," namely hypnotism and imitation (46). Public shows of magnetizers and hypnotists in the 1880s and 1890s were simultaneously scientific demonstrations, supposed manifestations of spiritual phenomena, and popular spectacle. The vagueness of the border between magnetism as spiritual power and as psychological power, combined with the belief of some psychiatrists that public demonstrations by magnetizers all too often led to insanity, made for an impassioned debate around 1900.

In *Magnétiseurs et médecins*, Dr. Joseph-Rémi-Léopold Delboeuf defends public shows of magnetizers and hypnotists against the panegyrics of psychiatrists for whom science is merely the *pretext* for these theatrical exhibitions. Delboeuf, a Belgian, was a participant in the Nancy school, but was also a philosopher and mathematician who wrote on psychophysics in 1883.[3] The very same psychiatrists also used hypnotism in treatment and experiments (which were perhaps just as deleterious to their patients' well-being) but, of course, they did not do so under a fairground tent or in theaters. And, since their *aims* (scientific knowledge as opposed to entertainment) were supposedly quite different, they intended to keep the distinction between the theater and the amphitheater as sharp as possible. Like Charcot and Azam in France, a Swiss psychiatrist, Dr. Ladame (in a book entitled *La Névrose hypnotique ou le Magnétisme dévoilé* [*Hypnotic Neurosis, or Magnetism Unveiled*]), denounced the outbreak in several large Swiss towns of a sort of *manie hypnotique active* in the wake of the public demonstrations of magnetizers. The practices of "*travelling magnetizers and charlatans*" are held responsible for the outbreak of severe problems of the nervous system and especially of symptoms found in hysteria. Indeed, many spectators had recurrent experiences of catalepsy, hallucination, or other symptoms of hysteria long after the magnetizer and his somnambulist had left town, and several people in France and Switzerland had to be admitted to hospitals as a result of these shows. Ladame reports that in February 1881 he witnessed members of the audience fall spontaneously into hypnotic trance during a conference he was giving on the subject; these young men had been hypnotized a few months earlier by the century's most famous magnetizer, Donato (in Delboeuf, *Magnétiseurs et médecins* 45). Donato was in fact charged with several grave incidents by Dr. Cesare Lombroso: a hypnotized army officer nearly became mad; a young man became an imbecile; a train employee was taken with convulsions and "*folie furieuse*."

What makes doctors especially indignant is that the most celebrated magnetizers are "solely concerned with the desire *to amuse or entertain the public*, [by producing] phenomena having the appearance of the supernatural (*le merveilleux*)." They are the possessors of "une force fascinatrice *surnaturelle*" (Ladame, in Delboeuf 11; italics mine). Notice that Ladame debunks the capability of the magnetizer to produce supernatural phenomena, yet the fascination exercised is itself supernatural. This confusion arises from an important shift: belief in spiritual phenomena has diminished, but this same vector of belief producing awe and fear has been redirected to technologies and instruments that transform perception and to individuals capable of controlling our perception and our body. The demonstrations of induced catalepsy are one example; magnetic transfer of hysterical anesthesia from one side of the body to another at the Salpêtrière—or transfers between individuals at La Charité Hospital—is another. It almost seemed as though science was going the supernatural one better. Azam ruefully refers to the faddish attraction that experiments like these enjoyed among the public.

"Magnetic fluid" is composed of electricity and magnetic attraction;[4] it effects a mutual influence between heavenly bodies, the earth, and living beings, and it accounts for the influence of the magnetizer's movements or thoughts on another person. The magnetizer's power resides in the "superabundance of magnetic fluid [which] spreads into his surroundings and penetrates people"; in the "domination of his will . . . in his imperious gesture, in his superhuman tenacity [regarding his goals]" (Roche 42, 48). "Will develops the magnetic fluid" and magnetizers use it constantly; "they exercise suggestion on their entourage: one feels, guesses and executes this will without word or gesture entering in" (49).[5] According to Dr. Ladame:

> The hypnotized Subject is delivered up as a spectacle to the crowd which is alive with unhealthy emotions, . . . abruptly put under a spell of fascination, hallucinated to complete madness . . . at the risk of

> compromising his mental or physical health. . . . Public hypnosis is the clinic of mental illnesses transported onto the stage *to amuse and entertain* the public. [These shows are] *the display of symptoms of insanity and of major neuroses whose comic character is exploited.* One surrounds [the phenomena] with *frightening and mysterious atmosphere* suitable to . . . *throw terror into weak brains.* (in Delboeuf 40–41; italics mine).

Aspects of insanity and hysteria can make the public laugh, but the last laugh will be on them when the aftereffects of these entertaining tableaux are felt. The supernatural character of the spectacle is what terrifies them, not (apparently) mental illness. Yet, as Azam wrote, it is precisely in watching shows like these that appear *merveilleux*—and are both frightening and fascinating—that "the door is opened" in those predisposed individuals with "weak brains" to alienation and hysteria (353). "Insane asylums are peopled with unfortunate souls that the cult of the supernatural has made mad" (23); "religious excitation [creates a predisposition] that has an influence on the nervous system of many individuals" (Dagonet 20). One of the principal revelations of the Charcot school was to show that what had previously been taken for possession by the devil and other supernatural, religious, and convulsionary states (in or out of convents) were in fact cases of hysteria (see Goldstein for the anti-clerical import of this takeover by science). Manifestations of the supernatural in magnetism "amuse and entertain," like Robertson's phantasmagoria did and like the films of Georges Méliès soon would, but in the case of magnetism, it is absolutely clear that they also inspire fear, awe, and—in some—madness. Not all doctors are alarmed: Dr. Léon Tétard states in the January 1887 *Revue d'hypnotisme* that "hypnotic experiments can be of educational benefit to those who don't have the opportunity to witness experiments by competent doctors, [and that] they do not constitute the multiple dangers for public health and morality that have recently been pointed out" (in Delboeuf 20). Yet the very need for making this sort of affirmation allows one to gauge the weight carried—and the fears engendered —by the opposite view. Even popular manuals for amateur magnetizers contained warnings: catalepsy "is not without danger, and one is closer to a cadaver than one thinks. This phenomenon should thus only be produced as a last resort to convince the incredulous" (St.-Jean 51). Here is a warning against attempting hypnosis on hysterics. "Your suggestions could . . . cause an attack, either subsequently or immediately, that you might not be able to control" (Roche 116–17). Serious medical practitioners were more specific as to the reasons: "Hypnotic practices cause hysterical manifestations, in every aspect the same as those which occur spontaneously, manifestations such as artificial somnambulism, catalepsy, or automatisms" (Regnard 243). The great medical practitioner of suggestion, Alfred Binet, also warned of its dangers: "It causes very major and unpleasant nervous phenomena in some people, and in addition it gives subjects habits of automatisms and a servile attitude" (*La Suggestibilité* 1).

But what really angered the medical profession was its supposed debt to theatrical magnetizers: "It's ridiculous to claim that these showmen have guided Drs. Charcot, Dumontpallier, Mesnet, and Bernheim in their clinical studies on hysteria, hypnotism and somnambulism" (Ladame, in Delboeuf 11). However, the contrary is true: magnetizers can learn from psychiatrists. An 1887 lecture-demonstration by Donato favorably impressed a number of doctors present. The experiments were done "more scientifically, and we consider this as a direct result of the research of the School of Nancy, of the hospital of la Pitié, of the Salpêtrière" (in Delboeuf 20).

Donato distinctly conceived of his role as that of a popularizer of psychological science: he saw himself both as a man of science and as a man of the theater. His experiments are presented "from a scientific viewpoint and show that the remarkable effects of magnetic fluid belong solely to the domain of physiology" (Delboeuf 96). Yet, the extraordinary impression made on Donato's spectators, their utter astonishment, does not lessen with the demonstration that magnetism is not supernatural but scientific; if anything, people are even more dumbfounded, now that they know it is their own bodies which are the source and the seat of these bizarre phenomena. The presence of science doesn't completely eradicate prior images of the supernatural in the popular imagination. (Ladame writes that "an imagination exalted by the delirium of magnetic fever would easily see [the somnambulist] as an angel fallen into the devil's power" [in Delboeuf 97].) Magnetism, like early cinema, contains all the elements necessary to create a fusion of the two. That is how science comes to be endowed with the same *prestige* as the marvelous (and *prestige* is the key to describing and understanding the magnetist's powers). Here is a description of Donato and his somnambulist, Mlle Lucile, written by a Mr. Strohl for the newspaper the *Val-de-Ruz* (30 October 1880):[6] "She is as immobile as a statue. A 'pass' from the magnetizer along her spine makes her experience a violent contraction of every muscle. She falls onto the stage, as rigid as an iron rod." Members of the audience, curious to verify her condition, come up on the stage, and then two men pick her up, placing her head on one chair and the heels of her feet on a second chair. "She stays in that position for ten minutes like a plank of wood [and] Donato affirms that she can stay like that for hours on end. *Our readers know that one sees cases in medicine that are exactly the same*, following traumatic accidents that engender tetanus. A simple 'pass' suffices for her to regain the suppleness of her members" (in Delboeuf 97; italics mine). Her "colossal muscular force" in the state of "lethargic sleep" is demonstrated, when, in response to a non-verbal command from Donato—transmitted by thought only—she knocks a vigorous man to the ground and pulls apart another four men who try to block her path. Finally, the magnetizer communicates emotional and physiological states to her, which she lives out before the audience: ecstasy, fear, anger, sadness, joy, laughter, deafness. "The scene of ecstasy is truly moving: the somnambulist's face takes on an expression of melancholy that is so touching that one can notice an involuntary tear from many a female spectator" (98). An analogy between the somnambulist's expressive power and that of the actor begs to be made. It *was* made: we will soon have a chance to consider it here. The precise similarities with poses, expressions, and physical hyperesthesia in hysterical patients are striking. This must have been evident to almost every reader of the *Val-de-Ruz* newspaper for Strohl to have made the aside that "our readers know." If, in a small Swiss town in the year 1880, medical cases of hysterical tetanus were well known and could be visualized by readers, one can only imagine how widespread close familiarity with states of catalepsy and the effects of hypnosis on hysterical patients was by the late 1880s after hundreds of articles had appeared and sensational cases such as the 1890 trial of Gabrielle Bompart had been at the center of national controversy. (Bompart claimed to have committed the murder of her husband under hypnosis, specifically, while under the hypnotic spell of her lover.) While Bompart's case was the most highly publicized—like the O. J. Simpson case a hundred years later, it was called "the case of the century"—there were dozens of criminal cases in fin-de-siècle France whose defense relied solely on the plea of posthypnotic suggestion.

Other popular commands given to somnambulists or volunteers from the audience under suggestion were: hallucinating a bouquet of flowers to be smelled, a glass of alcohol or a noxious liquid to be swallowed, or a lover to embrace. Audience members were made to experience insect bites, or were suddenly transformed into persons of the opposite sex, into children, or into monkeys; physical difficulties were imposed, such as the impossibility of raising one's arm, opening one's eyes, or sitting down ("Your legs are stiff... stiff... very stiff... they are singularly stiff... you are paralyzed!" [Roche 109]). Inducing cataleptic rigidity is the most typical feat of magnetizers' demonstrations, despite St.-Jean's warning, cited earlier. (Despite the appearance of anesthetic rigidity, the somnambulistic state is characterized by enormous motor and emotional excitation, and this hyperesthesia is one more trait that somnambulists share with hysterics.) The handwriting of somnambulists could be made to change as they "became" different individuals. One of the most spectacular feats was to introduce a hypnotized subject into the cage of a wild animal. The otherwise staunch defender of stage hypnotism, Delboeuf, underlines that he was one of the first (in 1887) in Belgium to protest against "this stupid and *immoral* spectacle of the introduction of hypnotized people, or those pretending to be so, into the cages of wild and ferocious animals. . . . Such exhibitions have nothing in common with hypnosis but the name. You might just as well throw in front of a lion's maw—and the spectacle would be exactly the same—a legless man or a nursing infant" (Delboeuf 114). The wild animal "attraction" was responsible for having exhibitions of hypnosis and magnetism outlawed in many towns, as was the Bompart "case of the century," as well as the multitude of thefts and other crimes committed under hypnosis. Although sensational cases such as these didn't surface in the twentieth century, as recently as December 1994 in London, an "important matter of public safety" was brought before Parliament's House of Commons: the "unchecked mesmeric powers of reckless stage hypnotists, and the growing roster of unwitting victims they were claiming across Britain." Despite the 1952 Hypnotism Act in that country, which gave local governments the authority to ban shows that were indecent or dangerous, such as the hypnotist "suspending a rigid, cataleptic body between two chairs, like a wooden plank," there remain "adverse consequences which some people might suffer after participating in performances of stage hypnotism," according to the Home Office minister Michael Forsyth. For example, a stage volunteer in his twenties was told he was an eight-year-old child, and nine months later he was still behaving like one. A twenty-four-year-old woman was told that a powerful electric charge was surging through her body; that night, she suddenly and inexplicably died. More difficult to verify: the headline in a recent London tabloid, "Hypnotist Made Me Have Sex With a Doll" (William E. Schmidt, *New York Times*, 22 January 1995).

Ladame informs us that one of the favorite posthypnotic suggestions of nineteenth-century magnetizers was to have their subjects perform pantomimes in a busy public square. Pantomime is associated in the popular imagination with the hypnotic state because of its dreamlike, silent, slowed-down movements, but also because of its "cataleptic" poses. Pantomime was present in café-concert performances, and it has often been pointed out that it informs the gestural language of early cinema; what has been not been noted is its link to magnetizers' shows.

Ladame notes that people have always sought out "spectacles of madness," but he specifies that it is particularly in the present period "of outrageous realism in novels" that the "representation of *clinics of mental pathology* in novels is no longer enough [for those] who are thirsty for *morbid pleasures and emotions: they want to see this clinic on the stage*" (in Delboeuf 41–42; italics mine). And, I would add, only a few years later on the screen. Certainly, the spectacle of hysteria was frequent in contemporary novels (of the Goncourt brothers, Flaubert, Huysmans, Maupassant, Lorrain, Rachilde, Claretie), as was that of somnambulism (du Maurier's *Trilby*, Stoker's *Dracula*, the Salpêtrière psychologist and physiologist Charles Richet's *Possession* and *Soeur Marthe*).[7] Further, hysteria as spectacle existed in the Grand Guignol theater[8] just as it did in the weekly lessons of Charcot at the Salpêtrière; as we'll see in the next chapter, it spelled success in the cabaret and café-concerts. Magnetizers' shows were simply one more theatrical representation of hysteria, and Ladame is absolutely right to note this aspect of their popularity. Given the ubiquity of representations of hysteria in the period, it is important to underline Ladame's next warning: the pernicious effects can appear several months later, *brought on by public spectacles that remind the spectator of the magnetizer's show*. The effects range from violent hysterical attacks, convulsions, and insanity (*folie furieuse*) to somnambulism, imbecility, and relapse into the hypnotic state of fascination by the sight of any brilliant light (this would obviously include film screenings). Practitioners of magnetism proudly concurred that posthypnotic suggestion could occur long after the subject has received the suggestion: "an individual unconsciously carries out acts . . . days and even months later" (Roche 58). Like the suggestion that remained active in the mind so as to produce a delayed reaction, acts that the body performed under hypnosis could also recur. Medical research explained why this recurrence was probable. Suggested movements are impressed on the motor centers and, at the same time, paralyze the higher centers. As Binet's, Féré's, and Richet's experiments demonstrated, when a movement is directed to an organ or region of the body, the brain "remembers, for a long period of time afterwards . . . all the effects, sensations, phenomena and manifestations originally directed to it" (Galopin 403), hence the likely recurrence of the negative effects of spectacles comprising movements that the spectator unconsciously imitates. Corporeal memory figures in acting theory as well.

Many of Donato's "astonished spectators"—those who volunteered as subjects and those who later experienced hypnotic effects—must have been "predisposed to hysteria," since "magnetic sleep is a particular nervous state [produced in] individuals with a great nervous sensibility, and particularly in hysterical women" (Delboeuf 94). Some doctors are more emphatic: the magnetizer's "medium" is simply "a sick person, an hysteric in the midst of an attack" (Galopin 403). Dr. Azam described the dangers of hypnosis in similar terms. The "clever *metteurs en scène*" of the shows take advantage of the public's credulousness because this public is "in general composed of believers and impassioned, emotional people whose nervous system is highly excitable." The exhibition of mentally disturbed subjects "has or can have deplorable results" because *the sight* of the extraordinary phenomena of hypnosis or suggestion, interpreted by someone skilled in exploiting them, only develops their tendencies" (354; italics mine). This belief—that the mere viewing of pathological or abnormal behavior will result in a similar pathology in the viewer—was, as we will see, widespread. Its importance for spectatorship in the period is crucial, yet it has not been taken into account in reconstructions of spectators' experience.

Meanwhile, Back in the Hospital Laboratory

The feats and poses taken by the somnambulist are exactly the same as those described by psychiatrists in observations of hysterics. Drs. Binet and Féré had noted that a simple gesture on the part of the psychiatrist sufficed for the hysteric to unconsciously adopt a pose, and facial expressions of sadness, joy, disdain, or fear appeared to be the direct *result* of certain positions of the body. (From around 1870, a more generalized scientific belief existed in France, Germany, and America that the body produces or intensifies the emotions it exhibits: we are sad *because* we are crying [see Fechner's *Ästhetik*; James; Bergson, *Essai*]). The experimenters have the patient hold an arm aloft and rigid (for up to one hour and twenty minutes), then watch the subject automatically repeat a gesture (up to 100 times!) or remain extended across the tops of two chairs. They also note a tendency for unconscious repetition to follow a movement by nervous reflex. Incessant gestural repetition, as we will see, will become a mainstay of cabaret and early film comedy. Other doctors amused themselves by making the patient hear the sound of bells, songs, fanfares, lift imaginary weights. These hallucinations are ordinarily violent, and as vivid as would be real sensations. "Dr. Bernheim makes a woman drink water and tells her that it is champagne," but this pleasant feeling doesn't last: he then informs his cataleptic patient that it was in fact ammonia! (*De la suggestion* 34). Dr. Bernheim "makes [the subject] attend an imaginary concert, smell specific odors, see animals, etc." (33–35). Music, in these experiments as in the novel *Trilby* considered later in these pages, is a particularly effective tool for making patients act out the emotions suggested. The doctor makes a gesture of fright as though seeing a wild animal, and the patient's body and expression imitate that fear; he suggests the idea of Paradise and the patient sees the Virgin and the saints. "Whether the subject is religious or profane, S . . . embroiders on the theme she's been given; that is because she has a vivid imagination and has read a great deal" (Bernheim, *Recueil* 221). Doctors are not immune to the fascination that the same images inspire at public shows of magnetizers. Enjoyment of the exploits and antics they themselves dream up for their patients is implied in these words of Dr. Charles Richet: the hypnotized subject offers "a curious spectacle." One that some patients are eager to provide; a patient afflicted with

Figure 1. Pose struck under suggestion in cataleptiform melancholia, from *Nouvelle Iconographie de la Salpêtrière*, vol. 3 (1890), plate 21. Photo Bibliothèque nationale de France, Paris.

"cataleptiform melancholia" (see Figure 1), suspected by his doctors of simulation, exhibits the characteristic motor phenomena of hysterics, often in the form of muscular rigidity or cataleptic states. As soon as a doctor starts to place his arm in a different position, he appears to guess what he's supposed to do, and completes the movement himself. This is simply an excess of "zeal to imitate."

Humans were not the only subjects in psychological experiments in suggestion: at the 1889 Meeting of Physiological Psychologists, Dr. Danilewsky reported on his success in producing hypnosis in snakes, turtles, frogs, rabbits, birds, and shellfish.[9]

Somnambulism—involuntary or artificially induced by hypnosis—is, as I've said, intimately related to the phenomenon of nineteenth-century hysteria, since the hysteric's second self surfaces in episodes of what psychiatrists perceived as somnambulistic states; the characteristic trait in hysteria is in fact this division in consciousness, noted as early as the 1830s by Dr. Leuret and explored in detail by Binet and Janet. The ideas introduced into the subject's mind while under hypnosis become rooted there, idées fixes split off from the conscious personality "like a foreign body" (Charcot, *Leçons* 17 November 1888). This tendency leads to abnormal states of consciousness (later called "hypnoid states" by Freud and Breuer). Thus, hypnosis produces the same state as an hysterical attack. The same relationship that exists between magnetizer and somnambulist exists between the unconscious, split-off side of the hysteric's personality and the other parts of the hysteric's personality. The magnetizer and his somnambulist are two people who act as one; the hysteric is one person who acts as two. "I am as though doubled, I put on a show for myself."[10] And, just as the somnambulist is the "slave" of the magnetizer's wishes, the hysteric is at the mercy of his or her unconscious desires, instincts, and perceptions. Since a foreign idea isolated from the rest of the psyche can easily be implanted in their mind, people who are highly susceptible to hypnosis/suggestion are therefore either hysterics or potential hysterics. Dr. Richet characterized somnambulism as a neurosis, a physiological malfunctioning (*Recherches* 272). We have seen, too, that the somnambulistic trance induced in exhibitions by magnetizers often developed into hysteria and produced a "magnetic fever" and hysteria in the spectators. Somnambulism and, to a somewhat lesser degree, susceptibility to suggestion, were therefore aligned with pathology. Charcot, who used hypnosis from the late 1870s to the mid-1880s, stated categorically that it could be produced only in hysterics. The celebrated psychiatrist from Nancy, Hippolyte Bernheim, maintained on the contrary that suggestibility is a universal phenomenon. Spectators in the period were caught in a double bind: whether a universal phenomenon or an hysterical symptom, succumbing to suggestion is risky business. All of the above notions were widely circulated in the press and became a part of popular knowledge.

Actors, Somnambulists, and Hysterics

Hysterics are eminently hypnotizable, and the hypnotizable subject, s/he who is susceptible to hysteria, is also the best endowed to succeed in an acting career (and, not surprisingly, the most likely to be capable of having a hypnotic power of fascination over the spectator and, potentially, communicating hysteria to the audience). In fact, acting talent is often compared to hypnosis in the nineteenth and early twentieth century. In other words, the "personal magnetism"—and we must now take the expression literally—of the performer consists in the talent for suggestion, for eliciting a repetition and imitation of his/her gestures or voice. We saw that the somnambulist's "talent" or capacity for expression, like the hysteric's, is akin to that of great actors, as Donato's spectator's "involuntary tear" made clear. In symmetry to the somnambulist's expressivity is the magnetizer's "great talent for stage direction (*grand talent de mise en scène*), which greatly contributes to making these showings (*séances*) eminently agreeable and interesting" (Strohl, in Delboeuf 96). Film screenings in France, it should be noted, are still called *séances*, meaning a seating, or showtime, but still carrying the echo of a spiritual séance. Dramatic ability takes on incredible energy under the influence of hypnotic suggestion. The psychiatrist or hypnotist has only to suggest a type, a character, for the person to objectify it and make its existence a reality. "It is not like someone hallucinating who is spectator to the images that unfold before the eyes; *it is like an actor* who, having become insane, imagines that the drama s/he is playing is a reality, not a fiction, and that s/he was transformed . . . into the person s/he is asked to play" (Richet, "La Personnalité" 228, italics mine; also cited in Souriau, *La Suggestion dans l'art* 304). Along similar lines, Gabriel Tarde states that the hypnotized subject is "an excellent actor [since s/he] incarnates the personality suggested to him/her so profoundly that it enters into the heart, the character, and is expressed by his/her poses, gestures, and language" (216 n).[11] (Stanislavsky's method comes directly out of nineteenth-century psychophysiology: the actor *becomes* the thing and *transmits* the thought to the spectator.) Even without totally losing oneself in the role, the actor's "double consciousness" draws on the unconscious memory of repeated sensations and movements. Diderot's *Paradoxe sur le comédien* (first published in its entirety in 1830), informed by the philosopher's knowledge of physiology, emphasizes the memory of repeated sensations and movements in the double consciousness of the actor, which allows him or her to be simultaneously in the role and outside of it. The notion of a "remarkable doubling of the personality in actors" (Souriau, *Suggestion* 290) is inflected in a stronger way at the end of the nineteenth century. Intense emotions that arise in actors as their "double" takes over must be monitored by the self, which has momentarily stepped away, "watching the beast carry on and roar; . . . if s/he doesn't keep watch, s/he is lost" (293). In his article entitled "Reflections on Diderot's paradox," Binet shares the results of a questionnaire that he had sent to nine actors (including Coquelin cadet, Mounet-Sully, and Mme Bartet). The responses led him to refute the paradox, for when a good actor "incarnates the character within himself, he ceases to double himself, he becomes another, he becomes the character" (293). Artistic emotion, according to Mme Bartet, "produces the same physical effects in the organism as if one were experiencing them in one's own life. . . . The physical emotion I am plunged into by certain roles stays with me after I leave the stage" (289). In the fin de siècle, hypnosis was used by some actors to attain a trancelike concentration on their role, to release creative energies "without voluntary participation" as the play worked on the actor's "cerebral system" (Roach 180).[12] That is why descriptions of the most famous somnambulists of the nineteenth century could easily be mistaken for descriptions of the most famous actors. For Souriau, Richet, Tarde, Schiller, and Martersteig, somnambulists and actors are intimately related at the base of their personality.

Friedrich von Schiller, writing in Mesmer's heyday, insisted that the first duty of the actor is to forget who and where he is (this behooves the public as well), in order to prevent artificiality and exaggeration in the expression of passion. For "if I am truly moved, I have little need to adjust my body to the tone of the passion, indeed it would be difficult—even impossible—to repress the spontaneous movements of my members."

> The actor is, up to a certain point, in the state of a somnambulist, and I see between them a striking analogy. If the latter, although he appears to have no consciousness of what he is doing, can, in his nocturnal walks, when all his external senses are sleeping . . . , assure each of his steps with the most inconceivable precision, against a danger that would

> demand, awake, the greatest presence of mind, . . . No matter how great the actor's absence of perception (of which illusion alone makes him capable) shouldn't there remain, without his being conscious of it, just as with the somnambulist, a certain sense of the present that would lead him without difficulty along the abyss of exaggeration and inappropriateness? (830–31)

Richard Boleslavsky, in an acting manual dating from 1933, credits "the French psychologist, Théodule Ribot, [as] the first to speak of [unconscious memory]" in terms of a "memory of affects." It is this "special memory for feelings, which works unconsciously" that the actor must draw on (36). A more radical view of the actor's link to the unconscious was held by the journalist, medical doctor, and anti-modernist Max Nordau: "Actors are distinguished by a greater vigor of the automatic activity of their centers [and] can only give semi-conscious or unconscious emotions to the crowd" (*Psychophysiologie* 164). Moreover, Nordau sees a "complete coincidence of the clinical picture of hysteria with the description [in *Degeneration*] of the peculiarities of the fin-de-siècle public" (*Degeneration* 26). As exaggerated as Nordau's views may be, they are sometimes accurate reflections of the average person's perceptions. Yet, if an anti-theatrical prejudice would have it that performers are "sick,"[13] and if the anti-avant-garde, reactionary doomsayer of cultural degeneration would have it that their public is hysterical, performance of pathology is not synonymous with being ill. The paradox of the actor's dual consciousness or double personality is paradoxical in an additional way to the point of view I'm taking here: it is a trait shared with the great majority of hysterics, but in the case of performers it is what allows them distance and indemnity from the hysterical or otherwise disturbed character portrayed. There are notable exceptions, and the two states that are meant to be kept separate can fuse. Maurice Rollinat was one of these exceptions.

In 1879 Dr. Paul Grellety invited over some friends "who were eager to witness the magnetic experiments of Donato" (*Souvenirs de Rollinat* 10). Once this initial curiosity of theirs had been satisfied, the host presented them with an unknown singer-poet, soon to become a star of the Chat Noir cabaret and the toast of Paris: Maurice Rollinat. Both men were natives of the Berry region. Rollinat was, in fact, Grellety's patient. Like scores of artists of his generation, he was very interested in recent psychological discoveries. He attended Charcot's weekly lessons for two years, and in the last years before his death, hysterical, addicted to morphine, and interned in a psychiatric hospital, he consulted Dr. Gilbert Ballet (who specialized in male hysteria) and Dr. Paul Dheur (the author of a major work on hallucination). When Rollinat's volume of poetry, *Les Névroses*, was published, articles in the press attributed his own neurosis *to autosuggestion and to imitation*. Writing about "Rollinat's delirium," Dr. Charles Guilbert called it "a sort of auto-suggestion wherein Rollinat wanted to incorporate the feelings of another, [for example], Baudelaire" (Miannay 377). Here is Grellety's account of the effect Rollinat had on the group assembled at his home that evening in 1879: "I see their astonished expressions listening to Rollinat and his friends . . . take turns emitting their strange elucubrations. . . . The astonished and dumbstruck public (frightening note: they are almost all of them dead) seemed to be wondering if they weren't victims of an hallucination" (ibid.). It interests me that Grellety spontaneously juxtaposed the two performers (the magnetizer Donato and the singer Rollinat) and their different but very similar forms of entertainment—as though a natural continuity existed between them. As I argue here, it does.

Imitation and Contagion

Other doctors vociferously warned of the danger of the contagion of somnambulism from magnetizers' shows, along with the danger of hallucinations from prestidigitators' shows in fairs, and of epilepsy *from the mere sight of an epileptic attack*. "There is no doubt that [epilepsy] can be engendered by imitation," and in fact this cause is perhaps more frequent than one might think: "as a result one must pay the most careful attention to preventing children, adolescents, and impressionable women from witnessing epileptic attacks" (Simon, *Hygiène* 24–25). One cannot easily imagine the fear that the idea of becoming an epileptic was capable of inspiring in the nineteenth century, since now the illness is no longer categorized as a form of insanity. In 1876, however, Dr. Henri Dagonet, who was a medical doctor at the Paris School of Medicine before becoming head doctor in 1867 at the Sainte Anne asylum in Paris, wrote that "the delirium of epileptics consists primarily of a maniacal state of excitement, sometimes extremely violent, of a somber character, which renders these patients very dangerous (521). In addition to having hallucinations and convulsions, "epileptics are irascible, subject to impulsive behavior that makes them dangerous. . . . The epileptic sees his intelligence decline each day, and in a more or less short period of time, he falls into a sort of stupor which usually ends in true dementia" (Bourneville, discussing Charcot's work, in Dagonet, 521). A doctor in the 1860s was even capable of stating that if a man with no previous mental pathology and who was not an alcoholic committed suicide or murder, one could say that the man was an epileptic in the midst of an attack (in Dagonet 514).[14] The belief that, through the automatisms of the nervous system, the onlooker's body would involuntarily mime epileptics, hysterics, and somnambulists therefore had very menacing overtones. The implications for spectatorship in a period where performances drew on the movements present in these pathologies need to be examined. In Chapter 1, we looked at some of the psychophysiological theories that explained this mimeticism.

To summarize these theories: according to research in the fin de siècle by physiologists and psychiatrists like Binet, Ribot, Henry, Richet, and Féré, the perception of movement causes a corresponding movement in the viewer's breathing, in the vascular system, in the eye muscles, and even down to a virtual recreation of the movement in the musculature of the body. At the same time as we perceive an object, our "internal machinery" re-creates it: "There is no idea without virtual, then real, movement" (Henry, *Esthétique scientifique* 2). What the nerves have assimilated continues to live in them, according to Ribot, Maudsley, and many others. A phenomenon similar to hypnotic suggestion would therefore take place not only in magnetizers' shows, but also in the cabaret and in film screenings. And this would hold true for all spectators, not only those who are "nervous" or "predisposed to hysteria." And that is precisely what researchers in the early twentieth century stated in regard to film audiences, as I will show in Chapter 5.

As Donald Crafton has written, "Fairy and trick films astounded viewers with their dreamlike fantasies, hallucinatory colors, and antirational special-effects photography. Spectators experienced near total identification with the screen images, as though they were witnessing real events" (*Emile Cohl*, 110).

One might put it another way: it is as though the spectators have been "put into a hallucinatory state by hypnotism [and their] brain [has become] a mirror faithfully reflecting the images that [the magnetizer] establishes in his own brain" (Roche 122–23).[15] I'm again citing from the manual on magnetism, but it only requires a slight change of angle to apply this to the effect produced by filmmakers like Cohl or Méliès. Their "astounded viewers" are the same "astonished spectators" of Donato's public shows of magnetism. The dynamic of identification is key in both forms of spectacle, because it will foster imitation. Hysterics, thus, are not the only ones whose bodies mime what they see: all our bodies do. In other words, the effect on the turn-of-the-century spectator was produced through a quasi-hypnotic experience and through internal physical mimicry, the body helplessly copying either the spasms and convulsions of epilepsy and hysteria, or the lethargy and trancelike catalepsy of somnambulism and hysteria.

A person magnetized by spectacle can, in turn, push his or her imitation of the performer so far that the person in turn "becomes a medium for imitation himself and magnetizes a third party, who, in turn . . . and so forth" (Tarde 91). Fear of contagion is the crucial link between hysteria and popular entertainment. Contagion occurs through the transmission of the electric shock or "jolts" (*secousses*) from performer to spectator, and this is achieved through the miming of hysteria.

Extreme physical reactions and mimetic gestures in spectators are tied to hypnotism and magnetism in journalistic reviews of popular spectacle. The can-can causes "more than one [spectator to] stick out his tongue and twist his arms craving more, *hypnotized* by the hectic transports" (Edgar Baes, in Lebensztejn 69; emphasis mine). Mimes want to render the public "delirious . . . totally overwhelmed (*bouleversé*), the nerves twisted. . . . You would have said that the spectators were *a troupe of hysterics suddenly hypnotized*" (Richepin, *Braves gens* 501; emphasis mine). "Come find a spasm at the scientific-magnetic-spiritist spectacle reads the poster's invitation to the "Cabaret of Death" *Le Néant* (Malthête-Méliès, *L'enchanteur*).[16]

Dr. Augustin Galopin had the magnetic power of the performer in mind when he warned against the hysteria engendered in the public by singers and actors. First of all, actors are "bundles of nerves" in whose ranks one finds the greatest number of male hysterics (125). Artists then "communicate to their fellow citizens an electro-magnetic spark from the incandescent foyer that consumes and devours [them] so quickly" (126). Galopin gives an example of "hysterical contagion" in a theater in Metz (128), and goes on to state in the concluding section of the book that "hysterical contagion is demonstrated and proven by science and by the facts" (391).[17] Doctors with reputations considerably more tested than Galopin's even believed that it was possible to communicate varied neuropathic states *at a distance* from a person who was awake to a person under hypnosis" (Jules-Bernard Luys, in Gauchet 203 n. 15). Accounts and studies of *cures* at a distance were not at all rare in the 1870s and 80s.

"Social mimeticism . . . impels us [to imitate those who surround us]. . . . A form of madness by imitation exists. There are epidemic sicknesses of the mind just as there are of the body" (Regnard x). These sicknesses make up the title of Dr. Regnard's 1887 book: *Les Maladies épidémies de l'esprit: Sorcellerie, magnétisme, morphinisme, délire des grandeurs*. "The acts of laughing, yawning, spread with an irresistible pull (*entraînement*) in a gathering. The influence of imitation as cause of convulsive epidemics is linked to this fact. There are few doctors who have not observed examples of hysterical contagion; medical literature abounds in facts of this sort" (Dagonet 19).

> The frequent sight of certain people pushes one, little by little, to reproduce their poses and gestures. Tics are contagious, external qualities and defects transmit themselves, and even thoughts are modified by contact with certain individuals. How can these mysterious influences and reciprocity of action be explained? Authors have held that, in nature, the molecules of all bodies are animated by incessant vibrations, and that in subjects who are placed in identical conditions, the two nervous systems end up vibrating in unison. (20)

This theory is similar to the theory of animal magnetism, only here the notion of a universal fluid is replaced by the notion of universal vibration. In the popular imagination, from the 1840s on, there was an amalgamation of notions about galvanic electricity and notions about animal magnetism (see note 4), and these ideas link magnetizers' shows, cabaret and caf'conc' spectacle. Some psychiatrists and physiologists believed that the "first basis of our existence [was] animal electricity" and that "a brain composed of defective batteries . . . produces sparks and shocks (*secousses*) that bring about insanity by . . . the violent combustion of the phosphorescent element of the cerebral pulp" (Galopin 116). By 1890, however, it would be generally accepted that the influence causing the irresistible impulse to imitation originates in the unconscious mind, and not the "cerebral pulp."

The universal trait of imitation continued to be considered as one of the primary earmarks of hysteria. Dr. Pierre Briquet was the first to underline that the faculty for imitation is one of the privileged domains of hysterics; it is an expression of the somnambulistic personality. The 1849 *Journal of Magnetism* describes a young somnambulist who had only to be put into contact with someone in order to "immediately become that person's double. She mirrors their gestures, pose, voice, and repeats their every word. If they sing, she sings; if they laugh, she laughs" (Binet, *Altérations* 152). According to Gilles de la Tourette, the hysteric's passion for imitation can be seen in "the eagerness with which he yields to all the suggestions of writers and artists" (in Nordau, *Degeneration* 26). This observation corroborates the idea of a form of reciprocity between hysteria and artistic representation. Imitation is the means by which hysteria is spread, since an hysteric has only to see a gesture in order to unconsciously imitate it (Briquet 371). It was, in fact, when the non-psychotic epileptics and hysterics were housed together at the Salpêtrière that hysterics took on traits of epilepsy because of their tendency to imitation, as Ilza Veith points out in *Hysteria: The History of a Disease* (230–31). The most imitated acts in the epilepsy/hysteria ward at the Salpêtrière were convulsive movements and hysterical yawning (yawning continuously for several hours or days). Yet, according to the Henry, Tarde and others, the phenomenon of imitation is not limited to hysterics: *the sight of any gesture makes us want to imitate it*. "There is an innate tendency to imitation in the nervous system" (Maudsley, in Tarde 95). Here is another case where an accepted fact of abnormal psychology or physiology is, in reality, a general condition.[18] Hippolyte Bernheim wrote that "every suggested idea [tends to] become act . . . movement, sensation, emotion, organic act" (*De la suggestion* 27). Gustave Le Bon, the widely read psychologist and former doctor in the French Army, took up this notion of the transformation of ideas into acts when he characterized the individual in a crowd as dominated by the unconscious personality: "He is no longer himself, but an automaton" (19). "Contagion is a phenomenon . . . that must be linked to hypnotic phenomena. . . . Having lost his conscious personality, [the individual] obeys all the suggestions of the operator [who has hypnotized him]" (17–18). In addition, the crowd gives out a "magnetic influence." "With the brain paralyzed, the subject becomes the slave of all the unconscious activities that the hypnotist directs as he pleases. The conscious personality has vanished" (18). Le Bon draws on research in nervous reflex, on hypnosis, and on microbiology: "By their power, which is solely destructive, [crowds] function like microbes that activate the dissolution of enfeebled or dead bodies" (12). One begins to understand why the figures of the automaton and the somnambulist appear so frequently in mass spectacle and novels in the period: they are a mirror of the fears that these theories inspired in the general public.

When Trilby, the most well-known fictional nineteenth-century somnambulist, becomes a performer, she in turn magnetizes the awestruck crowd: the sympathetic vibrations that run between Trilby and her spectators affect their breathing and their heart rates. Some become hysterical, and the hero falls into an hypnotic trance. In the novel, which is studied at the end of this chapter, the site of contagion is designated as a popular spectacle.

Binet wrote that "gesture, pose . . . often suffices to produce irrestible suggestions" (*Suggestion* 10). Tarde asked: "Why should we be astonished, after all, by the unilateral and passive imitation of the somnambulist? A given act performed by any one of us gives those who witness it the more or less unconscious idea to imitate it" (86). Arm and leg movements are especially contagious, but so is vocal intonation. Tarde gives the examples of a gentleman who imitates the slang and swagger of a proletariat, and the *femme du monde* who reproduces the intonations of an actress or singer (94). It seems clear to me that these instances would notably occur after coming out of a cabaret or caf'conc' spectacle. (Anyone who has not been able to resist trying out a few dance steps on exiting a Fred Astaire and Ginger Rogers movie will understand and agree with nineteenth-century physiology and with Tarde.) Citing Maudsley, Tarde notes that the somnambulist is capable of unconsciously reading the mind [of the person who is exercising the hypnotic suggestion] *by an unconscious imitation of the pose and expression of the person whose muscular contractions s/he copies instinctively and precisely*" (85; italics mine). Tarde's description of the magnetizer's *prestige* (charismatic force and power over others) also calls to mind what we've already observed as a trait of actors and performers in general: "In the magnetized Subject there is a potential force of belief and desire immobilized in memories of all kind, asleep but not dead . . . which the magnetizer has the power to open up" (85).[19] We are magnetized by what astonishes and captivates us, according to Tarde. For example, someone from a rural area arriving in Paris for the first time is "struck with a stupor comparable to the state of catalepsy. . . . In this state of attention so exclusive and strong, of imagination so strong and passive, they . . . fall under the magical charm of their new milieu" (91). Moreover, even sophisticated Parisians living in "an intense and varied society that furnishes spectacles and concerts" are subject to the torpor and hyperexcitability that characterizes somnambulism: "their mind, simultaneously drowsy and more and more overexcited, I repeat, turns into a somnambulist's. That is the mental state proper to many urbanites. The movement and noise of the streets, the store displays, the frenetic and impulsive agitation of their existence, have the effect on them of magnetic passes" (ibid.).

The alternation between lethargy and agitation seems to be characteristic of Second Empire cabaret audiences in the 1860s and 1870s (just as it is of somnambulists and hysterics): "The general physiognomy of the [café-concert] audience is a sort of troubled torpor: in our day, these people are only alive when they're shocked, shaken up (*ne vivent plus que de secousses*) and the big reason for the success of certain 'artists' is that they give a stronger shock" (Veuillot 150). There is an extraordinarily frequent recourse to the word *secousse*, shock, in describing the effect of cabaret performances on the spectator. Like the public shows of magnetizers whose powerful ill-effects can appear several months later, the "epileptic" movements of cabaret performers described in the following chapter can foster unconscious imitation for some time afterward.

Paul-Max Simon, after signaling the dangers of witnessing an epileptic attack, goes on to write that "sometimes hysterical attacks due to imitation [occur] in such a great number of subjects that the word *epidemic* has been used with some justification." The spread of mental illness, in 1881, is "more noticeable each day" (*Hygiène* 26). Among the supposed causes for its spread were, we've seen, magnetizers' shows, the sight of an epileptic attack, and some theatre performances. The barricades of the 1871 Paris Commune were also judged to be a breeding ground for hysteria. Even magic shows put on by fairground performers where "the imagination is struck too vividly" [are] an all-too-frequent cause of convulsions and subsequent forms of nervous illness" (48). Moreover, the "contagion of mutual example" is a fact of life in social situations, especially when people experience certain desires and beliefs together—for example: "the visual or auditory *sensation felt in the theater in the midst of an attentive crowd at the same spectacle*. . . . The intensity that desire or belief attains in the individual when it is felt by everyone" around him/her is enormous (Tarde 158), and the disintegration of individuality is produced "from underneath" (xv). Thomas Mann gives us a dramatic depiction of the phenomenon of contagion in *Mario the Magician*. The "satanic figure" of the hypnotist in this short story, whom the narrator qualifies as "the most powerful hypnotist I've ever seen," is a "deformed being." His physical abnormality and pathological gait will often reappear as traits of magnetizers and of comics in cabaret and early cinema. "For now he made them dance . . . and the dancing lent a dissolute, topsy-turvy air to the scene, a drunken abdication of critical [judgment] . . . lank limbs flying in all directions. Other recruits were not long in coming forward. . . . The jerking and twitching of the refractory youth's limbs had at last got the upper hand [as he] joined the row of puppets on the stage" (440–42).[20]

The "drunken abdication" of critical judgment and accompanying abandonment to automatic gestures (i.e., impulse and instinct)[21] are precisely what late-nineteenth- and early-twentieth-century audiences avidly seek—and vicariously find—in the cabaret, in pantomime, in Grand Guignol, and in early film comedies.[22] Their bodies, impelled to imitate other bodies, rediscover "the pleasure of muscular life" that Coquelin spoke of and *this* is what magnetizes them.

Trilby

The best-selling novel of the Victorian period was a melodramatic love story about magnetism. The magnetizer was named Svengali and his somnambulist, Trilby; their names became synonymous with these figures. Even today, people who have never heard of the novel and know nothing about magnetism or hypnotism recognize the name Svengali. Similarly, the commonly used expression "to make a pass" derives from magnetism, and knowing this casts a rather different light on it. The bilingual and binational George du Maurier wrote *Trilby* in 1894. It first appeared in installments in *Harper's Magazine*, and the same year was published in a volume by Harper and Brothers. It was adapted several times for the theater and three times for the screen (in 1922, 1931, and 1954).[23] It not only offers a dramatized "case study" of the double consciousness of a somnambulist, but a representation of spectatorship in relation to it. The setting is nineteenth-century Bohemian Paris, portions of the dialogue are in French, and the diabolical origin of the magnetizer's power is represented by Svengali's dark Otherness and extremely libidinal character—clearly identified in the novel with his Jewishness. The producers of all three film versions correctly perceived that the main character was not Trilby, and correspondingly entitled the film *Svengali* (the 1931 American film version directed by Archie Mayo and starring John Barrymore and Marion Marsh is analyzed in Chapter 5). From 1894 to 1900, the phenomenon of *Trilby*-mania held sway over Europe and America. "Svengali and Svengalism were lugged unceremoniously into all the petty details of our every-day life and talk."[24] The incredible popularity of the figures of Trilby and Svengali can only be ascribed to the equally overwhelming popularity and fascination of magnetism itself. Because these two fictional characters remain the paradigmatic examples for all future representations of the phenomenon, and because the text has everything to do with spectacle and spectatorship, the specific manner in which these roles are represented in the novel can tell us much about popular notions about magnetism and magnetizers.

Three young Englishmen, Taffy, Sandy, and "Little Billee," are artists living the stereotypical Bohemian Left Bank existence, surrounded by "the bygone mysteries of Paris" and fantasizing about "love, wickedness, and crime" as Englishmen in Paris will. Trilby is a young artist's model. Svengali and Gecko are musicians. Both are outsiders: Gecko is a Gypsy and Svengali is a sinister-looking man "of Jewish aspect . . . very shabby and dirty," whose black shoulder-length hair and beard framed a thin, sallow face (Du Maurier 12). When he plays the piano, the "susceptible audience of three [is] all but crazed with delight and wonder" (28). The tone is set for the important theme of spectatorship by this first depiction of it. The aspects of his musical performance are elaborated upon when "this truly phenomenal artist" plays a little pennywhistle: the "grace, power, pathos, and passion" resides in the music's capacity to *evoke and mingle* human emotions of tenderness and anguish. "Such thrilling, vibrating, piercing tenderness, now loud and full, a shrill scream of anguish, now soft as a whisper . . . more human almost than the human voice itself . . . perfection" (30). Now his audience is "dumbstruck." He is also responsible for Gecko's violin playing, since—Svengali explains—"it is as though it were *me* singing" when he plays the violin, "his adoring eyes fixed in reverence on his master" (29). Svengali's dialogue is often in French, transcribed to include a heavy German accent, literally imparting to the English or American reader the foreignness of both the arty, moral nonchalance of the Parisian milieu (dangerous for Bourgeois mores) and the German-Jewishness of the sinister magnetizer.

> [His] vicious imaginations . . . look tame in English print, [but they] sounded much more ghastly in French, pronounced in the Hebrew-German accent, and uttered in his hoarse, rasping, nasal, throaty rook's caw, his big yellow teeth baring themselves in a mongrel canine snarl, his heavy upper eyelids drooping over his insolent black eyes. (136)

In addition to the foreign layer of Svengali's Otherness, there is its *otherworldly* layer. To Trilby, Svengali sometimes seems a "powerful demon" and he weighs on her "like an incubus," yet she often dreams about him. Figures of the supernatural from the underworld of Hades easily impress themselves on the unconscious mind of the hysteric and become part of her dream world, according to writers like Regnard and Azam. Is this an early indication in the text that Trilby has an hysterical personality? That would explain her "particularly impressionable nature, as was shown by her quick and easy susceptibility to Svengali's hypnotic influence." Little Billee is called the "Captain of Purity," in contrast to Svengali, who is made to represent animality: dirt, earthiness, libido, sexual magnetism, immorality—all aspects of Low, subsumed under Svengali's Jewishness and its racially inferior status to the English, embodied in Billee. Yet even Billee is not immune to the power of the lower faculties over reason: not only is he "highly-strung, emotional, over-excitable, over-sensitive, and quite uncontrolled" (340), as we are told three-quarters through the novel, but when his family and friends conspire to prevent him from marrying Trilby, he has an epileptic seizure that ends in the "brain fever" of his "weak wandering wits" (204, 206). The additional information that he has "a drop or two" of Jewish blood perhaps "explains" not only Billee's nervous pathology but also his artistic genius, ironically linking him to Svengali.[25] Trilby interests Svengali because of the innate capacity of her vocal apparatus; innate (after all, her name already contains the trills that will later emanate from her), but unrealized, for she is tone-deaf. *He* of course, can sing *through* her body, and that is just what he will do. Trilby's physical complaints of migraine and neuralgia in the eyes (extremely common hysterical symptoms) play into his hands. He magnetizes away her pain with passes and counterpasses on her head, face, and neck, telling her that the pain has now gone into his body, inviting her to come see him whenever she suffers from these pains. It is only at this point in the novel (one-sixth of the way through) that the word "spellbound" appears, and it has not yet been explicitly used in relation to performer/spectator. The way has been prepared, though, by the emphasis on Svengali's incredibly powerful idea of the self: "I and nobody else, I Svengali, I, I, *I*!" (32). Just as the figure of the magnetizer has been suggested earlier, the figure of the somnambulist has already begun to take shape through Trilby's nervous symptoms and through other traits, for example, the doubling of a split personality. "Trilby speaking English and Trilby speaking French were two different beings" (94). The Scotch Trilby is absolutely "like a lady," in both mannerisms and speech, but enter a Frenchman and "a transformation effected itself immediately—a new incarnation of Trilbyness—so droll and amusing that it was difficult to decide which of her two incarnations was the most attractive" (96). She is demonstrative and flirtatious, always wanting "to be told one was fond of her," yet sometimes sullen and angry (ibid.); these are traits of the hysterical woman, according to nineteenth-century medical diagnosis. What is more, she is categorized as a "cancan dancing *quartier-latin grisette*." She also belongs to the realm of the Low, since she poses "naked and unashamed —in this respect an absolute savage" (98), mirroring the "primitive" cast of Svengali's sexuality. Her "singularly impressionable nature [is] shown by her quick and ready susceptibility to Svengali's hypnotic influence." Finally, the rigidly held poses of the artist's model remind one of the cataleptic poses of somnambulists and hysterics, as Elaine Showalter points out in a masterful introduction to the novel.[26]

Five years after Trilby's departure and Billee's illness, the three Englishmen return to Paris. There is an interesting interlude on foot fetishism when they return to their old studio and together contemplate the framed sketch of Trilby's left foot by Billee. The theme of High and Low comes into play in the way of a reversal: what is usually low—the foot—is in Trilby's perfectly formed case, an example of "high physical distinction, happy evolution, and supreme development" (19–20). There must be "no handing down to posterity of hidden uglinesses and weaknesses, and worse!" The intrusion of evolution theory, here at the outset of the novel, may at first seem peculiar but, in introducing the theme of High and Low, it leads very naturally into the period's concerns about a weak will and the subsequent upsurge of involuntary acts and unconscious or "savage" behavior in somnambulism, degeneration, and hysteria. In fact, all three men possess casts of Trilby's hands and feet. If this curious emphasis in the text inevitably evokes fetishism, it can also evoke the phantasy of separate body parts in hysteria that I've mentioned in relation to somnambulism. (Trilby later exclaims that, rather than "cut"—in the sense of "snub"—Little Billee, she would rather "cut [herself] into little pieces" [388]). The drawing is embellished by a poem that includes these verses (in French): "Poor Trilby . . . I'm her foot . . . I was a twin: what happened to my brother? Alas! Alas! Love has led us astray" (Pauvre Trilby, Je suis son pied. J'étais jumeau: qu'est devenu mon frère? Hélas! Hélas! L'Amour nous égara") (302). Interestingly enough, the talking foot recalls its double and laments their division into two separate entities. Logical enough for a foot, logical too for the hysterical or somnambulistic personality. And the fully developed somnambulist is about to make her appearance now in the novel.

The setting is the circus, the very setting I chose for the beginning of this chapter by citing Coquelin on the magnetized crowd at the Cirque d'Hiver. Svengali performs an overture, and then a woman appears whose "grey eyes looked straight at Svengali" (316). Trilby is now "la Svengali," and the mirroring or continuity through the communication of magnetic fluid between the two beings is now explicit. The three astonished friends experience something "so strange and uncanny about [seeing her there], so oppressive, so anxious" (317). This is an appropriate response to the figure of a somnambulist, as Freud remarks in his essay on "The Uncanny." The intonation of her voice is incomparably pure, and its seduction has a "strangely sympathetic quality" (318). The "great sensation" that Trilby produces in the audience—what makes her absolutely distinct from all other singers—is the communication of emotion that vibrates sympathetically like a sensation in each member of the audience. By mere tone and "slight, subtle changes in the quality of the sound—too quick and elusive to be taken count of, but *to be felt with, oh, what poignant sympathy*!" (321; italics mine).[27] The effect on Billee is even more sympathetic; he himself sinks into a somnambulistic trance state: "he believed himself to be fast asleep and in a dream" (ibid.). Trilby's phenomenal success as a performer is due to the power of magnetism to make the performer believe that she *is* the characters she incarnates, and second, to the utter concentration of interest the magnetizer commands through his somnambulist. It is not the melody, the lyrics, or the meaning of the song ("Au Clair de la lune"!), but rather "the spell of such a voice as that" (323), for the singer is "*Svengali*, and you shall hear nothing, see nothing, think of nothing, but *Svengali, Svengali, Svengali*!" (ibid.). The applause is "frantic," and when she sings "Chanson de printemps" by Gounod, the composer "seemed very hysterical" (324). Little Billee is blissful and his smile is "almost idiotic in its rapture!" (326). The emotions communicated in "Marlborough s'en va-t-en guerre" become personal anxieties for the spectators, affecting their breathing and heart rate, rendering them "almost sick with the sense of impending calamity"; at the conclusion, the audience of five or six thousand people is crying before it "bursts once more into madness" (326, 328). The finale is a vocalized rendition of Chopin's A-flat Impromptu that transmits "all the sights and scents and sounds that are the birthright of happy children, *happy savages* in favored climes" and those "who hear it feel it all, and remember it with her. *It is irresistible; it forces itself on you*" (330; italics mine). The effect of Svengali's art and the magnetic pull it exerts on spectators is summed up in the novel's concluding sentence: "hankering after the moon," as opposed to a "useful, humdrum, happy existence" (464). And so we see that the choice of the children's song "Au Clair de la lune," containing the somnambulist figure of the very *lunaire* mime, Pierrot, is not totally fortuitous. The somnambulist's capacities and talents are far greater than those of the ordinary mortal, and this is what thrills audiences: themselves caught in the magnetic spell cast by the performer, they participate in the "more than human" exploits and the intensity of emotion expressed by the somnambulist as performer. In *Trilby*, there is a confusion between the "divine and ineffable" beauty of Trilby's voice, and the childlike or primitive sensations that penetrate the spectator, which would normally be in contrast to a spiritualizing or elevating art that snubs sensation, and especially those linked to the primitive or low, the extraordinary and involuntary visceral experience in the body. Du Maurier wants it both ways. And the phenomenon of magnetism allows for the oxymoronic experience. Moreover, he wants to make it clear that this has to do with *psychopathology* and not the diabolical or otherwise supernatural realm previously underlined, so he now "cites" the reactions of music critics to la Svengali's Paris debut (Berlioz, Gautier, and Wagner ["Herr Blagner, as I will christian him"]). "Blagner's" review is a diatribe against "Svengalismus." What the composer objects to are the "*acrobatics* of the vocal chords, a *hysteric* appeal to *morbid* Gallic 'sentimentalismus'; [a] *monstruous* development of a *phenomenal* larynx, [and a] *degrading* cultivation and practice of the *abnormalismus* of a mere *physical peculiarity*" (334).[28] All of the words I've italicized belong to the vocabulary of nineteenth-century hysterical symptoms.

Little Billee feels jealousy, joined to feelings of awe for the couple's "genius" and "splendor," which maddens him to the point that he longs "for his old familiar brain disease to come back" (338). Indeed it does, but at a later point in the novel, when Trilby dies with "that ruffian's name on her lips . . . as if he were calling her from the t-t-tomb!" But it is in the character of Trilby that the novel's theme of nervous pathology is explored in the most accurate detail. In fact, the last seventy-five pages read like a case observation of double consciousness, illustrated by the double personality of the somnambulist. The differences between the two personalities are so great that *certain recognition* of Trilby only occurs when the three artists see a stereoscopic photograph of the singer with her prominently placed, sandaled left foot. After the spell has been broken by Svengali's sudden death, and Trilby has reverted to her original personality, the narrator refers to her as "*this* Trilby" (380). The "nervous shock" caused by the somnambulist's sudden awakening gives the impression that that she has gone mad. This impression is caused by the fact that she cannot remember anything connected with her somnambulist experiences, the periods in which she was "another person," but also because all of her energy seems to have been drained from her with the magnetizer's death. It is at this point in the novel that the somnambulistic episodes are recounted in flashbacks. However, it is only in the last six pages that the misunderstanding about Trilby's having "gone out of her senses" is dissipated by Gecko (456).

> I will tell you a secret. *There were two Trilbys.* There was the Trilby you knew, who could not sing one single note in tune. She was an angel of paradise.[. . .]And that was the Trilby who loved your brother, madame. [. . .]But all at once,[. . .]with one wave of his hand over her—with one look of his eye—with a word—Svengali could turn her into the other Trilby, *his* Trilby—and make her do whatever he liked . . . you might have run a red-hot needle into her and she would not have felt it. . . .
>
> He had but to say 'Dors!' [Sleep!] and she suddenly become an unconscious Trilby of marble, who could produce wonderful sounds . . . think his thoughts and wish his wishes—and love him at his bidding with a strange unreal factitious love . . . just his own love for himself turned inside out—à l'envers—and reflected back on him, as from a mirror . . . *un écho, un simulacre, quoi*![. . .]
>
> That Trilby was just a singing machine[. . .]just the unconscious voice that Svengali sang with.[. . .]
>
> When Svengali's Trilby was singing—or seemed to *you* as if she were singing—*our* Trilby had ceased to exist . . . *our* Trilby was fast asleep . . . in fact, *our* Trilby was *dead*. . . .
>
> Ach! what an existence![. . .]what adventures! Things to fill a book—a dozen books—Those five happy years—with those two Trilbys! (457–60; emphasis and non-bracketed breaks in the text)

Du Maurier *has* of course filled a book with the two Trilbys, and saved the most sensational for the conclusion, the scientific explanation[29]—so widely known that the Gypsy violinist Gecko is charged with its narration, replete with terms one would find in psychiatric case studies of the period (machine, unconscious, echo, simulacrum)—so widely known that every reader at the end of the nineteenth century is also in on "the secret" and has been eagerly waiting for the delicious thrill of reading the detailed exposition in the text.

Trilby's somnambulistic personality was what made her into a "singing machine." In the next chapter, we will see to what extent the mechanical body proliferated in popular entertainment at the end of the nineteenth century. This may be seen as a reflection of the anxieties surrounding the mechanization of work, and also as a reflection of new, mechanized forms of entertainment, but in the cabaret the figure of the mechanical body had a more immediate referent. As it did in *Trilby*, it expressed the outing of the corporeal unconscious.

A passage toward the end of *Trilby* allows one to guess just how powerful the film image of a hypnotizer might be a few years later: the heroine is mesmerized one last time *after* the death of Svengali *by a large photograph* of the conductor, baton in hand, "looking straight out of the picture, *straight at you* . . . all made up of importance and authority, and his big black eyes . . . full of stern command" (430; italics mine). Trilby sings "encore une fois," as though Svengali had commanded it. After this ineffably beautiful performance, she weakly utters the name Svengali three times and dies. If the photographic image could operate as efficiently as real presence, then certainly the *moving* picture would be even more potent, especially, as the text notes, when the gaze is directed out at *us*, just as it will be in the films we are going to look at in Chapter 5.

Unlike actors in dramatic roles, the cabaret comics and singers described in the next chapter were self-taught. They did not belong to a "school" of acting. It is highly doubtful that they had read Diderot, but they were certainly as well informed about hypnotism and hysteria as the average person. As we have begun to see, that information was far from negligible.

CHAPTER THREE

The Cabaret and the Body Out of Control

A psychiatrist threatened that our generation would wind up in the same boat as disarticulated beings; he was probably leaving a café-concert when he made that dire prophesy. A good half of the hit songs of the period belong to the home for the agitated (*le trémoussoir*) of the late Dr. Charcot. They tremble and jiggle (*trépident*). They have gesticulatory hysteria.

— GEORGES MONTORGEUIL, *Les Demi-Cabots*

Epilepsy as Performance Style in the Cabaret and Caf'Conc'

In 1896 Jules Claretie suggested a new thesis topic to university professors: the influence of the Chat Noir cabaret on the mystical *état d'âme* of the French at the fin-de-siècle. He was referring to the suggestive and dreamlike *mises en scène* of the Théâtre d'Ombres (the Shadow Theater) as a formative influence on Symbolism in literature and in the theater, and, more broadly, its influence on the general return to mysticism. I too am proposing a new "thesis" on the influence of the Chat Noir and of numerous other cabarets and café-concerts on the fin-de-siècle mentality: convulsive body language and hysterical tics and grimaces there formed the basis for a new aesthetic in popular spectacle and in "high art." Reciprocally, late-nineteenth-century cabaret and café-concert performance style was very much influenced by medical discourse surrounding epilepsy and hysteria, and by popularized depictions of the nervous disorders in newspapers and magazines (see R. B. Gordon, "Le Caf'conc'").

The contortions and other painful extremes of cabaret performers, as well as of mimes and clowns in the same period, were responding to the demand, from midcentury on, for strong sensations. This demand was met in popular entertainment at the same time that it became a focus of the medical gaze. With the popularization of hypnotism, somnambulism, and medical observations of hysterics, mass spectacle borrowed more and more from images of the body in these altered states of consciousness.

Briefly put, the question is this: is the café-concert hysterical because hysteria is everywhere in the period, or does it offer itself up as a model to potential hysterics who couldn't resist imitating the grimaces and convulsive movements that would characterize the *Nouvelle Iconographie photographique de la Salpêtrière*? More than one of Charcot's hysterics when s/he left the hospital, "cured" or not, went on to make a living as a street singer, or in the case of Jane Avril, as a Moulin Rouge dancer. While it is perhaps impossible to precisely trace the crisscross of influences with perfect assurance, what is certain is that the phenomenon of hysteria in the café-concert and cabaret preceded the furor of public attention garnered by psychiatric notions concerning the neurosis.

The traditional cabaret program consisted of songs, monologues, and poetry, and one often found marionettes or puppets there. The Chat Noir introduced shadow plays in 1888, and before the turn of the century, the tableaux vivants, mimes, magnetizers, musical revues, and comic sketches with dwarfs or clowns that had previously been the domain of the café-concert began appearing in cabaret programs as well. The size of the caf'conc' stage, in general larger and embellished with a decor that included a semicircle of seated women (up until the 1870s), provided for even more spectacular fare, such as acrobats and ballets, in addition to the attractions mentioned above. Music-halls "previously designated by the name cafés-concerts" carried on this tradition (see Paraf). Cabarets à attractions, such as Le Néant (see page 90), appeared in the fin-de-siècle. The *beuglant*, a type of neighborhood cabaret where rowdy audience participation was the norm, began to die out at the turn of the century.[1]

There were many different genres and styles of singer in the cabaret and caf'conc'. The Comic Trouper in military uniform was invented by Ouvrard, and its most famous exponent was Polin, whose song "I'm Afflicted with Anatomy" can still be seen in a Gaumont *phono-scène* (*phono-scènes* were post-synchronized sound films first shown at the 1900 Universal Exposition, or World Fair, by Gaumont). There was also the Monologuist, the Sentimental singer, the Realist singer, who imitated proletarian street singers, and the Patriotic singer. The genres that have a connection to hysteria or to degeneration are the Idiot Comic; the Alcoholic; the eccentric Gommeux (performers with outrageous gestures and dress); the "Scieurs" (singers of inept, nonsensical ditties); the Gambilleurs or Gambadeurs (singers like Paulus and Kam Hill who illustrated their songs with leaps, gambols, and kicks); Epileptic singers; singers with limps; and Phenomena, who owed most of their success to a physical deformity (for example, Siamese twins, hunchbacks, armless singers, or dwarfs) or to a bizarre talent such as that of the Homme-Aquarium, who could swallow several liters of water, including the frogs and fish residing therein. One of the most grotesque Phenomena was the hideous Brunin, the human skeleton who sang, meowed, barked, and cavorted dressed in a tutu. The acrobatic and comic talents of Little Tich, an English "gnome" (as Jean Lorrain called him) were considerable, but his "difformity" (Bizet 118) counted for much in his huge success at the turn of the century in Paris. Wearing outsized shoes and encumbered by yards of fabric around a tiny frame, Tich created a hilariously grotesque parody of Loïe Fuller's famous serpentine dance.[2] Endowed with an inventive comic genius, "if he falls to the floor, he starts to swim. There is no movement that doesn't give way to another comical movement. . . . Seeing him after the war, the public cried out: it's Charlot. In fact, he certainly contributed to the genial comedy of cinema with his silhouette and his primitive character" (20). To this list, one should add the performers of the late 1890s whose extreme *bizarrerie* did not even require that they sing or dance: the Pétomane, for example, whose talented sphincter could extinguish a candle from a distance of thirty centimeters and could whistle popular tunes and imitate "the fart of the mother-in-law," of "the bride on her wedding night and the morning after," as well as numerous animal cries. The Pétomane, dressed in tails and satin breeches, offered the most elegant variation on the theme of scatology that had always been present in cabaret and caf'conc' songs. In 1892, the year he opened his two-year run at the Moulin Rouge, he was studied by a physiologist working under Charles Richet.

Doctors were interested in exploring the "scientific importance" of Joseph Pujol's "musical anus" (Nohain and Caradec 46). The Pétomane was "a very modern, fin-de-siècle fellow," according to a review in the 25 September 1892 issue of *Gil Blas Illustré* (82). There was also the Pendu (the hanging man), a thin man with shaven head, "mouth twisted in a bitter grimace, hands contracted alongside his thighs, veins of the head and hands swollen," whose act consisted solely in being exhibited at the Concert Duclerc hung by the neck from a rope three meters long (V. Tranel, in Romi 39). But the most popular performers of the café-concert and cabaret between 1870 and 1900 jerked and twisted their bodies in bizarre contortions, imitating either the dislocations and gesticulations of a marionette or those of an epileptic, their faces alive with grimaces and mechanical tics.

As codified by Charcot, the epileptoid (characterized by convulsive movements) is the first stage of the major hysterical attack. Clownism (where the body contorts itself into all sorts of acrobatic poses) is the second stage. The last two stages consist of passionate poses (*attitudes passionnelles*), including catalepsy, then delirium and hallucination. The body's contortions in the first two stages of the hysterical attack formed an integral part of café-concert performance style and could also be seen at the circus, in marionette shows, and in pantomime. Poses struck in the third stage could also be seen in pantomime. Charcot, moreover, refers to clowns and acrobats in defining these stages, and Janet's famous characterization of the hysteric's theatricality was literally enacted by those chosen by Charcot to perform for the famous Tuesday Lessons at the Salpêtrière. The question of influence is therefore not unidirectional.

The fascination with convulsive, epileptic body language first became evident and was first given aesthetic form in the Parisian cabaret and café-concert. One of the seminal literary-artistic groups of the early 1880s was called the Epileptic Red Herrings, and the adjective "epileptic" was frequently used to describe cabaret performers in newspaper reviews. A new genre called "epileptic singers" came into being (see book jacket). I believe that the genre was representative of a remarkable contemporary phenomenon based on the fascination of writers, artists, scientists, and the public for hysteria. In its restructuring of the body, hysteria created a new form of expression in the arts. By inventing genres like the epileptic singer and the idiot comic, late-nineteenth-century cabaret and caf'conc' encouraged their audiences to see a correlation between idiocy, hysteria, loss of control, and laughter. There are good reasons that the Parisian cabaret and café-concert between 1870 and 1895 should be the principal site for this radically new aesthetic and ethos that would later (in Futurism, in Dada, and in German Expressionism) be recognized as typifying modernity. The aspects of the music-hall that were glorified in the Futurist Manifesto of 1913 are precisely those that dumbfounded or delighted commentators on the cabaret in the last quarter of the nineteenth century—for example, "the constant invention of new elements of stupor," "cascades of uncontrollable hilarity [and] profound analogies between humanity, the animal world, and the mechanical world," its "primitive, wild" character, the "grotesque mechanics of the clowns," and the "contortions and grimaces of future humanity." Marinetti's desire to "transform the Music-Hall into a Theater of Stupor [and] Psychofolie" was already close to being a fait accompli in the late-nineteenth-century cabaret. Nor did the Futurists fail to grasp the crucial importance of the spectator's participation in this spectacle, something I shall be emphasizing throughout this chapter. The vital exchange of energy between performer and spectator and the unique mingling of classes among these spectators (T. J. Clark describes this well in *Painting* 205–58) created a volatile ambiance where unconscious imitation was difficult to resist and potentially dangerous, not only because of the dangers of miming hysterical symptoms, but because the carnivalesque atmosphere and the anarchy of the body in cabaret performance resonated with political anarchy.[3] In reality, socialist and anarchist themes constituted a small portion of cabaret and caf'conc' repertoire; Jules Jouy sang his songs of social protest at the Chat Noir, and Aristide Bruant sang of prostitutes and hoodlums in the *faubourgs*, but other singer-composers in the same tradition were relegated to *goguettes* and song-cellars with limited audiences. Only around 1900 did the caf'conc' become a true entertainment for the masses; before that time, that was true only for the *beuglants*, and the *goguettes* in the *faubourgs*, as well as for the Bal populaire of the Moulin Rouge. That did not prevent the correlation—anarchy of the body = political revolution—from being made, however. At the turn of the century, "apaches"—a name first attributed to Paris street gangs, but which was soon expanded to cover violence, disorder, and terror—frequented the Lapin Agile cabaret in

Montmartre, and there were occasional violent disputes. That didn't prevent poets, writers, and painters like Utrillo, Mac Orlan, Paul Fort, and Francis Carco from patronizing it. The fear of anarchy in such settings has to do precisely with the theories of imitation and contagion discussed in the last chapter. Anarchist bombs exploded in Paris between 1892 and 1894, the year that President of the Republic Carnot was assassinated. Robert Nye has shown how, thanks to the medicalization of criminology, crime and madness were conflated in the period: biophysiology served to characterize political acts of anarchy in the same way as they did violent street crime.[4] "By the turn of the century, a medical outlook of *bio-pouvoir* had thoroughly penetrated popular consciousness" (170).

Music is particularly apt to elicit "a series of visceral reflexes" (D'Udine 67), and music can determine "grave hysterical phenomena" in some individuals (Galopin 129). As mentioned in the previous chapter, Gustave Le Bon reiterated notions like these and gave them a more sociopolitical orientation: "The disappearance of the conscious personality, predominance of the unconscious personality, orientation of feelings and ideas by way of suggestion and contagion [and] a tendency to transform ideas immediately into acts, these are the principal characteristics of the individual in a crowd. He is no longer himself but an automaton" (19). In addition, the extraordinary combination of dissimilar genres in cabaret shows where "high" and "low" converge in one place (Verlaine and Rollinat read their poetry before or after puppet shows and illusionists) seemed to mirror the blurring of boundaries (not only of class, but between performer and spectator). Some of the examples given by Gabriel Tarde in *Les Lois de l'imitation*—the gentleman who imitates the slang and swagger of a proletariat and the femme du monde who reproduces the intonations of a singer (94)—would surely have occurred after leaving a cabaret or caf'conc'.

The very composition of the cabaret program, with its abrupt shifts from one genre (and mood) to another, is "neurotic"; it resembles the emotional mobility of hysterics and what doctors tagged as the "aesthetic of degenerates": "exaggerated, paradoxical or incoherent. Often the burlesque is found alongside the grandiose" (Grellety, *Névrosés* 18).

In cabaret performance, the dislocations of the body express liberation and anarchic freedom, but also the disorders of pathology and pain. These movements are frenetic, angular, and "mechanical," accompanied by tics and grimaces.[5] Dr. Pierre Janet wrote in 1903 that the hysteric almost always claimed to feel "mechanical," like an automaton. "All of our patients use the same language, the words *machines*, *automatons*, *mechanical* return again and again" (*Les Obsessions* 283). Automatisms, remember, are the outward signs the body furnishes of the unconscious. An observation of a male epileptic at the Salpêtrière could easily describe a marionette: "He raises the right arm, seems to pull on strings with his left hand that he fixedly gazes at; his arms tremble and then fall. He remains rigid" (Féré, "Yawning" 164). Alfred Jarry's *Ubu Roi* was initially performed by marionettes (first in a friend's attic in 1888, and later at the Théâtre de l'Oeuvre in 1896, the year Méliès made his first films).[6] The Jarry scholar Henri Béhar underlines the guignolesque nature of *Ubu Roi*: "Guignol poses [and gestures are] used to express all sorts of sentiments." For example, when angry, Guignol shakes his famous stick; laughter "is accompanied by extreme physical agitation: 'Everyone is twisted and doubled over. Many die laughing'. . . . Jarry made every effort to give the same shape and volume to his characters as to a marionette" (55, 56). It is absolutely clear that Jarry used the corporeal exaggerations of marionettes in *Ubu* to emphasize the anarchic and aggressive nature of the play. The cruelty and nutty ferocity of Mère and Père Ubu were perfectly expressed by the dislocated, disarticulated, mechanical, and abrupt movements of these *pantins*. Jarry, making himself the double of Ubu in everyday life, moved like a marionette. In addition, he "spoke Ubu . . . a language where each syllable is detached, in monotone, a sort of mechanical speech." The humor of this language "had the cadence of a machine" (Tzara 69). "We feel attracted toward these living marionettes, these decors, this electricity" writes Maurice Vaucaire of the caf'conc' in the 1886 poem "Café Chantant." Why does the tremendous popularity of marionettes and puppets (as well as an ongoing fascination, inherited from the previous century, with mechanical dolls and other automata) in theater, in cabaret, and in early film comedy coincide with the popular fascination with hysteria? Marionettes are a mirror for the phenomenon of automatisms. The public sees itself in these figures whose strings are pulled by someone behind the scenes, suggesting the unseen, unconscious will of the second personality, just as they are pulled by someone on stage in public shows of magnetizers and hypnotists. In addition, their attraction also lies in the mechanical movements and dislocations of the body and in their capacity for violence and aggression: exactly as is the case for an hysteric, a puppet or a doll is allowed to express primitive impulses, to defy authority, to be violent. (Aggressivity and a feeling of disintegration are common to hysteria.) The hysterical body in its "cataleptic plasticity" or in its convulsive disarticulations can do almost everything that a marionette can. Recent writers on film, such as Paul Coates, have underlined the relationship between modernism and the body as machine in Expressionist cinema, but they have not seen that the phenomenon of the mechanical body as spectacle was first represented in cabaret performance, and that, there, it evoked representations of hysteria. (See the Appendix for the depiction of the mechanical body in early German cinema, both Expressionist and in comedies.) The human reduced to the mechanical makes spectators laugh, and the more troubling the image, the louder the laughter.

In 1891 the authorization is given allowing performers to wear military uniforms on stage, and the genre of the comic trooper is born. The creator of the genre, Ouvrard, makes especial use of knocking knees and pointing fingers in his stage mimic. He is "a seeker of mechanical tics," "Oh! the angles everywhere on this puny body, something automatic in the gestures . . . a mouth that splits open in a tormented grin (*rictus*); an astonishing mask culminating in two points: on top, the cranium, on the bottom, the chin: . . . diabolically planted on a packet of nerves" (Montorgueil and Jean d'Arc, in Caradec and Weill 138). But Ouvrard could not have existed had there been no Paulus.

In 1871 Paulus (né Paul Habans) introduced an original version of comic song combined with movements that were, I intend to show, hysterical. Until Paulus arrived on the scene, according to the journalist Georges Montorgueil (1857–1933)—who was a keen observer of Parisian life and, in particular, popular entertainments—artists sang rigidly upright and allowed themselves only "a minimal pantomime of the fingers." Beginning with Paulus, gesture in the performances of caf'conc' singers was a "pantomime destined to become more and more outrageous" until it became "gesticulatory hysteria" (Montorgueil et al. 14–15). As the Goncourts' 13 January 1865 diary entry shows, frenetic movement accompanied comic songs six years before Paulus appeared on the scene (and ten years before the creation of the genre of *chanteuse épileptique*): "A comic . . . sang senseless things, interrupted by barnyard cries and an epileptic gesticulation—the St. Vitus dance of idiocy. The room was enthused to the point of delirium" (*Journal* 4). It must have been rare, though, because Ouvrard confirms Montorgueil's statement: "Paulus, when he launched this new genre [of acrobatic song], overturned every tradition and the café-concert underwent, in less than six months, a complete transformation: you had to have movement, always movement. . . . The public watched the legs" (15–16). Mechanical or frenetic gesture was, thus, from Paulus onward, the key to success and, as I hope to prove, the essential characteristic of a caf'conc' aesthetics. According to Paulus's memoir, *Trente ans de café-concert*, he was inspired by a group of comic dancers, "Les Clodoches" and by the disarticulations of Holden's marionettes. The Clodoches were four eccentric dancers who had invented a new quadrille. They were very much in fashion in 1866, and in 1868 when they performed the "Grand Quadrille de l'Oeil crevé" at the Eldorado, they became "wildly famous throughout France" (Paulus 39–40). In 1880 Paulus had perfected his style "gambillard," and by 1886 his popularity was at its peak, where it remained, with a short period of decline in the late 1890s, until 1900. His nickname was "le gambadeur" (one who frolics, jumps, and hops around) and his jerky, syncopated style was described as an "imitation of the dislocations and gesticulations of a marionette." The public "took great pleasure in seeing marionettes in his person" (Montorgueil et al. 15). When Paulus is compared to a marionette, one can guess that underneath the Southern good humor of his texts lies the aggressiveness of the anarchic or hysterical body. With Paulus, a song became an opportunity for gymnastic display. "He throws his head back while agitating his arms and hands. He jumps around, winking mysteriously, marking every clash of the cymbals with his head" (Chadourne 231). In "Chaussée Clignancourt" he recounts meeting a young woman in Montmartre "with the gestures of someone being exorcized" (230). Dr. Charles Féré's male epileptic patient, described here, could have been a stand-in for Paulus: he possesses an extreme facial mobility; his mouth "deviates to the right at the same time as it opens wide and his eyes wink or close" (facial asymmetry is a common hysterical trait: see Figures 2 and 3).[7] His head rotates to the right while his members flex and extend themselves

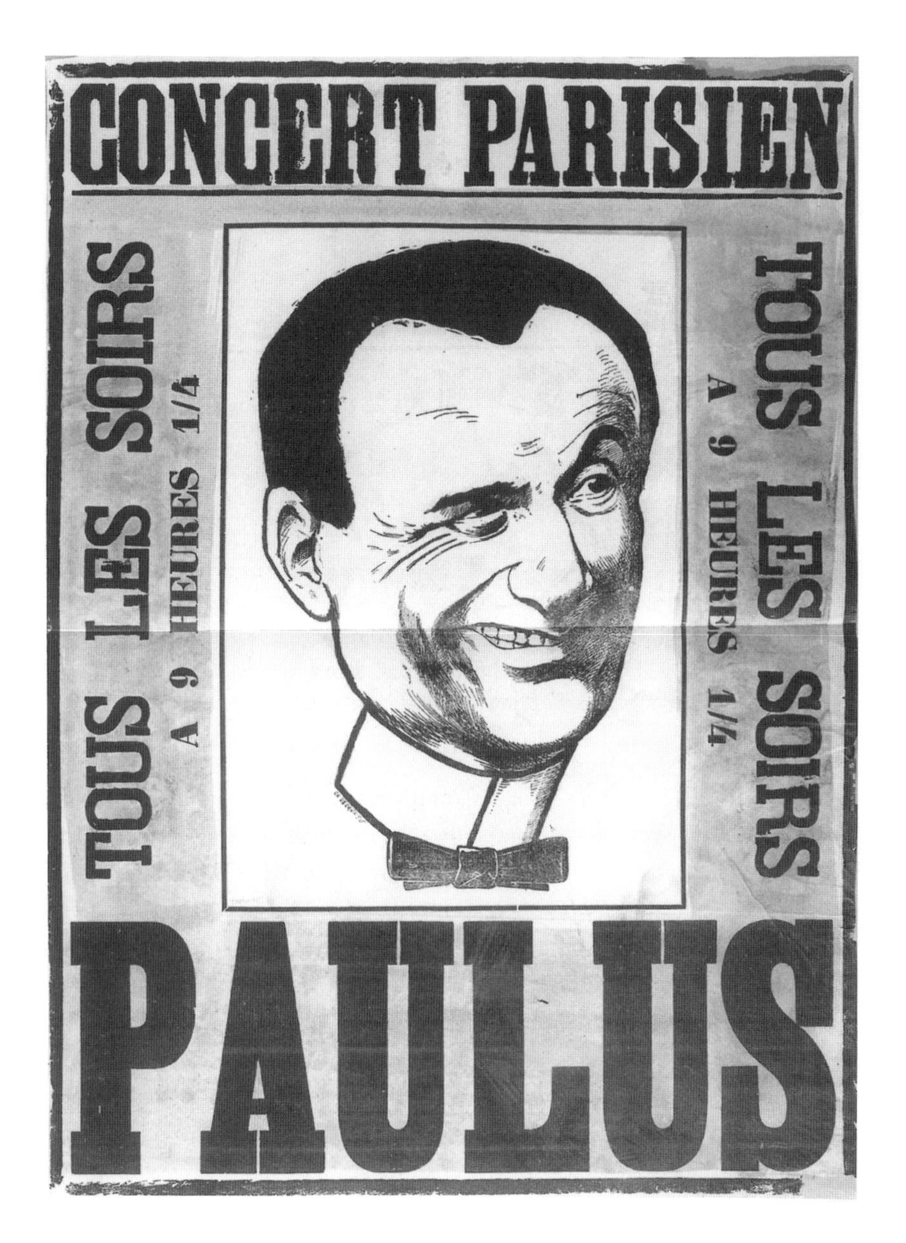

Figure 2. Poster of Paulus at the Concert Parisien in 1882. Phototèque des Musées de la Ville de Paris.

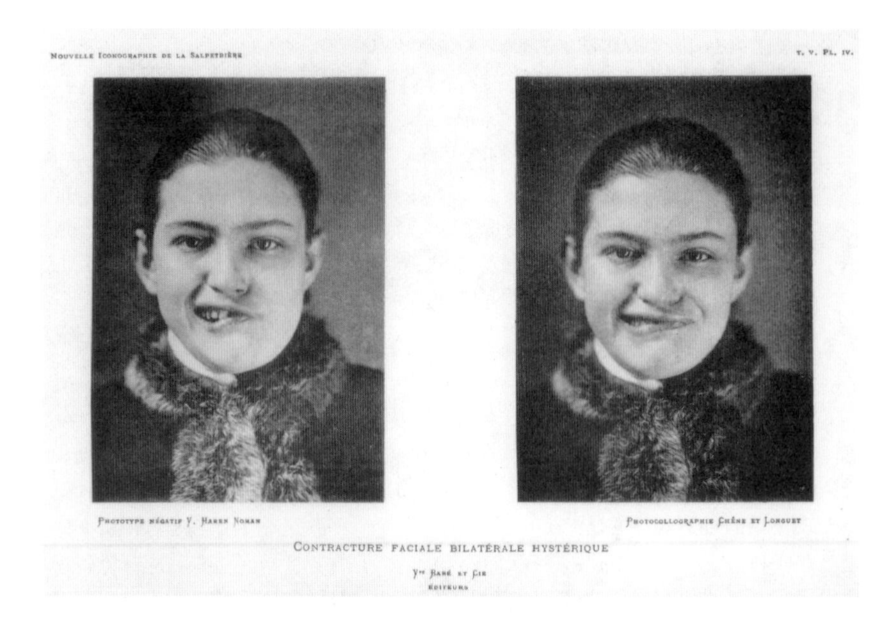

Figure 3. Hysterical bilateral facial contracture, from *Nouvelle Iconographie de la Salpêtrière*, vol. 5 (1892), plate 4. Photo Bibliothèque nationale de France, Paris.

in all directions ("Yawning" 164). Countless imitators of Paulus followed, just as they had for Thérésa (see below). In the first musicals of Ernst Lubitsch, one can see how much a part of this tradition Maurice Chevalier was. And, in fact, Chevalier, who was fascinated as a child by the acrobats and singers he saw, started out in a cabaret (the Café des Trois Lions, according to his great friend Mistinguett, who adds that he went by the name of Patapouf at the time). There, he "awkwardly rolled his mechanical body around" (roulait gauchement les mécaniques) (Mistinguett 149). "Chevalier is the very archetype—one could say historic type—of the Café-Concert singer. . . . [In the beginning], he was one of those comics who try to make you laugh by the eccentricity of their costume. . . . He had that 'stiff ambulation' in his gait that wasn't exempt from vulgarity, and he grimaced with his entire elastic face" (Bizet 137).

According to a psychiatrist who wrote his doctoral thesis on male hysteria, the popular image of the asylum was of people running, jumping, leaping, gamboling, shouting, insulting, and hitting each other" (Roubinovitch,

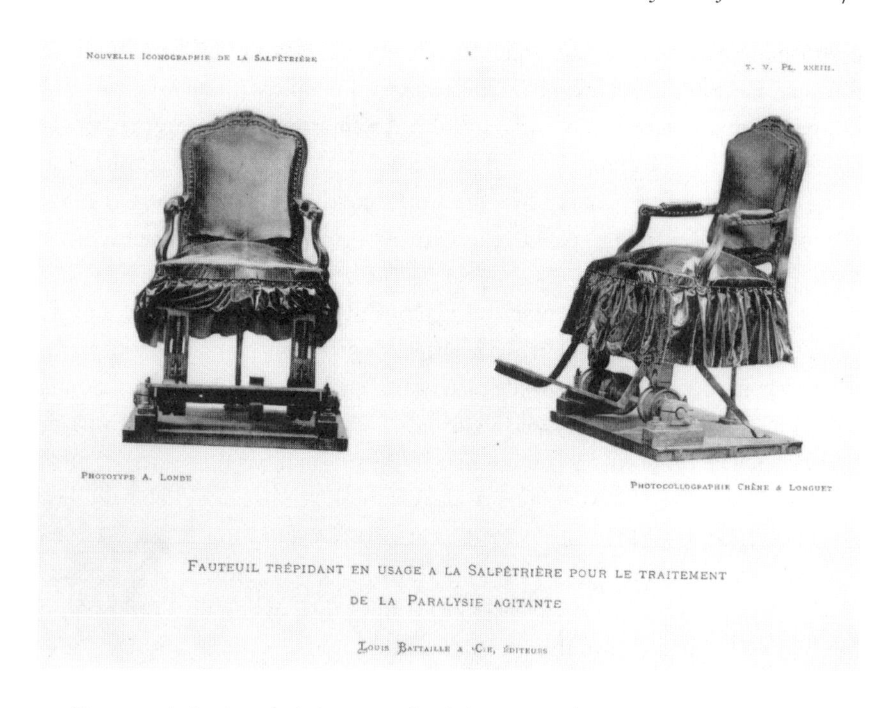

Figure 4. Agitating chair in use at the Saltpêtrière, from *Nouvelle Iconographie de la Salpêtrière*, vol. 5 (1892), plate 33. Photo Bibliothèque nationale de France, Paris.

"L'Hystérie" *fascicule* 7). His patients exhibited a wide array of corporeal symptoms: rigidity, contractures of the hands, the *arc de cercle*, bulging eyeballs, convulsive facial tics and asymmetry, grimaces, violent contortions of the extremities, extravagant poses, and chaotic gesticulations. Trembling, especially of the leg and foot, was a constant sign of male hysteria; when seated, a patient's foot taps a rapid tattoo on the floor (103, 109). This rhythmic movement of the foot is called "trepidation," and it is a word that one encounters in innumerable descriptions of cabaret performances. Trepidation, remember, is also used homeopathically in the treatment of hysteria: patients are strapped into the "trepidation chair" at the Salpêtrière Hospital and treated to the same movements, this time controlled by their doctors (see Figure 4). One didn't have to go to Charenton or to the Salpêtrière to witness such a spectacle; all of these movements could be seen nightly on the stages of café-concerts and cabarets. Paulus had a huge hit in the song "Derrière l'omnibus," during the performance of which he ran along the stage in pursuit of a bus. In addition to running, jumping, and kicking, he impersonated people with nervous tics and limps (limping was also a common hysterical symptom)—for example, in "La Boiteuse" (The Limping Girl), "L'Invalide," and "La Noce des Infirmes" (The Wedding of the Lame).[8] In the first song, "The little lame girl from Alençon is adored by the army regiment. As soon as he sees her cute little foot, the sergeant takes out his spyglass." (The comic trooper Polin also sang this song, and a grimacing, agitated Harry Fragson sang "Limping Love": "Walking, she dances the polka.") Georges Montorgueil explained that Paulus's "success was largely due to his pirouettes, . . . his prancing, his imitations of various forms of infirmity, of the crippled and of the invalid. This was an entirely new art that had to be learned" (Montorgueil et al. 15–16). Paulus was one of the great popular stars of the café-concert because, like Mlle Bécat, "that epileptic doll [who] bleated and twisted her hips in those inept convulsions that procured a quasi-celebrity" for her (see Figure 5) (Huysmans, "L'Exposition" 227),[9] he was able to represent for the public a non-threatening figure of the phenomenon that fascinated and frightened them: hysteria.

Huysmans was commenting on the lithographs of singers that Degas exhibited in the 1881 Salon des Indépendents. These singers, who remind Huysmans of Mlle Bécat, "hold out their paws which move like the paws of imbecilic monkey figurines" (*magots de Saxe*: a *magot* can also mean a deformed man, or a man as ugly as a baboon) (ibid.). Animality, automata, and epilepsy: a trio of characteristics that will be seen more and more frequently on caf'conc' stages. Emilie Bécat "inaugurated the epileptic genre in her debut in the summer of 1875" at Les Ambassadeurs (Paulus 214). Polaire would later claim to have invented the genre in the early 1890s, as would Mistinguett in her memoirs, but, as Degas's lithographs and Huysmans's commentary on them lead us to suspect, and as Paulus's memoir confirms, the genre had existed for almost two decades.[10] The epileptic genre emerged at precisely the same time as did the sharp rise in cases of hysteria, feeding into and capitalizing on a cultural phenomenon that was just getting underway. The parallel genre of the epileptic comic can be dated back to Réval's creation of the "eccentric comic" at the Eldorado in 1869; the resemblance it bears to the genre of the "epileptic comic" can be seen in Méliès's films *The King of Makeup* and *Tom Tight and Dum-Dum*. At the beginning of the twen-

Figure 5. "Mlle Bécat aux Ambassadeurs," lithograph by Degas (1877–1878). Lithograph transferred from three monotypes, 352 x 272 mm. (sheet). Museum of Fine Arts, Boston. Gift of George P. Gardner.

tieth century, the best-known epileptic comics of the café-concert were Sinoël and Darius M. Bécat's convulsive gestures and leaps were described by Paulus: "Quicksilver seemed to run through her veins; she ran, bounded, twisted herself with suggestive gestures [in] a short dress that showed off her calves" (214). Her repertoire consisted of off-color songs and absurd songs like "The Turbot and the Shrimp." Mlle Bécat enjoyed tremendous success from 1875 to 1884. Her costume as well as her epileptic movements would be imitated by a host of scantily, if extravagantly, clothed young chanteuses with small voices and big hopes: they were called *gommeuses*.

"Epileptic performers" were not, of course, epileptics themselves. Despite the "electricity" and "nervousness" of performers that doctors and journalists cited here alluded to, epileptic comics, singers, and *gommeuses* were miming epilepsy, not experiencing it. Performers are not by definition sick. There *were* negative repercussions of the body's repetitions of these movements among some of the more "serious" or intellectual artistic representatives of pathology as art such as Nina de Villard, and the relation between sickness and the performance of it gets more complicated when one considers Maurice Rollinat, as I do later in this chapter. The leading actor of the Grand Guignol theater also noted the severe effects the roles he played had on his nerves. But, despite these individual examples, performers who capitalized so successfully on physical and mental infirmities on stage were not doomed to mental asylums. My focus is on the spectator's internal response to perceived movement on stage and on screen, and the effects (miming of symptom, for example) that it was presumed to produce in the nineteenth century. Accounts of the caf'conc' public below seem to confirm that these effects were in fact produced.[11]

Like their male counterparts, the *gommeux*, *gommeuses* were "eccentric singers" whose particular characteristics consisted in the extravagant silliness of the costume and coiffure (underwear and an enormous hat were of major importance for the *gommeuse*). Raising their voluminous skirts, they cavorted and contorted their bodies with epileptic gestures and movements; they "shook, leapt around, twisted, and stuck their tongue out" (Romi 21). Jean Durand's 1911 film, *Dancing Girl*, is about a *gommeuse épileptique*. A contemporary described the category of "*nervous* or *epileptic*" singers who take "the slightest pretext to agitate themselves, twist themselves, to become boneless. One can't comprehend a word they say, their pronunciation is so rapid, jerky;

but everything in these women signifies: "That tickles me, gives me an itch, irritates my senses . . . True torpedoes, with whom contact seems dangerous" (Chadourne 244). From 1878 to the end of the century, the *gommeuse* was one of the biggest draws in Parisian nightlife. When Violette came on stage at the Eldorado in the 1880s, the audience yelled, "'Take off your knickers!... ' 'Higher!... '. . . . 'Give us a look!'" (Guilbert, *La Chanson de ma vie* 149). Paulus described Marie Heps in 1879 as "frisky, exciting, whose ample charms are ogled" (in Caradec and Weill 174). The *gommeuse* is a sensual object because of "her protruding bosom, her round arms . . . her legs that frisk about with zest—everything about her denotes love of laughter, [she is a] symbol of madness, of Parisian life" (Chadourne 240). "The hip-twisting . . . a certain way . . . of raising the leg or of twisting oneself about like eels compensate, for many people, for the inane subject matter, the idiocy of the lyrics" (280). Despite the décolleté, the lavish display of undergarments and the sexual content of the songs, the erotic appeal of the *gommeuse* is, at best, a curious one. "With the contortions of a strangling chicken, a woman . . . bleated out a popular song" (Renault and Le Rouge 116). "Mlles Violette, Gilette, Heps are true female Pauluses! . . . Mlle Abdala, taking advantage of her exceptionally skinny physique, made the grimace into an art form (poussa la grimace jusqu'au chef-d'oeuvre)" (ibid.). The curious mixture of contorted corporeal poses, comical grimaces, and unabashed sexuality in lyric, movement, and dress may be difficult to understand today. It had certainly never been seen before on stage. Yet the very same mix existed in the hysterical attacks of a great many female patients at the Salpêtrière. What the male spectator savored, according to many accounts, was the amount of flesh bared. Clowning and contortions did not seem to detract from his experience of sexual pleasure. Mistinguett (who went on to become France's most popular singer of the *entre-deux-guerres* period) began as a *gommeuse*. At the Casino de Paris, she sang "La Môme de Paris"—an "idiotic song [with] such immense gusto, making gestures with such wild abandon that I might have been unrolling yards of invisible satin" (20). She abandoned the style after leaving the Eldorado in 1907, after having performed there for ten years. "I was tired of the daily epilepsy, of sitting on the prompter's box, the better to gesticulate" (41). A review published when she left the Eldorado helps us to understand what had appealed so strongly to audiences.

> One will miss her genre, because this nervous little slip of a woman . . . brought into singing a new element: electricity. At the slightest word or gesture, she appeared to be set into motion by a spring, shaken by a mysterious battery that made her sprint and gambol, comically shake her arms, her legs, her hair . . . bounding . . . pirouetting, accompanied by violent clashes of the cymbals. . . . It was her facial expressions, her gambades and her high-pitched-voice that made us laugh! ("Fantasio," Mistinguett dossier in the Fonds Rondel)

Max Viterbo, a reviewer of the "nervous" *gommeuse* Foscolo, who "wasn't afraid to make herself ridiculous and ugly," would regret that there were no more women comics in the young generation. But in 1908, the public's demand for the thrill of this form of attraction was dying out, just as Charcotian hysteria had been supplanted by new medical nosographies, and hysteria itself had been supplanted by the milder nervous disorder, neurasthenia. This form of attraction had been carried over into film (see Chapter 6), but by 1912, "epileptic" film comics would be, by and large, a thing of the past.

In the last decade of the nineteenth century, the *gommeuse* was the rage of Paris, and, in particular, the "nervous" or "epileptic" *gommeuse*. "If you haven't seen Naya, the eccentric, hyperbolic gommeuse, you are not Parisian for two cents" ("Profils d'Artistes et de Mondaines," 1892 newspaper article in Fonds Rondel, dossier "Naya"). Eugénie Fougère and "La Belle Otero" were *gommeuses*. But the most famous epileptic singer was Polaire, the wasp-waisted brunette who, like Mistinguett, went on to make films, and who was the inseparable companion of Colette and Willy, both of whom actively participated in the caf'conc' and music-hall. Willy describes Polaire dancing: "Vivacious, the entire little body jiggles, like a little steam-engine. Her arms nervously extended, fists clenched in front of her, the pretty androgynous head flung backwards, she arches that famous waist, . . . and from her mouth, more voluptuous than classical, a gargling of laughter flies forth" (in Caradec 132–33). And in the 1904 *Danseuses*, Willy wrote that the cake-walk "remained a dance of epileptic savages—and like a representation of colic and the illustration of Vomito Negro, until the day that Polaire was good enough to dance it on the stage of the Mathurins" (in Caradec 170). (I will return to the amalgam of epilepsy, savages, and the cake-walk in Chapter 6.) Polaire's acting is discussed by admirers (resident psychiatrists in an asylum) in Willy's novel of the same year, *La Môme Picrate*: "Polaire, by her exclusively modern complexion, has a calling: to incarnate today's characters, and even tomorrow's. She brings us novelty. . . . Polaire is a type. . . . To translate a bit of this neurosis that smiles or tenses up on the contemporary Mona Lisa's lips, Polaire is served by an absolutely marvelous physique. You've noticed the quivering of this vibrant, slim and supple body" (249, 251).[12] In her *Mémoires*, Polaire (née Emilie-Marie Bouchau) wrote that "her instinct caused her . . . to sing with clenched fists, and with even her toes twitching in her shoes . . . bent over backward as though cut in two by [my] flexible waist . . . with nervous, exasperated movements" (in Condemi 152–53). Every part of her body, from the contracture of the hands to the twitching feet and the *arc de cercle*, conforms to the picture of nineteenth-century hysteria. And Jean Lorrain, Decadent novelist, critic, and connoisseur in all forms of sexuality, described Polaire this way:

> Polaire! the agitating and agitated Polaire . . . in a blouse tight enough to bring on the spasm (of orgasm). . . . What devilish mimicry, what a coffee grinder and what a belly dance! . . . Polaire hops around, trembles, quivers, dances with her hips, pelvis, and navel, mimes all forms of shocks and shaking, twists, leans over backward in the form of an arc, becomes upright, twists her . . . , rolls her eyes up into her head, meows, is in ecstasy and . . . swoons . . . and to what music and what lyrics! (279)

The commentary in Colette's *Mes apprentissages* concisely expresses the association of this performance style with pathology: "I had applauded Polaire in her epilepsy"; "Polaire sang [an obscene song, "Portrait du petit chat"] while tensing her whole body, quivering like a wasp stuck on fly paper, and smiling with a convulsive mouth as if she had just drunk lime juice" (in Romi 48).

The hyperbole of one writer on the café-concert in 1896 points up the effects of this style on performer and public alike. The music works on the nerves of the "animalistically aggressive" singers, on "their poor nerves" and makes their torsos vibrate . . . like the movements of ancient madness. . . . A music that is so mad, moreover. . . . In the repeated refrains especially, it is imbecility that they pound into the skulls [of the public]" (Coquiot 17). In fact, the raison d'être of the café-concert is "to do away with all decency. For most of the public, it is the Bicêtre asylum where their madness is free to express itself. . . . Even the posters plastered over the walls of Paris "glorify the gesture of a cretin; make one laugh at physical deformities, celebrate a famous ham's cachexia of the brain" (ibid.). The model of epilepsy and *hystéro-épilepsie* for a specific performance style is part of a larger discourse on the café-concert as a (titillating and dangerous) locus of pathology.

The central place occupied by nervous pathology in the caf'conc' repertoire is nothing short of astounding, and our favorite song has got to be the *gommeuse* Alice de Tender's "La Parisienne épileptique," on the Eldorado program in both 1899 and 1900. I've already mentioned the vogue for songs about women with a limp, a pathology of movement associated with hysteria and whose jerky, asymmetrical rhythm seems to have excited a number of men; another corporeal abnormality in fashion was the hunchback: "The Little Parisian Hunchback" (1869), "The Hump" (1898), "The Little Hunchbacked Girl" (1906), which also play on sexual enjoyment more than on pathos. Then there is the aging seducer's fate in "The Story of the Little Old Man": he follows so many women on the streets of Paris that he wears his legs down to the thighs. "He wore down his hind paws and became legless" (Il s'usa tout à fait les pattes, et devint cul-de-jatte). The dance craze of 1902–1906, the cake-walk, assimilated nervous pathologies like St. Vitus's Dance (see Chapter 6). The references to nerves are, in fact, everywhere: Stiv-Hall's "Nerveuse" (1898), Dutard's "Too Nervous" (1904), Mlle Valois's "Tata's Tic" (1896) and Mlle Lidia's "Mechanical Doll" (1896), Galipaux's monologue "A Man with a Tic" (1905), and Lucy Muger's "Electrocuted" ("I jump like a wild woman") the same year. The contagion of nervous disorders is underlined in a song by Strit in "When I Follow Cocottes": he marries a Cocotte (a woman of easy virtue) who has St. Vitus's Dance. He becomes a "moron" because he "constantly stands in front of the mirror, seized by the little nervous tic of my wife, I dance." Then there are the songs about neurasthenia; Dranem's "I'm a Neurasthenic" is the most famous, but there is a long list. In Dranem's monologue, "Family Doctor," we learn that "the most fashionable sickness is neurasthenia." In the 1905 "The Little Nervous Woman," Muguette de Trévy sang, "Don't tickle me like that, I'm a little woman who's excessively nervous. . . . In reality, the blood of a turnip runs through my veins:

But the fashion today, the grand chic, is to appear neurasthenic." Dalbret's 1906 "Neurasthenia" deserves to be quoted at length:

> Progress and fashion have just given us a new method to replace snobbism and spiritism. . . . It's neurasthenia; everyone has it. . . . What rules the world? It's neurasthenia. . . . Most society women, in order to calm their nerves, want to try the whole gamut of perverse pleasures. . . . And neurasthenia turns one into a somnambulist. . . . Even the princes of science, doctors, have all got it. . . . It makes you lose your memory. . . . It's an invisible force that drives humanity: it's impossible for anyone to resist it. . . . The brain of lovely persons is too electrified. . . . It's the reason that women on their own ask for it [sex] all the time, they want it. . . . They become hysterics, it's neurasthenia. . . . Satyrs, black masses, come from that state. As a result of singing about this mess, I've caught it and now I'm insane (*détraqué*). . . . The authors of this song caught it when they were children. It's neurasthenia; if they are more idiotic than lyric opera composers, it's neurasthenia.

Is neurasthenia, and hysteria before it, largely a phenomenon of fashion, as this song implies? Certainly they became trendy afflictions, and the café-concert was very instrumental in making them so. The popularity of this entertainment leads me to think that it was as instrumental as the popular press in making hysteria and neurasthenia household words. There can be no doubt about the attraction of the epileptic performer and of songs about nervous disorders and corporeal pathologies. And the appeal of adopting some of the characteristics of these maladies is evoked in some of the songs I've cited. Yet, the fashion of a manageable malady (with rather mild symptoms?) is very different from the medical cases that abounded at the time. The theories of comedy discussed in Chapter 1 propose explanations of laughter at physical deformity, idiocy, and madness. Along with the notion of identification with the alienated Double is the recurrent idea of the sense of superiority that the sight of the afflicted offers to spectators. "The element common to all laugh-inducing situations is the presence of a *masterable* discrepancy or incongruity (Storey, *Mimesis* 163). This may well be true in the case of representations of epilepsy and idiocy. Yet, if neurasthenia is everywhere, spectators can not distance themselves from it; their laughter may be what the Goncourt brothers, in their 1865 diary entry on the epileptic comic singer, called an "unhealthy laughter," participating, reveling in the pathology. "There is a rottenness of stupidity in the public and a laughter that is so unhealthy that it will take a great and violent event, bloodshed, to change the air." (Six years later, the uprising of the Commune took place.) André Chadourne wrote in 1889 that the public "is thirsty for these songs . . . it can't get enough. And cases of pathology like this are met with more often than one would think" (277). The irresistible pull of fashion, of modernity, governed the caf'conc' public, and nothing is more "modern" than the nervous pathology whose contagious, jerky rhythms and movements define popular song in the period.

Before Epileptic Gesture

If these gestures and movements also existed prior to 1865, they were not construed as referring to nervous pathology; this is clear from the reactions to them and descriptions of them in newspaper reviews and books on popular culture that date from the last half of the century. The comic singer at the Eldorado who put the Goncourt brothers in mind of epilepsy appeared in 1865, and the widespread popularity of "outrageous" pantomime accompanying song began, as we saw, with Paulus in 1871 and Emilie Bécat in 1875, who created the epileptic genre. It would be foolhardy to proclaim that the café-concert had an absolute monopoly on these kinds of epileptic and hysterical movements, gestures, and facial tics. The caf'conc' spectacle was the first to *emphasize* jerky, syncopated movements, which I further characterize in Chapter 4 as the zigzag. The public there perceived these movements as new; spectators described the shocks to their bodies, choosing the verb *trépider* and the noun *secousse* again and again. Literary personalities proclaimed that it was modern and, in fact, that it typified modernity (Huysmans; Lorrain; Barbey d'Aurevilly; Wolff, in Guiches 94–95). Granted, the media, then as now, had a large part in creating the perception of novelty. What *is* certain is that the success of the epileptic singing style was so overwhelming that scores of imitators in the cabaret and caf'conc' quickly made it a phenomenon that—if it was not confined to these spectacles,—it was *perceived* as exclusively linked to the cabaret/caf'conc' spectacle, and permanently identified with them historically. And it is just as certain that the style fell out of fashion in France at around the same time that the fascination with hysteria died out. These movements may also have been present in ballet,[13] in *commedia*, in circus clowning, and in pantomime. I have chosen to examine the case of pantomime in particular, since it was one of the avowed inspirations for the cabaret aesthetic described here. Yet, as we will see in the next chapter, even the leaps, kicks, and somersaults of French pantomime were still perceived as gracious and *sympathique*.

High and Low

> In the lower depths of society are the blind forces of the automatism.
>
> —JULES-BERNARD LUYS, neurologist

Why the desire to vicariously experience the convulsive spasms of epilepsy and hysteria in one's own body, or to be put into a trancelike state? There was an expectation that going to the caf'conc' would be a very *physical* experience, the body jolted by extreme sensations and pulsating to unusual rhythms. Either irregular rhythms (such as those seen in the staccato, angular, spasmodic, or violent marionette-like gestures) or stultifyingly repetitious rhythms (such as those in the idiotic and inept refrains and movements of comiques idiots). Either the spasms and convulsions of epilepsy and hysteria, or the lethargy and trancelike catalepsy of somnambulism and hysteria. The total domination of body over mind, of sensation over reason and reflection, had—and has—a tremendous appeal in popular entertainment. In the last quarter of the nineteenth century, however, this appeal had additional implications, as has been previously discussed. The terms "mechanical movement and gesture" and "electrical discharge" constantly resurface in psychiatric documents of the fin de siècle (just as they do in literary texts). Café-concert performance style deliberately appeals to the lower faculties. At stated in Chapter 1, it was "popular" entertainment, mass entertainment par excellence (even though its audience was hardly confined to the working classes), "low" art as opposed to "high" culture, and that has to do as much with the psychiatric and physiological theories discussed in this book as it does with sociopolitical factors. In fact, the sociopolitical was, as we've seen, very much dependent on the psychiatric and physiological (as well as on theories of biological, psychological, and social evolution) for its arguments. High and Low take on new meaning in light of nineteenth-century physiological and psychiatric theories. Here is what Jean Lorrain had to say about the *beuglant*, a type of cabaret where rowdy audience participation such as "bleating," shouting, and singing along was the norm: "Thanks to the beuglants, we are headed toward all that is low. Everything that dirties ideas, feelings, and pure instinct fills us with happiness and shakes us with joy" (in Jacques-Charles, *Le Caf'conc'*). This view was expressed twenty years earlier (in 1872) by Jules Bonnassies, but enlarged to cover all café-concerts: "those vulgar establishments that encourage vice and debauchery. . . . The public, appetites whetted by sensual satisfactions . . . [and where] artists . . . go to deform their talent" (165–66). Even a lover of popular culture like Jean Richepin has his main character in *Braves gens: Roman parisien* exclaim that the café-concert "public and personnel were vulgar and low: not naïve, but a corrupted populace, and an imbecilic bourgeoisie; not artists to move such an audience, but grimacing individuals (*des grimaciers*)" (101). A night at the café-concert stimulated an "unhealthy nervousness."[14]

The spectator's physical experience is exciting and stimulating yet anxiety-producing; the experience of the body involuntarily imitating the convulsive movements and facial contortions that characterized epilepsy and hysteria could not help but remind spectators of the all-too-common attacks of these illnesses that found their way into the popular press. So, whereas the predominance of the lower over the higher faculties was thought to lead to hysteria, hallucination, and split personalities (double consciousness and double personality), it was to generate an absolutely new aesthetic form—one that was, above all, *magnetic*, a word used again and again to describe it.

In the Goncourts' novel *Manette Salomon* (1865), Anatole Bazoche is an exhibitionist and a mimic. At a masked ball, his faced floured like that of a Pierrot, he performs a dance that contains, in embryo, the majority of the characteristics of cabaret and caf'conc' performance from the mid-1860s to the end of the century (that is to say, the same period encompassing Charcot's celebrity).

> From every part of his person cruel caricatures of infirmities surged forth: he gave himself nervous tics that insanely skewed up his face, imitated, by limping, the clubfoot or the wooden leg, simulated . . . the foot of an apoplectic old man. He had gestures that spoke . . . that seemed to spread excrement, slang, disgust! He fell into . . . stupid beatitudes, idiotic ecstasies . . . interrupted by sudden bestial itches that made him beat his chest like a native of Tierra del Fuego. . . . He imparted to one of his hands a movement of mechanical rotation. . . . He parodied woman, he parodied love. . . . It was the infernal cancan of Paris, not the cancan of 1830, naïve, brutal, sensual, but the corrupted cancan, the snickering and ironic cancan, the epileptic cancan that spits like a blasphemy of the pleasure of the dance in the blasphemies of all time. . . .
>
> At the end . . . the women [who had climbed up onto their partners' shoulders to see better] were crying from laughing so hard. (249–51)

The involuntary facial and motor dysfunctions that made cabaret audiences hysterical with laughter fall into the same category as the bestial, the idiotic, and the disgusting: all variants of Low, and all symptoms associated with hysteria. Thérésa, who rose to stardom in 1864, is a big woman known for her ugliness, crowned by a "mouth [that] appears to circle around her head; for lips, cushions like a negro; the teeth of a shark" (Veuillot 149). She "acts out her song as much as she sings it . . . with her eyes, arms, shoulders, and hips, with daring. . . . The shock is violent" (ibid.). She was also known for the vulgarity of her songs and for her voice; she sang "perfectly inept [songs that contained] the flavor of the gutter, and the trick is to find in the gutter the tidbit that contains the real taste of the gutter. Parisians themselves are not all lacking in the flair that leads to this truffle" (ibid.). "The animal maw [of the public] has to be fed from now on with rotten meat" (151). Huysmans describes a caf'conc' where a comic trooper sang, in "a superhuman voice where gutter water crossed by the sound of horns gargled," about the results of eating too much melon. These scatological couplets made the enthusiastic public "double over, twisting their sides" ("Autour des fortifications" 428). Zola (changing only the names) describes the attraction for the bourgeoisie of Aristide Bruant's cabaret Le Mirliton as the spectacle of people "in heat, filthy, an irresistible attraction of opprobrium and disgust. . . . Hypnotized by contempt [and] what a frightening symptom, the condemned of tomorrow throwing themselves into the mud, voluntarily hastening their [mental] decomposition by this thirst for what is ignoble, sitting there, in the vomit of this dive" (in Richard 264). The Upper (class), hypnotized by the caf'conc' spectacle, is pulled down into the realm of the Lower. The degradation of the intellect by frequenting dives, cabarets, bars, and café-concerts came more and more into question from 1885 to the end of the century, when elegant Parisians went searching for cheap thrills in these places. In fact, what was disturbing for many commentators was the mix and consequent physical proximity of classes in the caf'conc' public: political figures, femmes du monde "rubbing elbows with a lot of modest folk, shop owners, salesmen, servants, and the inevitable bizarre, violent faces. . . . Without a barrier between them, in a shared, carefree atmosphere, the prostitute and the society woman, . . . masters and servants, honest people (well-bred) and hoodlums" (Talmeyr, in Richard 131). Léo Claretie attributes the "strange taste among good company for the riff-raff": hence the popularity of "slumming it" in dives and sordid bars, as well as the proliferation of realist and naturalist literature and theater where themes of alcoholism, crime, and prostitution abounded. Aristide Bruant, more than any other, capitalized on the fashionable taste for the "*canaille*" (low-life) in his song cycle *Dans la rue*, whose songs are set in the poor quarters of the Bastille, the Villette, and Menilmontant, and in which pimps beat up the pale waifs who work for them and streetcorner punks rob and knife the Bourgeois passing by. As for cabaret humor, "one ends up descending to a state of mind . . . where a clown's jokes, grimaces, contortions, and sudden idiotic expressions are sufficient to shake us with a salutary burst of laughter" (Lemaître, in Caradec and Weill 208). Edmond de Goncourt was horrified that the contagion had reached his own family, a "family without a single eccentricity." The vocabulary and humor of the caf'conc', "the entire repertoire of Thérésa, all the pratfalls of the Bouffes, the ditties and refrains of the low theater of our day, that's all you hear coming out of the mouth of the son and daughter of good families. . . . The world of honest people has stolen the expressions and humor of the other [world]; and I wonder whether [the former] isn't being slowly and daily led by this contagion of low sentiments, of unhealthy irony, droll and stupefying, to an intellectual and moral abasement never before witnessed in society" (Goncourt Brothers, *Journal*, année 1866, 217–18).

In addition to observing that the greatest number of male hysterics were to be found among performers who were "bundles of nerves," some psychiatrists and physiologists believed that the laws "of human and animal movement emanate[d] from the continuous current of dynamic electricity," and that "a brain composed of defective batteries produces sparks and shocks (*étincelles et secousses*) that bring about insanity . . . by the violent combustion of the phosphorescent element of the cerebral pulp" (Galopin 116, 125) (see Chapter 2). (We are reminded of the description of the magnetizer Donato with his "fascinating, almost phosphorescent gaze" [Delboeuf 96]): one of the most famous actresses and monologuists of her day, Gabrielle Réjane, was described as "the muse of hystero-epilepsy" and as "nerves and eyes, that's Réjane. . . . The modernity of this actress is adorable" (Champsaur, *Paris* 54). We remember Lucy Muger's hit song "Electrocuted." Nothing is more modern than nerves. Saying that actors were "bundles of nerves" or emphasizing the electricity emanating from them often translated into seeing them as hysterics, subjects who complained of the electric currents that traversed their bodies during attacks. The public craves the strong shocks of this electric experience. Movement in the performance style of cabaret, like that of early French film comedy, was *directed* toward the production of shocks, as dozens of journalistic and literary accounts that contain the words *des secousses* will attest. Sought after, but associated with mental disorders, the electric jolt is communicated by the performer to the spectator; it is "an electro-magnetic spark from their electrified imagination, the incandescent foyer that consumes and devours them so quickly" (Galopin 126).[15] Certainly one can question the scientific validity of notions like these, but what emerges clearly from contemporary observations on the cabaret cited in this chapter (which continue in the section below on the public) is that the repetition of nervous, convulsive, mechanical movement produced a state that could only be characterized as a simulacrum of pathology, as quasi-pathological.

The Comic Monologue

The comic monologue was a genre inseparable from the cabaret, invented (along with the phonograph) by a member of the Hydropathe group, Charles

Cros. It was in 1867 that Cros first read his "Pickled Herring"; it was soon to be on everyone's lips. By 1880, the monologue was enjoying a tremendous vogue with "all variety of audiences" (Forestier 258). The "extraordinarily Parisian" monologue is one of the "most original expressions of modern gaiety" because it reaches the spleen directly (Coquelin, *Le Monologue moderne* 12) and because it has to with madness. For Jules Claretie, Charles Cros is the best representative of this bizarre form of comedy, dizzying and intensely mad ("d'une folie intense") (in Goudeau). For some, the comic monologue was "execrable and, worse, intolerable. . . . The pleasure that the public finds or pretends to find in these ineptitudes is absolutely incomprehensible. Nothing is better proof of the power of fashion over the minds of the crowd" (Francisque Sarcey, in Forestier 259). If I am right, however, it is the reverse that took place: it was the spirit of the masses that exercised its power over fashion.

Some cabaret personalities explicitly warned others against impersonating hysterics in their gestures, thus confirming my argument that the tendency was to do just that. The most famous practitioner of the monologue, Coquelin ainé, gave the following advice:

> You come on stage with the physiognomy of one who is a bit overwhelmed, the body slightly automatic; . . . be concentrated, obsessed, very anxious and worried, but not hallucinated: you are a theatrical subject, not a medical subject. You belong to the stage, not to Doctor Charcot. (Coquelin and Coquelin 92)

Evidently, comics needed to hear this warning or admonition. However, Coquelin also wrote that to make an impression on the spectators the monologuist had to convey "the stupefaction of a man who is bewildered by (whose head is spinning from) the things he's recounting [and that] this man should be alternatively phlegmatic and suddenly carried away by excitement" (*Le Monologue moderne* 21). This is a fairly good description of an hysteric. Moreover, his brother, Coquelin cadet, "made the public dizzy with his insane capers, his extravagant gestures, and his terrifying grimaces" (Meizeroy 105). Many monologues turn on pathology, like Henri de Noussanne's 1895 "The Tic" and Galipaux's "Man with a Tic." For Ernest Coquelin, "the absolute incarnation" of the modern monologue is Cros's "Obsession." In this monologue (performed by Coquelin) the obsessed person comes on stage and announces, "Oh! I'm really sick." Two days earlier he'd been to the theater and heard a song that he hasn't been able to get out of his mind. He walks in cadence to it, he rings the concierge's bell in rhythm to it, he washes to it, and so on. The tune becomes a form of echolalia (an hysterical verbal tic consisting of repeating the last syllable of words). He takes the "train, trin, trin, trin," while his head splits ("éclate, klat, klat, klat, klat); [he] arrives à la Gare Saint-Lazare, zar, zar, zar, like a madman (comme un fou, fou, fou!), Oh, this melody (cet air, tère, tère, tère, tère!"). He throws himself into the Seine as a last resort to stop repeating the melody. Unfortunately, he is rescued and when he recovers consciousness, he "expels the water, but not the *air*! lère, lère, lère, lère." The humor in this monologue is based on involuntary impulse to imitate and repeat a rhythm, an intonation heard in a song, a phenomenon that is universal, according to Tarde and is illustrated by the films to be analyzed here, but which can easily become pathological, obsessional. Dr. Pierre Janet's *Les Obsessions et la psychasthénie* contains several like examples of linguistic repetition. In another of Cros's monologues, "La famille Dubois," everyone is named Dubois, and the repetition of the name drives the interlocutor crazy: "I screamed, furious [at the name Dubois]." The recurrence of a single idea, an "idée fixe" was considered by Janet as the lesion characterizing hysteria. Ernest Coquelin held that the comical is born, among other things, of "uninterrupted verbiage and of the idée fixe" (Cros and Corbière 261).

The very definition of the genre of the comic monologue emphasizes pathology: "a kind of one-person vaudeville, mixed with fantasy and satire, with a little enormity (extravagant exaggeration), as in Rabelaisian farce, but with a modern twist, which, precisely in what it contains of madness, corresponds to the state of our nerves" (Coquelin and Coquelin 75). The same audiences who appreciated the Coquelin brothers also applauded "a starving madman who recited . . . an hysterical sonnet, a macabre ballad, an idiotic monologue" (Champsaur, *Paris* 103). As will become more and more clear, modernity in the cabaret and theater is another word for pathology.[16]

The theme of madness runs through the fin-de-siècle cabaret from the Hydropathes founded in 1878, a name that recalls the cold showers of the asylum,[17] to the Epileptic Red Herrings and the Incohérents (to cite only the artistic groups whose names made this theme visible), to the epileptic singers and "comiques idiots" I've described. The spirit of the cabaret, *le fumisme*, is defined by Emile Goudeau, chef of the Hydropathes, as "a species of inner madness externally manifested by imperturbable buffooneries" (100). *Parce Domine*, Willette's mural decorating a wall of the Chat Noir, depicts an exuberant procession descending from Montmartre to the Seine; frenetic Pierrots and adolescents at the outset, become faded and crumbling figures at the end who appear mad and tubercular. Jean Goudeski implies the link between madness and reciting verse in cabarets in this poem: "He's the monsieur who recites verses . . . / Certainly, the vocation isn't rosy / And I would have a lot less neuroses / If I could write in prose" (in Richard 270). Montorgueil's association of the cabaret shows of the 1880s with the psychiatrist's prognostic that his generation would end up "in the bag of *désarticulés*," people who had joints and members that seemed detached or askew, seems more and more logical.

Pathology also infiltrated the theater of Grand Guignol, from the 1905 "Une Leçon à la Salpêtrière"[18] and "L'Obsession" (among five, possibly eight, plays written by the psychiatrist Alfred Binet with André de Lorde), which included "The Horrible Experiment," "Crime in an Insane Asylum," and "Le Laboratoire des hallucinations." Other plays that turn on pathology are "Tics," "A Concert in the Insane Asylum," and "The Mad Ones" (Les Détraquées, written by Dr. Joseph Babinsky and Pierre Palau). These plays represented a new genre, "Théâtre Médical," created by André de Lorde. De Lorde, librarian of the Bibliothèque de l'Arsenal and curator at the Bibliothèque Sainte-Geneviève, as well as author of some of the most repugnant scenes imaginable in theater, proclaimed that his "vocation [was] to study physiological cases . . . like a doctor studies a sick person" (M. Gordon xxxviii). He was the first to set plays in insane asylums and hospital operating rooms. In "Une Leçon," Dr. Marbois is a candidate to succeed Charcot at the Institut de France. The play begins in a lab where interns are dissecting the brain of an old alcoholic with Jacksonian epilepsy. "Here's his brain! —Oh! he had a big one for an imbecile!—It's always like that." A supposedly hysterical female patient has been maimed in an operation performed by one of the interns, Nicolo, and is later brought on stage for one of the famous Tuesday lessons at the hospital. She takes her vengeance on the intern by throwing sulfuric acid at his face. Nicolo, convulsed with pain and screaming in terror, shows his horrible visage to the audience, burned bright red with the sulfuric acid that has just been thrown on him. The interns run back and forth "like madmen." The Grand Guignol audience shouted out loud (as they did in the caf'conc' and *beuglant*, and as they had in melodrama), and a house physician was always present and often needed. The doctors and mad scientists on stage "operated" viscerally on the bodies of the spectators, hypnotized by the horror and gore. "Horror was to be immediately and physically shocking, even sickening" (M. Gordon 18). I've mentioned the shared content of sexuality, crime, and nastiness in the *rosse* plays that filled out the Grand Guignol program and in the songs of Aristide Bruant (and Fursy). There is another parallel to be drawn: the master of the genre, Oscar Méténier,[19] found the "instinctive and savage actions [of his characters] superior to the vain pretensions of bourgeois theater-goers" (in M. Gordon 13). The adjectives "instinctive" and "savage" should alert us to the inherent resemblance between the *rosse* play and the medical plays: both take as their subject the corporeal unconscious. And it is therefore not surprising that the name Grand Guignol came from the puppet shows that inspired Alfred Jarry in precisely the same years. The crazy, violent behavior of puppets, with their dislocations and capacity for dismemberment, are perfectly in sync with the plots and *mises en scène* of the Grand Guignol. Puppets, as I've suggested, are not the masters of their actions or movements and are thus perfect symbols of the corporeal unconscious driven by primitive, instinctual forces. Other plays contained scenes of hypnotism, somnambulism, and madness, and their presence in the repertoire of the Grand Guignol theater with its mass appeal is yet another indication of just how widespread public knowledge of the pathologies of hysteria were.

In his 1883 *La Vie humoristique*, Coquelin cadet describes the gait of the most famous clown of his generation, Agoust, as the gait of a centipede accompanied by grimaces. The movements of the singer Baron are a "precious swaying of the hips, the gestures of a puppet, accompanied by a hypocritical smirk (*narquois*)" (57). His voice accounts for the other half of his popularity. He has a voice that would belong to the gargoyles of Notre Dame if they could speak; it "tears apart the eardrum. . . . It sounds like an iron pot bouncing off the tail of a howling dog [and] makes you laugh because of its sumptuous discordance" (55–56). What makes people laugh is "the exaggeration of the body's way of being [and] the magnification of any known sensation" (Coquelin, *Le Rire* 4).

Pain

The emphasis on pain in late-nineteenth-century spectatorship often goes along with the destruction of or resistance to language, as Elaine Scarry has noted in other cultural contexts in her book *The Body in Pain*. This is most obvious where language is of course totally absent—in pantomime—but other forms of contemporary spectacle dispense with language as well: in puppet shows, inarticulate cries that accompany the stick striking the head or the seat of the pants frequently punctuate sparse dialogue, and some of the most popular songs and monologues of the cabaret contain nonsense syllables or words whose syllables are strangely detached or repeated. The voice of the poet-singer Maurice Rollinat "cuts like a razor." The can-can or *chahut* as it was also called, pushes the body to the painful limits of the possible, eliciting shrieks (of joy or pain? or both?). This is the paradox that exists in hysteria. Hysterics seemed to relish painful sensations and derive pleasure from them. Yet the search for ever more intense sensations was a generalized phenomenon in what fin-de-siècle spectators demanded from their entertainment. The Grand Guignol Theater of cruelty is of course the best example of this, with its scenes of torture, rape, decapitation, and other forms of gore. What precisely is the tension between showing pain in the body and liberating the body, allowing it to express the previously inexpressible? Part of the answer is found in observations of hysterics, and part in accounts of the impact on the public of circus, pantomime, and caf'conc' performances. The incredible explosion of libido and joy is the other side of pain, and of two other fin-de-siècle obsessions: decomposition and death. Nothing, therefore, could have been a more fitting decoration for the Chat Noir cabaret than Willette's *Parce Domine*. In Dorville's cabaret Le Néant (Nothingness), the drinks, set on coffins, were served in skulls by "undertakers," and a skeleton hung prominently from the ceiling as a priest administered the last rites to those present. One could witness "his own decomposition, thanks to a play of mirrors; one sees his 'face turn green, crawl with vermin, and fall apart in the final disintegration'" (Richard, 123–24). Georges Méliès contributed a number of original illusions to this cabaret. Extreme reactions are the order of the day in cabaret: otherwise, no public.

Painful corporeal extremes are an essential facet of the comic, contributing to the element of surprise and astonishment that is so sought after. Theories of laughter between 1860 and 1900 all point out that *the unexpected* is an essential component of the comic, and some writers find it particularly characteristic of *modern* comedy. One of the principal sources of surprise in pantomime comes from the abrupt switches from grimaces and frenetic, epileptic contortions to deadpan and complete immobility. This contrast will later provide the basis of early film comedy. The same progression exists in the passage between the first two and the last two stages of the hysterical attack. Dr. Paul Richer's account could easily be mistaken for a description of the mimes, the Hanlon-Lees:

> The contortions consist in strange, unexpected, illogical poses; the [hyperbolic] movements [are] rapid oscillations between [for example] a series of exaggerated salutations, extremely acrobatic somersaults and *sauts de carpe* [flat on one's back, without the use of the hands, one springs from the pelvis to the upright position], tumbling (*culbutes*), always repeated several times, often preceded by automatic cries like a train whistle. . . . The third period, passionate or sculptural poses [illustrate] a drama, sad or gay. (*L'Art et la médecine* 149–50)

In the 1870s, Dr. J. Falret asserted that convulsive movements and involuntary vacillations of the eyeballs are symptoms that the nervous illness is incurable. Patients with chronic mania suffer from constant agitation and violent impulses; they are prone to sudden laughter and frequent grimaces, as is illustrated in Figure 6. The patient in this photograph is constantly in motion; she can't stay in one place. Occasionally, she tears her clothes. She talks to herself all the time, but her sentences are incoherent. Similarly, the "irresistible impulses" of hysterics make them commit "ridiculous or extravagant acts," such as breaking objects, shouting, or bursting into laughter (Dagonet 522). The grimaces that are characteristic of hysteria and manic disorders reappear in pantomime, performances of clowns, cabaret song, and early film comedy.

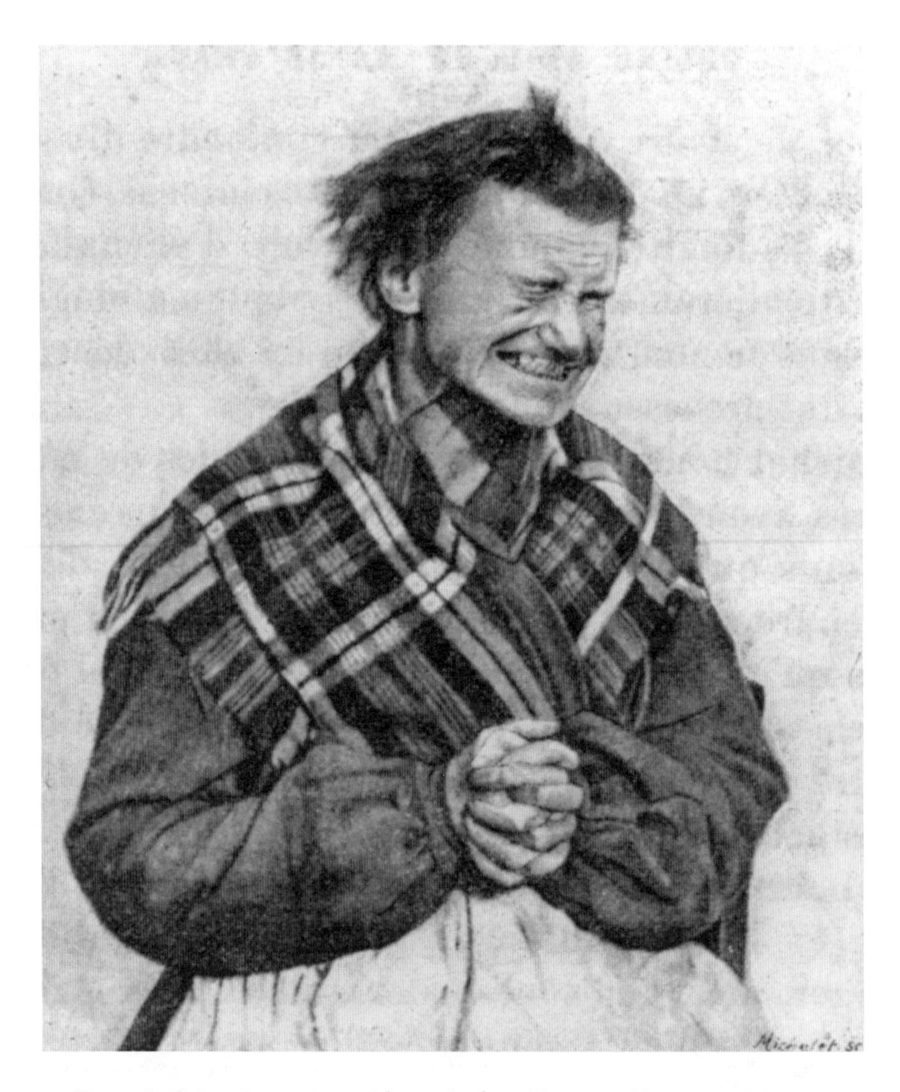

Figure 6. Grimacing patient with mania, from Dagonet, *Nouveau traité élémentaire des maladies mentales* (1876). Photo Bibliothèque nationale de France, Paris.

The Cabaret and Caf'Conc' Public

> The literature of the Cafés-Concerts is the expression of the tendencies of the crowd and a summary of the popular aesthetic. There is a totally direct contact between *la chanson* and the people, the masses.
>
> — LÉO CLARETIE, *1893*

> It is certain that today, primarily in the cities, hysteria is the illness in vogue. It is everywhere.
>
> — DR. PAUL-MAX SIMON, *1881*

Although the "gymnastics of song" made so popular by Paulus and others—the songs that Georges Montorgueil saw had "gesticulatory hysteria"—has its source in pantomime, and although it owes much to marionettes and the comedy team the Clodoches, it is nevertheless an original art form proper to the caf'conc' of the last thirty years of the nineteenth century.[20] The phenomenal success of the chanteuses Thérésa, Mlle Bécat, Polaire, and scores of others was above all due to the extravagant movements that accompanied their songs. Jean Lorrain, we remember, described Polaire as hopping around, trembling, quivering, and dancing "with her hips, pelvis, and navel, mim[ing] all sorts of shocks and shaking" as she leans over backward in the form of an arc before she rolls her eyes up into her head and swoons. "The room, immobilized with stupor, forgets to applaud; only the old gentlemen, reacting enthusiastically, remember to do so" (279). Stupor is a symptom of imbecility or idiocy, two varieties of mental pathology much written about in the 1870s and 1880s (see, for example, Jules Voisin's *Melancholia with Stupor and Cataleptic Stupid Melancholia*). The state of stupor is associated with epilepsy in the period (Dagonet 259), and Polaire's act induces a reaction of stupor in the public: not only her convulsive movements, but the content of her songs as well, for example, "Portrait of the Little Cat," which is cited by Colette.[21] T. J. Clark notes the liberating and dangerous forces of this sort of spectacle. "It couldn't be prudent to put so much emphasis on the . . . body. . . . Sexuality is linked to other forms of terror" (231–33).

Thérésa's public, "seeking strong shocks, vibrates passionately as she produces a shock wave with her unadulterated gut twisting" (Veuillot 150). The expression "*c'est tordant!*" (I split my sides laughing, or, literally: It twists my body), which continues to be commonly used in the French language is the mirror image of the physical contortions that provoked laughter in the French public between 1870 and 1912.

The degree and intensity of audience participation in cabaret spectacle of the nineteenth century was extraordinary. It is unequaled in any other form of entertainment: the spectacle was truly as much in the audience as it was on stage. The *visual* importance of the variety of spectators was understood and foregrounded by every visual artist who made the cabaret a theme: Toulouse-Lautrec, Ibels, Degas. The vivacity of the public, with its mix of social classes, professions, and attitudes often attracts and merits *more* attention in these paintings and prints than the performers. The public of the Chat Noir changed radically from its beginnings in 1881, when it was a "club" for poets, artists, and monologuists, as were several other artistic cabarets. In 1888, with the first shadow play of the Théâtre d'Ombres, *L'Epopée*, it became the rendezvous of the Tout-Paris (the upper classes, the influential, and the famous) and of wealthy foreign visitors, but also of a broader public. The Shadow Theater was composed of hundreds of silhouettes and gauze screens giving the appearance of considerable depth within the round aperture on stage; it foreshadowed cinema, and the last play, performed in 1896, would coincide with the first full year of film screenings.[22] Alongside the "artistic cabarets" there were the "cabarets à attractions," which were frequented more by the bourgeoisie than by the working-class public. Many café-concerts, on the other hand, continued to be inexpensive enough for the average working-class family to attend on Saturday night. "Viens, poupoule," sang Mayol: "Saturday night after work, the Parisian worker / Says to his wife, I'm taking you out to the Caf'conc'. Come, my little chicken, come my little chicken, come, / Remember that that's how I became a papa." Opinion held that the cabaret was primarily a venue for the elite, and that the caf'conc' was a show for the masses, an industrialized form of art. This did not prevent the same corporeal and vocal forms of expression from dominating in *both* places. Simply put, the powerful attraction of pathology as spectacle pervaded all classes of society.

The public participated in the show in several ways: visually, vocally, physically, and as "victim." Audiences often sang the refrain along with the performer, and in the *beuglant*, the public shouted and sang so loudly that the artists could scarcely be heard. Uproar like that was not confined to the *beuglants*, though, as Yvette Guilbert tells us: in the "tumultuous evenings" aux Ambassadeurs people came to shout, vociferate, and make an uproar/ruckus (faire du 'chahut')" (*La Chanson de ma vie* 149). At the Chat Noir, Rodolphe Salis inaugurated the style of provocation (later so widely imitated that it would be taken to be an inherent element of cabaret programs) that involved "greeting" his customers with derision as they entered his establishment. Bruant insulted them in the language of the street at the door of the Mirliton: "There you are, you bastards (*salauds*), you bunch of pigs!" He singled out spectators by gesture or word as he incorporated their least lovely traits into his songs, forcibly making the public a part of the show. Bruant's rude and vulgar jibes are what continued to bring the public to his cabaret in droves. Not masochism, but the desire to be a part of the spectacle. The public is also drawn to the anti-bourgeois nature of many songs and texts. Thumbing one's nose at convention took many forms: absurd and ludicrous texts, songs that were pure nonsense, erotic, obscene, or scatological subjects, social protest songs and *fumisme*. The physical participation of the spectator is the most interesting aspect of the café-concert and cabaret. In a short prose piece published in *Le Chat Noir* of 16 February 1884, Gladia (a young Parisian) is on her way to the "bastringue populaire," the Elysées Montmartre. "She already pictured herself lost among the noisy, colorful crowd, overflowing with energy . . . the cries, the pushing and bumping, feet in the air, legs bowed, arms outstretched, skirts raised, flesh-colored stockings glimpsed, waists grabbed with both hands, kisses exchanged . . . leaping in the harsh light of 60 gas beakers, whipped along by the banal sounds of a diabolical quadrille played by 30 panting musicians" (Lepelletier 230). The excitement of the crowd dancing the quadrille, or the wild thrill of the cancan, is not unlike descriptions of St. Vitus's Dance and "Tarentisme" noted in convulsive hysterical disorders. "Among the numerous singularities of sporadic hysterical outbreaks is a pronounced tendency to dance," notes Dr. Dagonet (20). Physical participation in the caf'conc' conformed to the physiological and psychological laws of imitation described in the previous chapters: it was contagious and habit-forming.

Often in the cabaret there was no stage, thus the singers and monologuists were literally on the same level as the audience. The absence of a physical separation between audience and performer obviously encouraged interaction: the public called out song titles, or the master of ceremonies did. And because most cabarets were populated by "regulars," artists and writers who knew each other, people called out from table to table and moved about. Bruant strolled up and down the aisle between the row of tables, and the patrons crowded up against the bar. Sometimes, he climbed up on a table to sing. As Lionel Richard notes, the use of slang, puns, and *coq à l'âne* (shifting abruptly from one idea to another) are another form of complicity between performer and public. There is a resurgence of the cabaret today in France (Achille Tonic is the troupe must faithful to the cabaret tradition of the late nineteenth century), just as there is of the circus, and direct contact with the spectator is an essential component of these shows.

Let us recall the Goncourts' description of the Eldorado audience's reaction to the comic singer whose nonsense lyrics were interspersed with "epileptic gestures—the St.-Vitus dance of idiocy. The audience was enthused to the point of delirium." The audience at the Moulin Rouge reacted similarly in 1892 to the performances of the Pétomane: "People were literally doubled up; women, suffocating with laughter, were carried off by nurses" (Jacques-Charles, in Nohain and Caradec 9); and "It was at the Moulin Rouge that I heard the longest spasms of laughter, the most hysterical attacks of hilarity" (Yvette Guilbert, in Nohain and Caradec 7). In the 1886 *Braves gens*, Richepin describes the mime's goal: "I'll drag them by the hair. . . . I'll turn [the audience's] intestines inside out, I'll pull on their exposed nerves and bone marrow. . . . Art commands it." The goal of the mime's gestures is therefore to render the public "delirious, . . . the nerves twisted. This change of attitudes, postures, in the public was brought about by the abrupt call of a single, unexpected note . . . drawn out in strident vibrations" (501). And the hysteria on stage is transmitted to the audience.

Why, one might well ask again, would the spectator *enjoy* such an experience? If one goes along with (for example) the Goncourt brothers, the answer lay in the "unhealthy" tastes of the masses; if one prefers to listen to Max Nordau (one of the most influential popularizers of the psychiatric theory of degeneration), the answer is in the "degenerate" tastes of the intellectual and artistic elite: pain and other intense sensations are sought after to stimulate a lethargic and decadent psyche. Certainly Nordau was right to discern the rhythms, movements, and abnormal sensations of hysteria in "modern art"; they underlie nearly all that is new in the arts of the fin de siècle.

The discourse on degeneration had wide currency in the fin de siècle, as indicated in Chapter 1, and neurasthenia, with its loss of physical vitality and attenuated hysterical symptoms, became "the malady of the century" in the first decade of the twentieth century. Bizarre character traits and an exacerbated originality of style and taste go hand in hand with emotionality and imbecility. Moreover, "degenerates are always in danger of becoming insane" (Marquezy 1144). Interestingly, from 1886 on, psychiatrists began to reclassify many cases of degeneration as male hysteria. The characteristics of degeneration and hysteria are continually emphasized by commentators on the cabaret.

Montmartre is described by Laurent Tailhade as "a province of . . . cheap vice where an overflow of lust spills out of the human beast" (in Richard 129). An article on the can-can at the Moulin Rouge in *La Revue Belge* makes it clear that the violent movement on stage produces a parallel physical reaction in the spectator: the dance is "nothing but a frenetic spasm of a panting gnome and a female ghoul in heat. . . . More than one [spectator] sticks out his tongue and twists his arms craving more, hypnotized by the hectic transports of a monstrous and degrading lack of decency" (Edgar Baes, in Lebensztejn 81). This form of spectacle was dangerous: the most well-known dancer of the Moulin Rouge was said to have the blood of a revolutionary, and the numerous descriptions of La Goulue underline her animal sensuality. The lower order—the instinctual, the corporeal unconscious—was inevitably linked to anarchy and revolution. This spirit, transmitted visually and rhythmically, imitated by the "hypnotized" crowds (made up by a good number of lower-class patrons) could only lead to trouble.

Yvette Guilbert and "La très moderne chanson, dit fin-de-siècle"

What Yvette Guilbert has to say about cabaret performance in *L'Art de chanter une chanson* will confirm much of what has been said in the previous pages. Since she was *not* one of the singers who made pathology the basis of her performance style, the resemblances between the photographs illustrating Guilbert's technique and those illustrating the theatrics of the patients of the Salpêtrière are all the more interesting (see Figure 7). This said, her silhouette and her presentation evoked for Henri Lavedan "some troubling automaton, a waxworks woman of Edgar Poe," and for Jean Richepin "the power of suggestion [in her songs is all the more] unexpected because it's her gesture that speaks, her physiognomy that vocalizes and her voice that gesticulates!" (both in Guilbert, *La Chanson de ma vie* 166–67). And she didn't hesitate to sing Maurice Donnay's "Eros vanné": "I am blond, my emerald eyes hypnotizing the neurotic ones. . . . I am the God of the Refined ones whose brain I derange."

How did Yvette Guilbert "acquire the facial [and the corporeal] mimicry" (41) of a corresponding idea? How did she make the outside mirror the inside? "In exteriorizing the palpitations of my heart, the (sensory) impressions . . . of my nerves, . . . by not being ashamed . . . to make my face ugly" (41). "You have to know how to deform your physical beauty in the interests of art [like the] jugglers and clowns [of the Middle Ages who] danced and sang in the streets and tried to make the public laugh by the contortions of their face and their body" (64–65). The singer's face and body mirror the interior thought and the language of the nerves in the same way that the hysteric makes the unconscious idea visible through the bodily symptom. The text of a song is only the trace, the "*fil rouge*" that leads to the underlying thought, the "soul of the couplets' body" (94). Yvette Guilbert's long friendship with Freud leads me to think that the choice of these images is not innocent. The words are often insignificant: everything is in the "acrobatics of juggling with the refrains." Gesture and pose must be "so expressive that they suggest what you are thinking" (103). Each character in the song "is a marionette set in motion by the gestures of the singer" (107). Then, not only the elite but the masses will see "the true meaning" and "*unconsciously* receive the beautiful gift" (60).

In one of the songs that serves as an example of technique, "Ah! que l'amour cause de peine!", the singer deforms her pronunciation, stutters, and skips over words "like an idiot" (130). The pathology of language is accompanied by pathological gait at the end of the song, when she exits very comically "*en tourniquet*" (ibid.).

Like the hysteric, the singer has to possess multiple personalities, "multiple brains, hearts, and souls" (153). And it is *magnetism* that is responsible

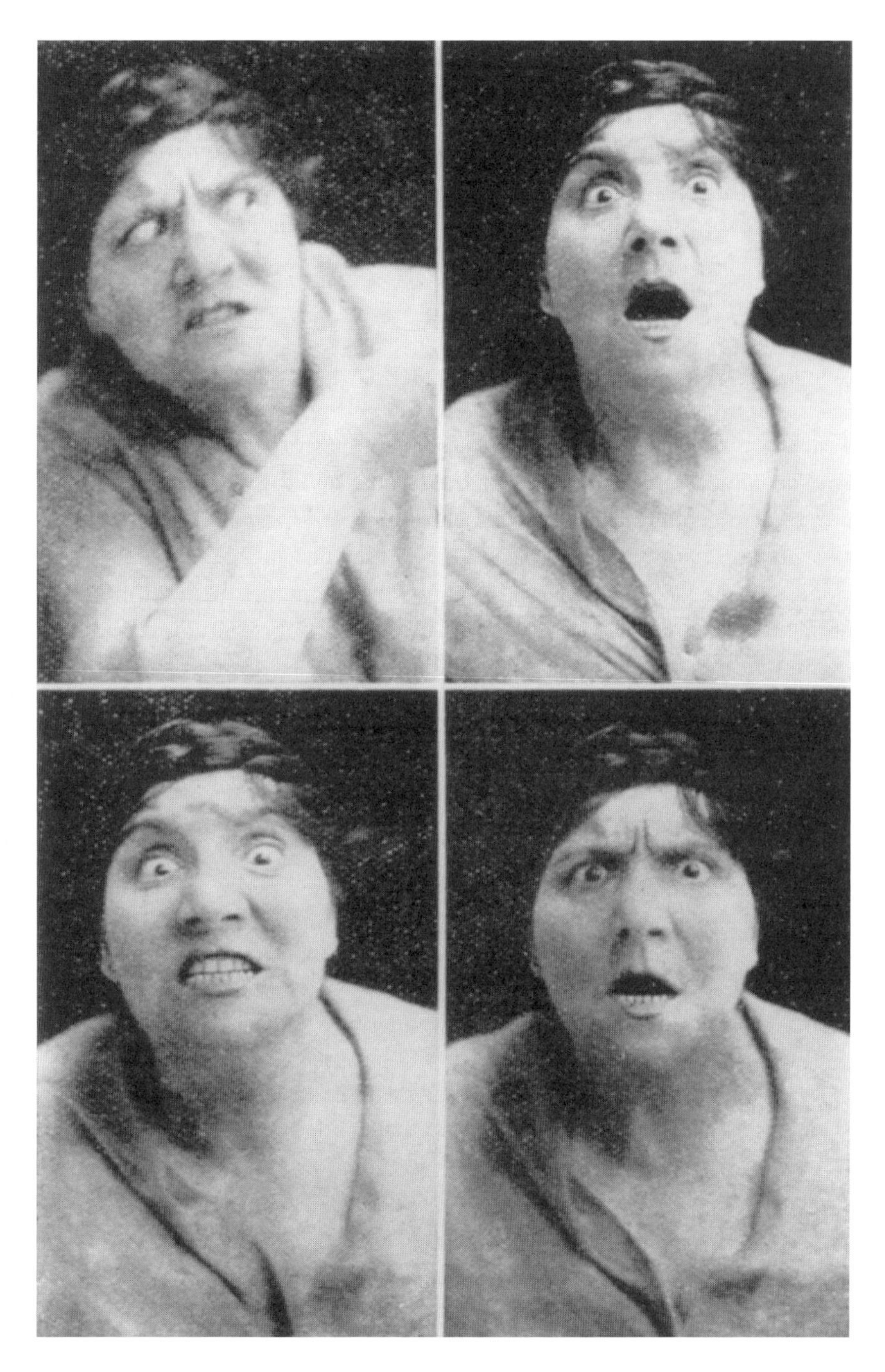

Figure 7. Yvette Guilbert, from *L'Art de chanter une chanson* (1928). Paris: Bernard Grasset, 1928.

for the artist's success. This "imperative power" that attracts things and people to itself is part of the personality and makes the artist's soul magnetic and irresistible. Briefly put, Guilbert understood that modern song was a distillation of the entire cabaret spectacle—acrobatics, juggling, marionettes, the idiot comic, pathological gait—of which gesture was the guiding force.

Life Imitates Art

Dr. Galopin had the magnetic power of the performer in mind when he warned against the hysteria engendered in the public by singers and actors. We remember that Maurice Rollinat, Hydropathe and author of *Les Névroses* and *L'Abîme*, exercised this power over his provincial audience to a supreme degree (see Chapter 2). "Those who saw him for the first time were stupefied . . . by his flashing eyes, his voice, his chaotic gestures . . . and the communicative heat he gave off" (Grellety, *Souvenirs de Rollinat* 9–10). His effect on a gathering of sophisticated Parisians was even greater. Rollinat's Parisian debut was in November of 1882 in Sarah Bernhardt's salon, and Albert Wolff's account of it the next day in the pages of the *Figaro* made him an instant celebrity.

> [The listeners] are frozen in terror. Truly, the extraordinary has leapt into the room. A nightmare of horror and beauty weighs on every breast. Faces are pale, the features tense, . . . the eyes are hallucinated by the spectacle of this head [that] appears like the Saint John of human madness. The song has ended. . . . Suddenly, . . . a frenetic ovation burst forth. . . . Now he has [his listeners'] fibers and nerves under his fingers. He plays on them at will . . . caresses them, enervates them, pinches them, exasperates them, makes them mad, and the audience no longer has any control over itself. He gives them the supreme [cerebral] commotion with "Troppmann's Soliloquy." Then all is delirium. All are on their feet. . . . AND IT'S FAME! (in Guiches 94–95)

In this fusion of hysteria and the supernatural, the parallels between Rollinat and the magnetizers of the period, who had the same control over their audience, are again evident.

Rollinat, singing his macabre, morbid poetry at the Chat Noir, had an intensely physical effect on audiences. Emile Goudeau spoke of Rollinat's "convulsions" while singing "Troppmann's Soliloquy," and added that Rollinat achieved his incredible success "by torturing the nerves of his audience" (166, 175). His "jerky, staccato voice got into your bone marrow [and] literally bewitched the public" (Valbel 87). His voice is that of a "devil made out of steel: sharpened steel that cuts and chills in cutting. His face is contorted in convulsive grimaces and his eyes stare in horror . . . he has *le diable au corps* . . . visionary of visions that he doesn't see. And so it is that we have one more modern poet" (Barbey d'Aurevilly, in *Le Constitutionnel* (Paris), 1 June 1882; and *Le Chat Noir*, 1 June 1882). The above allusion to hallucinating was not gratuitous: Rollinat suffered from hallucinations, and drinking didn't help. Dr. Valentin Magnan's 1874 *De l'alcoolisme* clearly linked alcohol's effect on nervous tissue to madness. Absinthe, according to Dr. P. M. Simon, could be the sole cause of epilepsy. Saying that Rollinat's body was inhabited by the Devil was simply another way of saying that it was hysterical, since cases of possession by the devil were shown in the nineteenth century to have been cases of hysteria. (A decade later, in the films of Méliès, the overlap between the diabolical and the hysterical would surface most clearly.)[23] The poet is largely indebted to psychiatry for his conception of "modern" forms of expression: as I stated in chapter 2, he attended Charcot's lessons for two years and was conversant with contemporary debates on hallucination and hysteria (Miannay 298). The poem "La rélique" provides one example: "Ton corps . . . / Toujours affamé de plaisir . . . se tordait dans l'alcove / Bouillant d'une hystérie irresistible et fauve" (Your body, Always starving for pleasure, was contorting itself in the [bedroom] alcove, boiling with an irresistible and wild hysteria) (Rollinat, *Les Névroses*).[24] Maurice Barrès wrote that Rollinat "grips language, brutalizes it, wounds it at times. . . . Without any intervention of the will, sensations are immediately translated in his brain into dramatic monologues. . . . He is unconscious. . . . A convulsionary. . . . Excessive, he brings on a cerebral congestion [and] if it gives way to inflammation . . . there is delirium" (34–36). In other words, the will has disappeared and the singer abandons himself to sensation (the hallmark of mental pathologies), and actually works himself up to the point of madness in his act. Rollinat's mental illness was amply documented in several accounts and medical studies. One of the first of these was written by his friend Dr. Grellety, who tells us that the singer-poet was sick, a "neuropathe in the broadest sense of the word with the notion of bizarre illness that the public attaches to it. [He] was subject to incessant yawning and itching without respite" (*Souvenirs de Rollinat* 17).

What was the effect on the *entertainer* of incorporating the gestures, tics, and visions of hysteria in his or her act? A remarkable number of performers in the cabaret (and in early cinema) became hysterics or neurasthenics and were prone to hallucinate. Rollinat died insane (in 1903 at age fifty-seven), as did Jules Jouy and Charles Cros's mistress, Nina de Villard. Villard was a musician and monologuist whose salon was "a workshop for insanity" (an atelier de détraquage), as the Goncourt brothers called it. According to Félicien Champsaur, she "wanted to be original, bizarre, and she consumed a considerable amount of absinthe." Her frequent nervous attacks became madness, and she could be seen at night "dancing, walking, with the characteristic movements and gestures of hysteria, calling for her lover who had left her" (*Paris* 104). She died insane in 1884 at the age of forty-one (Bersaucourt 89).[25] The Grand Guignol actor René Chimier lamented that one didn't play madmen, sadists, and people suffering from hallucinations every day with impunity. "I reached the point where I no longer had control over my nerves. I feared becoming really neurasthenic" (in M. Gordon xlv). André Gill, one of the greatest illustrators of the satiric press, Emile Cohl's maître, and the creator of the sign for the cabaret Le Lapin Agile which bears his name (à Gill), was committed to the Charenton asylum for hallucinations in 1881; he died there four years later. As the mime in Jean Richepin's novel proclaims, "Nothing will stop me; I'll fire up the machine [the body] again and again, even if I have to make my own furnace explode, set my brain on fire" (*Braves gens* 501).

Who's Acting?

If we assemble the plethora of references to convulsive agitation and epilepsy in the period, we see that suddenly hysteria was everywhere. In 1870 hysterics and epileptics were separated from the other patients at the Salpêtrière

Hospital; in the 1880s a good number of convulsive attacks were considered to be hysterical, and no "sure" method existed to distinguish epilepsy from hysteria before the 1895 *Studien über Hystérie* of Freud and Breuer. Epilepsy was "often complicated by a state of mental disorder that could take on different forms of madness, frequently presenting all the symptoms of dementia," according to Dr. Dagonet (639). Even as Charcot was underlining the tendency of hysterics to imitate everything they saw (first and foremost, they imitated the epileptics lodged in the same ward, but Charcot omitted this model) and everything that was suggested to them, psychiatrists refused to see that patients were willing actors in the *mises en scène* of the interns and photographers at the Salpêtrière, miming the symptoms they were supposed to be displaying. Much has been written on this subject. Cases at the Salpêtrière sometimes hovered squarely between symptoms of hysteria that the patient appeared to be simulating and the rehearsal of the gestures, poses, and grimaces of the cabaret repertoire. If the patient *is* a simulator, is s/he simulating hysteria or cabaret performance? Of course, who would obsessionally repeat the same cabaret act for hours and days and weeks on end if not an hysteric? The would-be caf'conc' star can't, perhaps, find a venue, but he *can* find an audience, and a captive one at that, at Charenton or at the Salpêtrière. The enormous prestige that the caf'conc' had among the working classes—the same classes who populated the Salpêtrière and Charenton—forces us to ask whether the sharp rise in cases of hysteria around 1875 and the continuing increase in the 1880s wasn't due in part to the phenomenon of mimetic behavior so prevalent in the cabaret and café-concert. Many psychiatric patients were keenly interested in the theater: one of Roubinovitch's patients who barely knew how to read composed a play in five acts.

Case observations of hysterics offer striking similarities with cabaret performance, as I've said. In photographs XX and XXI of volume 3 of the *Nouvelle Iconographie de la Salpêtrière*, we see a patient afflicted with "cataleptiform melancholia" whose poses evoke caf'conc' style (see Figure 1). The psychiatrists at the hospital suspected him of simulation, moreover, because of his "stereotyped gestures, special grimaces. . . . Sometimes he starts to sing a song, always the same one, and suddenly stops after a few words" (Sollier and Souques 123). Besides a look of stupor, this man has the characteristic motor symptoms of hysterics, "either in the form of convulsions . . . , or more often in the form of muscular rigidity or cataleptic states. . . . [His gestures, grimaces and words] correspond to an inner delirium, perhaps to hallucinations" (ibid.). His psychiatrists' comments are interesting: the patient isn't a "true cataleptic" because his members don't possess the "waxlike flexibility of true catatonics and cataleptics." Rather than hysteria, they see in this patient a "simple variety of melancholia with stupor and false catalepsy" (124). A few years later, Roubinovitch would conclusively demonstrate what had been suggested by Marquezy in 1888: male melancholics had been misdiagnosed and were in fact male hysterics.

Psychasthenics share some of the symptoms of epileptics and, in addition, suffer from vague and diffuse agitation, either motor or emotional and visceral (Janet, *Les Obsessions* 72). A twenty-eight-year-old male neurasthenic came home to find two cadavers in the next apartment: his neighbor had killed his wife, then himself. Despite the horror of the scene, the patient seemed calm and unemotional . . . until the next day, when he read a sensationalized account of the same scene in the newspaper *Le Petit Journal*. It was *then* that he was overcome with violent emotions. It is the representation, the *mise en spectacle* of the scene that provokes the hysterical symptoms that now ensue. Janet perceives the implications of this fact. It is not simply the delayed reaction (Freud's *nachträglich*) that accounts for the curiousness of the subject's reaction, but "the power of art . . . by which psychasthenics who are left cold by the real thing can be moved. . . . Psychasthenics always understand literary or artistic representations *better* than they do reality" (74). This, I believe, is revelatory of the power that cabaret, Grand Guignol, and film performance had on potential hysterics. Janet's patient translates the emotion he felt in reading the account: he is seized by extreme motor agitation: "he gesticulates, raises his arms to heaven, paces, runs. . . . He can't stay in one place, he constantly feels the need to gesticulate, shout, walk." Another of Janet's patients suffers from a bizarre new nervous illness, akathisia, or the impossibility of remaining seated. After a few minutes of being seated, he desperately contorts himself, stretches and spreads his legs, becoming rigid on the left side, and bends his head to the left shoulder; his whole body shakes and is traversed by sudden jolts (*secousses*), while sweat pours from him; he grips the chair with both hands and seems to be trying to hold on to it (76). Perpetual movement characterizes hysteria, epilepsy, and cabaret performance; writers on early cinema called it the essence of film.

Some of Janet's patients suffer *not* from their symptoms but from *the fear of having them*: that is to say, from the spectre of madness, the neurotic anxiety surrounding the impulse to imitate what one has seen (the traumatic scene that caused hysteria) rather from madness itself. A thirty-three-year-old woman feels dizzy from the powerful "emotion of fear that she might have an epileptic attack, become insane, have convulsions of the face if she looks up" (101).

Male Hysteria

Social marginality is to the male hysteric what eccentricity is to the female hysteric.[26] One of Charcot's hysterical patients, also labeled a victim of degeneration, performed as the "wild man" in a carnival, caged and devouring raw meat, lending credence to the link made in the period between hysteria and evolution theory. A more common form that social marginality took was that of street singer, a profession that was well represented among the inmates of Charenton and the Salpêtrière. Popular songs are linked to hysteria in the period, not only because of the accompanying gesticulation, but also because of the element of provocation and their antisocial nature. I'm referring to Bruant's songs about socially marginalized groups like *clochards* and hoodlums, the socialism and anarchism of Jules Jouy's and Jehan Rictus's songs that have to do with the injustices toward the lowest economic and social groups, Paulus's songs about people with physical disabilities, and the sexual innuendo and outright vulgarity (Leo Lelièvre's "Oh! les nichons!" [Oh! tits!, for example]) or the scatological lyrics that are prevalent in the repertoire.

A particularity of language in male hysteria also reveals itself here. The female hysteric communicates with her body and often suffers from aphasia. The male performer in the cabaret appropriates the body language and joins a narration to it. Yet, this narration is as different as it can possibly be from the narration that the paternalist psychiatrist attaches to the female hysteric's corporeal discourse. The parallel found in male hysteria is a loss of verbal coherence or meaning. One of Marquézy's male hysterics marked by mental degeneration often becomes obsessed by a word he has heard. The word takes hold of him and he repeats it incessantly (like the melody in Charles Cros's monologue "Obsession") until he has an hysterical attack with loss of consciousness. In texts sung by male cabaret singers, the deliberate ineptitude and an exalting jubilation in nonsense gives primacy to the body and gesture over the word, underlining the loss of the communicative function of language. Instead, the playful function takes over, where repetition, puns, stuttering, and even total verbal anarchy reign, just as in the "Syndrome S" of the psychiatrist Gatian de Clérambault, composed of motor and sensory phenomena and characterized by innumerable *psittacismes* (wordplay, nonsense, and verbal saws). The Saw (with a recurring formulaic or nonsense lyric) was one of the most characteristic musical genres in the fin-de-siècle cabaret: it "is a genre distinguished by deliberate incoherence or by its painful (*lancinante*; piercing like a needle) repetition. . . . The sought-for result is rather a sort of nervous irritation" (Léo Claretie, in Romi 37). Jean de Tinan explained its success by the "conditions of modern intellectual life" which render the Saw "an indispensable way of letting off steam" (ibid.). Examples include: the *gommeux* Libert's "L'Amant d'Amanda" or "Portraits de famille" ("Qui qui prend du chocolat? C'est papa. Qui qui boit son petit vin blanc? C'est maman"); or Brunin's "En voulez-vous des z'homards? Ah! les sales bêtes! Y z'ont du poil aux pattes!!!" (Do you want some lobsters? Oh! The filthy creatures! They have body hair on their paws!). But the ideal interpreter of inept verses was the performer who created the genre of the "comique idiot": Dranem. His hit "Oh! les petits pois" is the best-known example of the Saw: "Oh! peas, peas, peas, they're a very tender vegetable; peas, peas, peas, you don't eat them with your fingers." Dr. Dagonet describes the "nonsensical and incessant chattering, a characteristic rage to constantly talk, loud and stupid laughter, snickering and grimaces, extravagant declarations" of mania in imbeciles (282–83). Incoherent lyrics echo the dislocated fragmentation of the hysterical body, a body Parisian audiences couldn't get enough of.

The 1907–1908 Gaumont *phono-scènes* made of the songs "5 o'clock" and "Jiu-Jitsu" as performed by Dranem are perfect illustrations of cabaret performance style as pathology. In them, he enters the stage with little hops, wobbles to the center, and begins singing. Dranem's body language moves

Figure 8. Dranem, "Le 5 O'clock," from a Gaumont *phono-scène*. Courtesy Cinémathèque Gaumont.

between total lethargy (his eyes are even closed through most of the songs, as though he were in a somnambulistic state) and repeated, staccato hops back and forth with one leg rigid, as if it were anesthetized (see Figures 8 and 9). One of the traits in hysteria is the insistently repeated movement, and any repeated movement implies an automatism, a potentially pathological symptom. There is a marked difference most of the time between Dranem's right and left arm: one is rigid and immobile, fist clenched or hand in pocket, while the other is extremely agile, twirling a cane. Bourneville and Regnard describe a similar pose: "very marked contracture of the right hand whose fingers are clenched [while] the left hand falls limp" (*Iconographie* 1:66), and Drs. Binet and Féré remark that exaggeration of motor capacity is "an essentially pathological phenomenon [when] it exists on one side of

Figure 9. Dranem, "Jiu-Jitsu," from a Gaumont *phono-scène*. Courtesy Cinémathèque Gaumont.

the body" only (331). Dr. Dmitri Michaïlowski also describes a patient who holds one arm rigid while the other exhibits a contrasting rotation of the forearm (5:55). Dranem, knock-kneed, executes a little dance step that twists his body around backwards.[27]

Dranem's two biggest hits were "Oh, Peas!" and "I'm a Neurasthenic": "J'ai le bourdon, j'ai les intestins en accordion" (I'm having a fit of depression; my intestines are in the shape of an accordion). Dranem, like so many other stars of the café-concert, became a film comic around 1900. When he first saw himself on screen (in a Pathé film, *Dranem's Shoes*, with Ferdinand Zecca), he exclaimed happily "Never would I have believed myself to be so idiotic!" (in Coissac 414). It would be hard not to see a parallel with current tastes in mass entertainment in America in products such as *Dumb and Dumber* and *Beavis and Butthead.*

The appellation "comique idiot" was not neutral: a great many male hysterics and epileptics were also "imbeciles" or "idiots," and idiocy "always corresponds to a profound alteration of the skeleton" (Dagonet 386). Automatic acts constituted one of the characteristic forms of idiocy, which was thought to *result* from, among other causes, epilepsy. The movements of imbeciles with ataxia, similar to those of patients with hysterical chorea, are described in the *Nouvelle Iconographie de la Salpêtrière*: "The facial movements are truly extraordinary, giving birth to varied expressions, the most frequent of which is a wide grin." These expressive grimaces—which can attain a frequency of thirty-three jaw movements a minute, and can become "frightening"—correspond to the body's involuntary movements, which follow the most irregular and illogical progression. An imbecile with ataxia is knock-kneed and walks like a goose. In rhythmic hysterical chorea, the jolts (*secousses*) follow in regular intervals; some patients jump rhythmically as though dancing: this is called jumping chorea (Michaïlowski 5:59, 68, 253).

Dagonet remarked that there was, in these "spontaneous gestures of Idiots hints of the life of the psyche, something enigmatic *that singularly attracts the observer*. In some, a continual swaying of the body, . . . in others, constant shaking of the head . . . , clapping the hands" (386–87). This description fits Paulus, Dranem, and numerous others. Was their popularity, like that of Pierrot, indebted to this glimpse of the life of the psyche? I believe that it was.

Two films made circa 1910–1912 at the Salpêtrière Hospital,[28] which recorded the various gesticulations, grimaces, tics, and gaits of the seven male and female patients paraded before the camera, offer conclusive proof, when juxtaposed to documents on cabaret performance, of the analogy drawn in the pages of this chapter. There is the male hysteric who suffers from trembling, a female hysteric who limps and walks in circles while repeatedly touching the tips of her fingers, a woman who is constantly forced to catch her hand, which seems to have a will of its own, an hysteric in the throes of terror from a hallucination, a woman with hair clipped short talking to herself and grimacing at the camera, a man who discourses vehemently as he walks back and forth with giant steps while exhibiting a contracture of the hand, and a male hysteric with an aggressive look of provocation dragging one leg and walking rhythmically—sometimes backward, sometimes forward —in what looks like a complicated dance step. His movements correspond exactly to

Figures 10 and 11. Hysterical patient with ambulatory automatism, from a film made ca. 1910–1912 at the Saltpêtrière. Courtesy Cinémathèque Gaumont.

Dranem's (see Figures 10 and 11). This man also repeatedly points to his nose with his index finger, a gesture that was one of several used in experiments involving hypnotic suggestion and hysterics with catalepsy in order to demonstrate the power of unconscious repetition induced by suggestion and by automatic reflex. Other movements that experimenters like Drs. Binet and Féré communicated to their patients were: rotation of the forearm, flexing and extending the finger, and turning the two hands around each other. All of these gestures are found in the caf'conc' repertory. The repetitions of finger to nose can be seen in a comic monologue in the 1908 Gaumont film *Café-Chantant*, which also features a *gommeuse épileptique*.

Paul Margueritte attempted an explanation of the seduction exercised by Pierrot: "the expressive anxiety of beings who . . . while making themselves understood, don't succeed in explaining everything. . . . Figures passionate

and stupid at the same time" (in Storey, *Pierrots on the Stage*). It's almost as though he were defining the way that the exacerbated expressivity and metamorphoses of the hysteric elude all our attempts at logical explanation and all of our efforts to attach a meaning to them. And if Pierrot could mime hysteria, he could also mime the Master of the symptoms, their orchestrator: he could play the role of Azam's and Charcot's predecessors in *Pierrot magnétiseur*.

In the cabaret, the body becomes its own narrative, and it narrates pathology. Yet contortions and hysterical grimaces aren't an entirely negative phenomenon. They convey a release and excess of energy and afford a sensation of liberation. Liberation from the layers of inhibition that societal conventions and taboos place against bodily abandon, as well as rejections of images of illness, deformity, and ugliness. The layers of inhibition imposed over the "primitive"—or simply, the natural—self disappear in the electrified, nervous ambiance of the cabaret, allowing the "other" to surge forth. For the more sophisticated members of the public, this liberation was not only one of the body, but one of the mind and senses: they sensed that they were experiencing a new art form.

Modernity therefore owes much to the hysterical aesthetic of the cabaret and café-concert. Like the medical and cultural phenomenon of hysteria that it played a role in shaping and defining, it was the crossroads where literary and artistic Symbolism and Decadence met with popular culture. The hysterical caf'conc' aesthetic is a faithful reflection of the ethos of the last third of the nineteenth century.

CHAPTER FOUR

Pantomime and the Zigzag

One source of epileptic singing style was the Clodoches in 1866; another dates back to the English mime troupe the Hanlon-Lees, whose Paris debut was in 1867. Pantomime was a staple of the English music-hall, and would make its way from there onto Paris caf'conc' stages. Twenty years earlier, the Hanlons had begun in London as "entortilationists" and gymnasts. Now contortions and grimaces had been part of the clown's and mime's repertoire of expression in the eighteenth century and early-nineteenth century as well, but the intensity and ferocity of the Hanlons' performances was to mark the opening of a new era of gestural possibilities. It will be useful here to sketch out a brief evolution of gesture in pantomime, the art form that, along with marionettes and puppetry, contributed to the invention of epileptic gesture in the cabaret and café-concert.

English mimes had always been more brutal in their gestures than the gracious French mime. The character of Pierrot, called Clown in England, is a "fat, joyous butcher" in contrast to the "long, thin, so fine and so distinguished" French Pierrot who "lends himself to a delicate and witty pantomime," as the author of pantomimes, Champfleury, painted him in 1859 (164). The originality of the acrobatic French mime Mazurier (1798–1828) was celebrated throughout Europe, and his style of "ballet-pantomime" influenced the Hanlon-Lees (Winter). A continual exchange of clowns, dancers, and various fairground entertainers between the two countries in the 1820s meant that the English tradition of knockabout farce made incursions into French pantomime. Nonetheless, "the French Polichinelle [played by Mazurier] lacks a certain brutality in the distribution of blows that characterize Punch. . . . Mazurier's comic style is 'bien français': joyful, luminous and free from the macabre irony of the English" (Winter 139). So even when Mazurier's creations are "grotesque," they are "toujours sympathique" (143). One of his creations was the monkey, Jocko, a character that was immediately imitated in fairs, theaters, circuses, at the Funambules and all along the Boulevard du Temple. The Theater of Monkeys of Jacopo Corvi was one of the great fairground attractions in Paris between 1872 and 1914. Jocko had precursors: the troupe of trained monkeys presented in 1810 by the Jeux-Gymniques. But here is the very important difference with the monkeys that we will see in the films of Georges Méliès: Jocko is "affable" and "well-behaved" (140). His character did not destroy everything around him, nor did it carry implications of devolution.

Similarly, the most famous mime, Deburau père, may be "*peuple*" (lower class) but he is "gracious and witty," even as he hops around and grimaces. "Without exaggerated gestures, without contortions, . . . solely by the play of this pale physiognomy, . . . he knows how to render every impression. . . . What inimitable grace" (Félix Mornand, in Mawer 120). Deburau was far from immobile. He was one of the inventors of the "*Pantomime sautante*" (jumping pantomime), defined by Jules Janin as a slim plot mingled with corporeal exercises. The various emotions and characters are expressed by various forms of leaps and somersaults. This new genre obtained much success but was abandoned in midcentury. When Deburau hops, kicks, leaps, and executes "eccentric dances," thereby representing the "instinct of the people" (Janin 77) and "mimes slang" (Péricaud 157), the analogy with pathology is never made.

The extraordinary frenzy of the Hanlon-Lees, who were a revelation to Parisian audiences in 1867 despite the frequent appearances of other English mime troupes (such as the one Baudelaire described in 1842), was surely astounding, and the specific forms of movement in their act should be discussed here. The specific techniques accompanying certain gestures are described in their memoirs. The principal movement is whirling about (*tourbillonner*). Each blow, in addition, has its own movement: slaps are applied in a straight line, a box on the ear "describes a parabolical curved line. . . . And the fist blow is given in a straight line with a trigger-release at the end" ([Lesclide] 102). We can see that the spatial arcs and lines traced are not in the shape of the zigzag, which allowed one writer on pantomime in 1886 to describe a new aesthetic based on that figure (see below). According to the Hanlons, they realized their goal of combining gymnastics and pantomime in 1878, three years after the first appearance of Emilie Bécat.

In 1865 Henri Agoust joined the Hanlons, and they combined elements from the circus, the pantomimes of Deburau père, and English pantomime. They constructed their plays out of the dreams they related to each other. With their source in primitive fantasies, and their expression "throb[bing] in every nerve, quiver[ing] in every muscle," these performances could not help but "enthrall" audiences (in Storey, *Pierrots on the Stage* 185). At the end of his 1883 book, Ernest Coquelin describes several of the most famous pantomimes of the "Hanlons."

"Do mi sol do" and "Les Cascades du Diable" are among the pantomimes that belong to the *insane* genre (*le genre fou*) according to Coquelin. (Although I don't know what else one could call "Meat and Flour," where all the characters, including the little English pig, seem to be afflicted with a "diabolical St. Vitus's dance," and in which a sleeping woman is swallowed up by her bed, out of which an immense rat appears at the same time as the bedside candle grows to enormous proportions! Perhaps it's the aspect of utter cruelty and anarchy along with its "furious fantasy" that places "Les Cascades du diable" in an even more insane genre.)

Here is the scenario: the shades of Hell are sent up to earth dressed as *pierrots*, Colombine, dandies, and so on. The two *pierrots* terrorize a village, baking the village baker in his oven, dumping an old woman out of her wheelchair so they can take a ride in it, and setting the village on fire. In one scene, they stare lewdly at a giant woman made out of wood, who is undressing; when she strips to her corset they stretch out their hands to grab her, but she gives them a mighty slap and disappears. Suddenly an elephant captures a traveler with his trunk (the elephant's). The crowd cries out; the elephant gives the man back. Then there is "a truly exhilarating" scene with mannequins/dummies at the door of a cabin. A *pierrot*-doctor vaccinates a crowd of children who bray like a regiment of donkeys. A *pierrot* in the lantern of a lamppost makes the gaslighter's ladder disappear up into the glass. A huge chair with a hole in the seat is carried on stage and inside the chair it is "impossible to relate what's going on: a series of somersaults, slaps, planks of wood broken over heads, people jumping up into the air: mind-boggling magic and incoherence can't go any further than this." There is a magic staircase and a house that crumbles, and Colombine and Arlequino are found dancing on its ruins. The tableaux of the pantomime are totally unconnected but possess an "epic drôlerie" (Coquelin, *La Vie humoristique* 205–7). Another pantomime, "Do, Mi, Sol, Do" is a "critique of charivarico-cacaphonico-Wagnerian music." A conductor directs an orchestra, impervious to the musicians who keep trying to take over the podium. As they rush at him and manage to rip off the tails of his coat, he taps them over the head with his baton. Chaos ensues but then, miraculously, they calm down and begin to play. The emotions in the poses and facial expressions of the conductor are marvelous. "There follows a series of slaps, kicks in the . . . back, violins broken over noses, wigs that dance and fly away, violin necks that rise like specters or shoot off like machine-guns, gigantic legs that appear as though in an insane nightmare, serenades of musicians trying to sing while their hat is blown off by the wind, whistling trains that pass through." Finally, the conductor is lost in his score, while the musicians try every means to make him sit down. Impossible. They get an enormous cable that they tie to his legs; they pull on the cable like sailors, but it breaks and they all fall over . . . except for the conductor who wanders off in a dream (197–98). In "Le Frater de Village," an angry Pierrot, rejected by Colombine, decapitates several members of her family; the apotheosis of this violent frenzy is "a raining forth of frenetic gestures where slaps and kicks spread out like the sparks of a pinwheel" ([Lesclide] 111). Théodore de Banville, who prefaced the Hanlons' memoirs, describes the "violence of their leaps, of their contortions . . . [and] their gymnastic ferocity" (12). Indeed, they shocked and thrilled French audiences by their ferocity.

Yet, clowns and mimes, no matter how violent and frenetic, did not call forth associations with pathology. That association, however, will become more and more commonplace from 1879 on. Robert Storey writes that it was in the early eighties that "Pierrots of a disturbing *nervosisme* began to invade the salons, the music-halls, and circus" (*Pierrots on the Stage* 118); he cites Jules Chéret's statement that the "modern type, thrown into a life too great for his atavistically contracted brain" must be represented by Pierrot, whose mouth twitches in a grimace (121). Paul Margueritte asserted that his incarnation of Pierrot made him the victim of a *dédoublement de la personnalité* (Margueritte 24).[1] Mimes made him think of "somnambulists in the midst of an attack" (27). Margueritte was the author of pantomimes such as the immensely popular "Pierrot assassin de sa femme" (1881), first performed at Stéphane Mallarmé's home in Valvins, and in 1888 at the Théâtre Antoine. By tickling Columbine's feet, Pierrot makes her die laughing. Remorse "twists him in the same convulsive laughter and the same horror of the agonies of death as his victim. . . . He falls over backwards in a last jolt (*saccade*) of epilepsy, struck dead" (26). There is no laughter in this excerpt from "Fear" however: "Pierrot . . . shaking his leg . . . kicks desperately . . . with the convulsive quaking of a cornered animal . . . [and] utters a piercing cry of hysteria" (Storey, *Pierrots on the Stage* 133). Gestures and psychic drama have changed radically from the "gracious" and "*sympathique*" pantomime of Deburau, as well as from the primal, cruel but joyful anarchy of the Hanlons. The fin-de-siècle Pierrot now carries and portrays the anxious psyche and contorted postures of the hysteric.

Jean Richepin's mime will pinpoint the shape of gesture appropriate to this very modern expression of the times: "Gestural arabesques, downstrokes and upstrokes ending in spiral flourishes! Enough! Today we need heavy dark lines, and without flourishes. Zig, zag, paf!" (Richepin, *Braves gens* 95).

Seeing the Hanlons in 1879 gave Huysmans the idea of writing a pantomime with his friend Léon Hennique: "Pierrot sceptique," where Pierrot falls in love with a mannequin. The poet Théodore de Banville wondered how it was possible to reconcile the Hanlons' "eurythmy of poses" with their frenetic agitation. (Had he studied the photographic *Iconographie de la Sal-*

pêtrière, the answer would have been evident.) For Edmond de Goncourt in 1879, this English clowning had become, over the previous years, sinister and "terrifying."

> All of the anxieties and shivers that rise from contemporary society . . . [this clowning] makes its prey, to serve them up to the public in acrobatics. It has terrifying aspects for the spectator . . . merciless assimilations of the ugliness and infirmities of life, magnified . . . and which, in the fantasy of the spectacle, take the shape of a fantastic nightmare. . . . The frolicking and jumping doesn't try to amuse the eye, but rather manages to give birth to troubled astonishment and emotions of fear and almost painful surprises from this strange and unhealthy motion of body and muscle [with] visions of *Bedlam*, of Newcastle, of the *amphitheater of anatomy*, of the morgue. . . . These modern phantoms of the night . . . with the projection of their *dislocated* and grotesque shadows on this white wall . . . begin their *maniacal* tours de force, their *idiotic gesticulations*, the *agitated mimicry of a band of madmen*. (*Frères* 124–25; italics mine)

The "anxieties and shivers" of society that are translated into the acrobatics of the clowns are terrifying because the dislocations are clearly assimilated with the pathologies of the body and madness, underlined in the above passage. Goncourt later describes "a nightmare of everything impossible, unfeasible that the human body has accomplished" (246), a nightmare that pushes the contortions that composed part of circus and many café-concert acts even further, contortions such as the Irishman nicknamed "The Earthworm, the dislocated man, who, his legs folded backward around his neck, rolled himself into a ball and broke a peach pit with his buttocks" (118). This darkly fascinating aspect of clowning—the "strange and unhealthy motion of [the] body"—is the very same trait that attracted spectators to hysterics and to hypnotized subjects.

In a voice-over narration to his 1970 film *The Clowns*, Fellini explains the reactions of Federico, the child through whose eyes we are watching the circus show: "The clowns didn't make me laugh; they frightened me [with their] atrocious jokes, enigmas, and chalky faces." They remind him of lecherous village idiots, of all sorts of madmen with their "terrifying, exhilarating violence." It is not by chance that the Fratellinis perform in a mental asylum, and this extraordinary *mise en scène* of audience response is a model of the impulse to imitate, an impulse the inmates of course cannot resist, necessitating the intervention of the psychiatrist, who hypnotizes one of them back into his seat. In the final scene of the film, the gag of the giant mallet over the clown's head is redirected outward so that it becomes a huge mallet over the spectators' heads, breaking the camera lens and making it very clear that we feel the pain and viscerally experience the spectacle in our body.

Z for Modernity

The mimes in the novel *Les Frères Zemganno* were aware of the forceful connotations of the zigzag in the letter "Z." The astonishing nature of their final performance called for the adoption of a new name: Zemganno. "Zemganno... how original... it has a devil of a Z at the beginning, like a fanfare of ringing bells within a tempest of beating drums" (Goncourt 217).[2]

When Goncourt describes what was "new and inventive" in his fictional brothers' act in France, it is the theme of obsession and the twisted contortions and deformations of the body juxtaposed to its harmonious, beautiful gestures. As we will see, the arabesque is being painfully twisted like Art Nouveau vermicelli, but it is not yet abandoned in favor of the zigzag.

Subtly, the representation of corporeal pathology in the novel shifts to the description of the onset of mental pathology, as if to confirm that miming pathologies of hysteria leads to the involuntary repetition of these movements and, finally, to the illness itself.

> In the moments when he wasn't on stage, and even for the most ordinary actions, he felt his members twist into eccentric arabesques. More than that, alone, he was compelled to the gestures of a somnambulist and of one who is hallucinated, and that physiologists call "symbolic movements," gestures over which he didn't have absolute control. He surprised himself in the act of [casting shadow figures on the wall] with a contractured hand . . . pointlessly . . . and as if his body was obeying an impulse of weird magnetic currents and capricious forces of nature. (155–56)

These "symbolic movements" are the automatisms that signal hysteria, and that belong to the spectator's body as well, according to the nineteenth-century notion of a corporeal unconscious and the tendency to imitate what one sees. The predominance of automatic gesture always implies a corresponding loss of capacity for conscious activity:

> Then, little by little, in a state both vague and exalted, and as in a slight effacement of the reality around him and a sort of slumber of day-time thought, in his head, similar to that empty head where one sees a spoon scooping out the ideas one by one, the clown ended by only seeing the reflection of his white face that the mirror sent back to him, in his eyes the images of the monsters on his costume, and also the murmur of his diabolical violin remaining in his ears. (126)

The automatisms and magnetic current coursing through the dislocated body of Goncourt's mime reflect salient aspects of gesture in the cabaret and café-concert aesthetic. One important aspect, though, underlined in descriptions of Paulus and Ouvrard is missing: angularity.

Seven years later, the artistic modernity of angularity will be better appreciated by a writer very much involved in theater and in mime. Jean Richepin's novel about cabaret, mime, and music-hall performers, *Braves gens, roman parisien*, appeared in 1886 and enjoyed considerable commercial success. Richepin himself wrote pantomimes (Sarah Bernhardt played the role of Pierrot in his 1883 pantomime, "Pierrot assassin") and was a charter member of the Cercle Funambulesque between 1888 and 1898.[3] In addition, he participated in the Chat Noir cabaret and wrote for the journal. Richepin is thus an exceptionally reliable source and his ideas on pantomime should be taken seriously. In *Braves gens*, a new theory of pantomime is being proposed by the mime Tombre:

> Gestural arabesques, downstrokes and upstrokes ending in spiral flourishes! Enough! Today we need heavy dark lines, and without flourishes. Zig, zag, paf! The fist clenched, the fingers clamped shut convulsively, only the thumb free and rigidly separate, he described in the air angular figures with sudden breaks. (95)

Toward the end of the novel, the mimes' performance is described.

> A flood of light projected in livid letters: THE HAPPY ZIGZAGS. . . . The stage was completely naked . . . a void between the walls . . . one [mime], dislocated, made of rubber, slipped along the edge, seeming to slither with the twistings of a centipede, while the other, shrunken into a ball, seemed to slowly roll down from above. . . . The first reached the foot of the wall and glued itself there in a contortion in the form of a zigzag . . . giving the appearance of a centipede cut into three pieces by a whip. (459)

Later these movements are compared to "the slashes of a knife. Or rather, of a razor" (165), exactly like the cutting, razor-sharp voice of Maurice Rollinat singing at the Chat Noir, or like the cutting jokes under the heading "Zigzags" in the 1879 *Hydropathe* (issue no. 14), the journal of the club that counted among its members Rollinat and Charles Cros, and preceded the Chat Noir. All of these Zigzags are plays on words turning on physically violent transformations of the body (for example, decapitation is degrading: Fulbert's operation on Abelard—in other words, the castration of Abelard—plucked out the root of evil [*le mal*] / of the male [*le mâle*]). The literary group that Cros got together in 1883, taking up where the Hydropathes left off in the activity of thumbing its nose at convention, was baptized the Zutistes.

Pantomime, as we observed, had violent aspects at the Théâtre des Funambules between 1820 and 1860, as it certainly did in the pantomimes of the Hanlon-Lees a few years later, but as Goncourt's novel and the passages from Richepin's *Braves gens* demonstrate, the public didn't react in the same way. As far as I can see, that is because the movements of French mimes prior to the 1870s were based on the arabesque and only became epileptic around the same time that a marked increase in cases of hysteria occurred. And it was probably only in the 1880s, if we believe Richepin (and his authority in this domain is indisputable), that these movements espoused the radical angularity of the zigzag.

For Charcot, the zigzag was a form symptomatic of hysteria. It is found not only in the gestures of hysterics, but in their drawings, in their handwriting, and in the "dazzling scotoma" that intervene in their field of vision.

A drawing made by Charcot, himself under the influence of hashish (a drug shown by several psychiatrists—Moreau de Tours, Richet, Charcot—to produce the same symptoms as hysteria), exhibits the "zigzag contorted forms and jumbled hallucinations" that he was later to associate with the hysterical attack (Silverman 101). In experiments on automatic writing in hysterics, Binet noted the zigzag marks his patients produced, marks that revealed the latent depths of consciousness that remain unknown to the subject (*Altérations* x). Finally, it was the zigzag that came to Freud's mind to describe the path taken by the movements of unconscious energy (in Oughourlian 292).

The angularity of the zigzag expresses pain, pathology, and the violence of "cutting wit"; it is also a cipher for hysteria and for the unconscious.[4] The zigzag expresses these forces and the anarchy of epileptic gesture in the caf'conc' well before it appears in art and literature. We see it in the short stories of Guy de Maupassant: a poor soul locked up in an asylum has an uncontrollable gesture, a convulsive reaching for something with a zigzag motion. A father, who received a traumatic shock when he realized his daughter had been buried alive, relives the sensation in the automatic zigzag movement his hands make in *The Tic*. Maupassant was no stranger to hysteria; he was afflicted by an hysterical blindness, precisely the pathology that Binet studied in his experiments with automatic writing; he also suffered from hyperesthesia, and from hallucinations, including the vision of his own double. In the first volume of Hermann Broch's 1931 *The Somnambulists*, which takes place in 1888, a character is introduced solely in terms of his gait, and passersby, who are repulsed when they see him, react by laughing. This is the way the devil strolls along, a limping dog on three legs [with the cane]; it's a walk in a rectilinear zigzag (Broch 9–11). This character's aggressiveness is shown later in the novel as a mixture of despotism and hysteria.

The modernity of the zigzag form is highlighted in another passage from Richepin's novel, highly suggestive of cinema (a decade later) and of the telegraphic style of Blaise Cendrars's poetry (twenty-five years later).

> This synthesis, this imagery in action by suddenly immobilized poses, this summary of pantomime, that was absolute art, the supreme finality of my theories. Zig, zag, paf! an entire, fulgurating drama, speeding by

> like an express train, surging up like a landscape lit up by a flash of lightning! (*Braves gens* 477)

But (setting aside Rimbaud and Lautréamont) literature in 1886 was not yet ready to take the same risks as pantomime or cabaret and espouse the violence of the zigzag. Richepin is perfectly well aware of that fact when he writes: "One would have to graphically reproduce the manuscript of the mime, Tombre, with [its] hooks . . . , crosses . . . , lines crossed out with a violent stroke of the pen, spurts of ink flying off in zigzags toward the margins and exploding there in bombs. That would give some idea of the life that Tombre put into it in writing" (164).

Gesture is infinitely superior to the word as an expressive tool. "All of the butterflies of feelings and ideas that hover on the tips of the gesticulating fingers [of the mime] and which fly off in a crazy turbulence (*tourbillons*), isn't spearing them with the pins of stiff words tantamount to killing them?" Richepin asks in a wonderful little text entitled "La Gloire du geste" (The Glory of Gesture) (ix). Pierrot is the embodiment of appetite—digestive, erotic, narcissistic pleasure, unleashed fury—and spiritual yearning. As he "caresses his stomach, yawns, . . . winks, sneezes, . . . raises his arms to heaven, . . . sticks his index finger in his nose, his little finger in his ear, . . . shakes his cheeks with a convulsive tic that makes them tremble" (viii), he "embroiders life itself" (x) on the stage. Huysmans admires Théodore de Banville's style because it is acrobatic and disarticulated like the circus performers and mimes it portrays, and his own prose moves in this direction, at times emulating the hysterical attack described in the novel *En rade*, an electric quivering in the legs, the shock of the spark along the thighs, and its sudden discharge (117–19): "the sacred illness, the epilepsy of this world, the hysteria of this planet . . . arching over backwards, shaken . . . the cold Selene had fallen into catalepsy" (113). Were the Decadents creating an anarchistic style, as some claimed, one as free as the language of gesture? Writers like Huysmans experimented with patterns that mimed the irregular rhythms, jolts, and periods of immobility in hysteria, and those experiments exploded the novelistic form just as surely as the use of slang and neologisms exploded like an anarchist bomb in the midst of convoluted syntax.[5] Hysteria—the *modern* illness, the chic illness—is sought as a literary effect in the Decadence after having enjoyed an uninterrupted run of popularity for over a decade in the cabaret and café-concert.

At the Chat Noir, Mac-Nab was singing his poetry in a voice that was compared to that of a seal with a bad cold. His "Ballad of Circumflex Accents" demonstrates the mobility and the epileptic gymnastics of angular form at work in language. "Sometimes they seem occupied / Performing unbelievable gymnastics: / Taking fantastical forms. / Then they're long mosquitos / With arms and legs cut off. . . . In old Gothic manuscripts / They coiffe like a lampshade / The five vowels one by one / Which, under their vulture claws, / Make epileptic turns."

One of Jules Chéret's covers for the "Incoherent" books of Jules Lévy was *Paris qui Rit* (Paris Laughing), where the letter "R" of Rit cavorts on the page, gesturing in the form of the zigzag. Chéret's poster for the 1886 Exposition des Arts Incohérents—a celebration of lunacy, anarchy, and zaniness—is also structured by the zigzag, as are many of his posters for the Folies-Bergère and for the caf'conc' (see Figure 12). This choice of composition can be appreciated by comparing it to the hundreds of others in Chéret's output that are structured by the arabesque. Nothing was more appropriate to symbolize Incoherent humor, lunacy, and anarchy than the zigzag.

Willette's and Steinlen's drawings for *Le Chat Noir* also tend to show an evolution toward the zigzag. These droll and often cruel narratives—precursors of the first comic strips—either abandon their habitual horizontal progression from left to right to espouse the composition of the zigzag, or the horizontal narrative progression is retained but the silhouette of Willette's Pierrot, dressed in black like Steinlen's black cat, traces the zigzag across the page like the "Z" of Zorro.[6]

When, years later, Félicien Champsaur tried to verbally re-create the spirit of Montmartre that Willette's *Parce Domine* had visually encapsulated, he wanted his novel to be "the living fresco of a night of carnival . . . erotically enervated . . . an amusing canvas [of] part of Paris in funambulesque ascension. . . . A bacchanalia [through which he traces the] *exasperated zigzags* of the vice of living" (*Nuit* 9–11; emphasis mine).

In the convulsive and radical polarities of the fin de siècle, when the arabesque was twisting itself into the whiplash line of Art Nouveau, a new form of expression emerged in violent opposition to the arabesque. "Certain

Figure 12. Jules Chéret's Folies-Bergère poster, "La Musique de l'avenir par les Bozza." Fogg Museum, Harvard University.

decorative artists were exaggerating the whiplash line to produce a lightning-like line in the form of a zigzag, a leitmotif whose contagiousness and ill consequences were revealed by the Universal Exhibition" (Lahor 14). The zigzag was the other form of modernism that came out of the cabaret aesthetic. Its razor-sharp aggressivity would suit the aesthetic of the twentieth century even better—in Egon Schiele, Pechner, Schmidt-Rotloff, Max Beckmann, Kandinsky, and in Expressionist films like *The Cabinet of Dr. Caligari.* In the first decade of the new century, when the relationship between modern art and pathology was clearly perceived to play a predominant role, Urbain Gohier wrote:

> The scenes and characters in our paintings [are] drawn from life, in a neurasthenic, hysterical, epileptic, alcoholic humanity. . . . So these bizarre anatomies, these deformations, these contortions . . . are ours. Our painting is faithful . . . our descendants will have a precise idea of what men, society, and life today are in looking at our canvasses.

If these compositions are no longer perceived as hysterical, that is because we recognize them for what they are: the artistic expression of our century marked by fragmentation and violence. Dislocation is no longer the symptom of an abnormal state, but a dimension of our present culture.

CHAPTER FIVE

Hypnotism, Somnambulism, and Early Cinema

I hate Valentino! . . . I hate his patent-leather hair; I hate his Svengali glare; . . .
I hate him because he's an embezzler of hearts.

— DICK DORGAN, "A Song of Hate"

The dynamics of imitation, doubling, and automatisms (in particular, mechanical movement) found in hysteria and somnambulism are, to my mind, central to late-nineteenth-century and early-twentieth-century spectacle.

An advertisement for Du Maurier's first novel, *Peter Ibbetson* appears at the end of the 1894 edition of *Trilby*. Like *Trilby*, that novel was based on a double existence split between waking and dreaming and, like *Trilby*, it was adapted for the screen.[1] The ad contains the following press reviews: "Nothing more fascinating or curious has of late appeared. . . . *The tale will induce many of its readers to attempt Du Maurier's recipe for 'dreaming true'*. . . . [It] combine[s] . . . Oriental occultism and modern science. . . . This weird story grips the reader like a wraith and has in it a brilliant picture of French life" (italics mine). I have underlined the journalist's prediction that the reader will be *induced* (as in somnambulism) to imitate the unusual psychological states of the fictional hero. This sampling of reviews lists the components necessary to "*grip*" the audience: the object in question must be fascinating, curious, and weird. Magnetism, hypnotism, somnambulism, and hysteria were all of these (the first two were fascinating in the literal sense of *fascino* [the evil eye], here the spell of the magnetizer). And again, as with hysteria and magnetism, these qualities belong as much to the supernatural and the occult as they do to science. As I stated in Chapter 2, nowhere were science and the supernatural fused in the popular imagination more than in displays of hypnotism, magnetism, and somnabulism. The mixture of the two and the effect produced are immediately apparent in the marvelous films of Georges Méliès, but they are present in a great many films made between 1896 and 1912, from comedies to serials.

Magnetism and somnambulism are extremely frequent themes in films and in film criticism between 1896 and 1935.[2] Early films include Méliès's "Le Magnétiseur" (1897) and Gaumont's *Chez le magnétiseur* (1898); extend to genres as different as Feuillade's *Les Vampires* (1915–1916) (as well as *Bébé hypnotiseur*, in his comic "Bébé" series), Max Linder's *Max hypnotisé* (1910), André Deed's *Cretinetti hypnotizzatore* (1912), and Pathé's *Nick Winter et le voleur somnambule* (1911); and continue throughout the 1920s and 1930s, resonating with the aims of Surrealism. One might even argue that the exhilarating representation of anarchy in Jean Vigo's *Zéro de conduite* (1933) would be incomplete without the emblematic figure of a somnambulist at the outset of the film. If artistic and popular spectacles encouraged or *induced* imitation of unusual corporeal and feeling states, this tendency to mime hysterical or somnambulistic gesture was all the more compelling in the cinema, enhanced as it was by the hypnotic power of the flickering light on a luminous screen in a darkened room, and often underlined by the presence of a character in the role of mesmerist or hypnotist training his gaze out at the audience. The fixed gaze on a brilliant object has inspired an analogy between hypnotism and film spectatorship, from the writings of Ycham in 1912, to those of Jacques Brunius in 1954 ("the prolonged observation of a luminous point in space allows the subject to reach hypnotic sleep" [Brunius 8–9]), and, more recently, in the texts of Raymond Bellour.[3] "Cinema acts on the brain directly," wrote Antonin Artaud (in Ghali 346). Film is "*magnetizing*," wrote André Breton ("Comme dans un bois," in Kuenzli 8). "The collective hypnosis into which the cinema audience is plunged by light and shadow is very like a spiritualist seance," Jean Cocteau noted more than once, but in *this* variety of seance, the words uttered, which mediums attribute to a spirit, are "lifted out of our own pockets and come from the darkness within us [the audience]" (Cocteau 26, 41). Even outside of the darkened theater, cinema's hypnotic power continues to hold sway with its "fantastic advertisements, veritable lighthouses with giant lamps, [which] fascinate, hypnotize and subjugate the pedestrian attracted to a bright light" (G.-M. Coissac, in Crafton 98).

Why is early cinema thought to operate directly on the mind, and why is it so interested in *showing* what is going on inside the mind? Filmic representations of hypnotism and somnambulism are an important component of this persistent desire and effort on the part of filmmakers in early cinema. The continuing presence of hypnotism and magnetism in films, alongside the continuing critical discourse on their relationship, is testimony not only to the important place these themes enjoyed in the minds of filmmakers, but also to the hold they had over the popular imagination. As interesting as it is to note that this presence continues even today (for example, in Benoit Jacquot's 1998 film *Le Septième ciel*), my purpose here is more narrow: it is to show that the frequency of hypnotism and magnetism as theme and metaphor in early cinema is due to an ongoing belief in, fear of, or enthrallment with the unconscious automatisms of the body, the involuntary imitation that they trigger, and their potential for viewer contagion. Tom Gunning has emphasized the way that attractions in early films (in ways similar to the fairground attraction) highlight the role of the spectator: they "can only be thoroughly understood if these [formal] devices are conceived as addressing spectators in a specific manner" ("Now You See It" 5). By analyzing contemporary theories of unconscious physiological response and imitation, we can better understand the elements that make up the direct address to the spectator in the cinema of attractions. The staging of the relationship between hypnotist and somnambulist is, similarly, a specific form of address that also engages spectatorial response in a very precise way, not at all out of sync with the exhibitionist regime in the attraction. The constant allusions in cinema's first decades to hypnosis, suggestion, nerves, and "hunger for hypnosis" (see below) explain why fears about the domination of the lower faculties, nervous illness, and contagion should immediately arise in regard to cinema, just as they had in regard to the shows of magnetizers. The perceived similarities between the two forms of spectacle were just too striking not to inspire the uneasy thought that they could produce the same consequences.

Fleeting Suggestions and Early Film Criticism

The earliest filmmakers were, above all, illusionists and knew themselves to be so. The link between illusionism and hypnotism is discussed at the end of this chapter; here I want to briefly consider illusionism in relation to the well-worn question of film's reality effect. From Méliès's first film, "L'Escamotage d'une dame au Théâtre Robert-Houdin" (and Blackton's copycat American version, "The Vanishing Lady"), it is clear that the power of the filmmaker resides in the ability to play with the viewer's perception, making all forms of distortion and hallucinatory transformations seem as though they were the product of our troubled perception, and not as though they were being imposed on our gaze by a "magician." Yet from the point of view of the spectator's experience, the material circumstances of film are extremely evocative of spirit manifestations as well as of hallucination: "weightless images, reflections and projections, light and shadow floating mid-air" (Shaviro 17). From the point of view of the filmmaker, as set forth in a recent article by François Jost, the same techniques are used to represent an apparition or a mental phenomenon. There seems to be an underlying religiosity in dream phenomena (dreams, before Freud, are visions) and, by extension, in mental images. "Dreams are thus visions, close to supernatural apparitions; they conserve a magic power similar to clairvoyance" (Jost, "Métaphysique" 265). Jost reminds us that films were projected in fairs next to seances of magnetism, hypnotism, and thought transmission, and a clairvoyance show often took place between two films.

The "trick" is to show how the underlying stock of supernatural images continues to affect the spectator's film reception, and to what extent it is complicated by a parallel experience of mental and sensory pathology. What I want to do in this book is answer a question cogently posed by François Jost in this essay, taken up again in *Le Temps d'un regard*: "Why is early cinema so interested in representing what is happening inside the mind?" His answer, that mental images are inextricably bound up with religio-supernatural ideas is, to me, only a partial answer. Certainly, the apparition that supposedly emanates from outside the Subject and the hallucination of the mind are *shown* in the same way by the same techniques. The film spectator can't know if s/he is in the presence of the supernatural or having an hallucination. Jost shows that people (for example, Joan of Arc) who are experiencing an apparition are shown from the back, so that the apparition is clearly *our* image. (Of course, if the character were not in the frame at all, the image would belong even more to us.) Religion, hallucination, and cinema magic have "equal power to make images instantaneously appear [like an epiphany] which [literally] jump out into the eyes (*sautent aux yeux*) of the spectator" (*Le Temps* 271).

I couldn't agree more with François Jost. Nonetheless, the public of early cinema was just as much caught up in hallucinatory phenomena associated with hysteria as it was with the supernatural. By recreating perceptual pathologies, and by representing hysterical movement, cinema is representing "what goes on inside the mind," based on a physiological model of mind that ensured the most viscerally intense experience of the images on the screen. My understanding of the spectator's shock and astonishment, therefore, also differs from Tom Gunning's. The intense reactions to events on the screen are, on the one hand, the result of unconscious identification and the involuntary repetition by the body of the images and movements on the screen and, on the other, of a conscious awareness of the perceptual experience taking place, an "owning" of the perception of the images projected onto the screen. As scholars have noted, the medium of film is endowed with a magical aura not only because of its ability to reproduce "life itself" (as commentators in 1895 put it), but because it draws on the illusions perfected in magic shows, magic-lantern shows, spirit photography and, as I show elsewhere, the stereoscope. The magic of the illusion of reality and the illusionism of magical transformations are two possible applications of this cinematic power. My focus is on a third use: the creation and projection of hallucinatory images that spectators *must* take to be real because they are in fact really there. There before their eyes, there in their own body. However, perceptual disorders like optical illusions, double vision, and persistent afterimages were often the first, *and always the most important, warning sign of mental pathologies such as hysteria.* "Sensory illusions are the most palpable and striking symptom of mental alienation," wrote the physiologist Théodule Ribot in his review of James Sully's book, *On Illusions* (438). Afterimages (also called *spectres* in the nineteenth century) remaining on the retina were supposedly indistinguishable from hallucinations and could be superimposed over actual objects for as long as thirty minutes.[4] These optical spectres were feared as spectres of madness, and filmic superimpositions and double exposures could reproduce them more convincingly than any other medium had been able to until then. And whereas audiences would naturally place these visual illusions in the context of the magic show, stereoscopic spirit photos, and the magic lantern, the impact on their bodies would be very much intensified. In other words, convincing spectators that they "own" the *illusions* projected before them is tantamount to instilling an anxiety about mental instability. Thus, there is a simultaneous recognition of the pathological component of the reaction and the irresistible submission of the body to the experience.[5]

I agree with Gunning that the spectator's fear is not of the impending disaster (a train hurtling toward the audience) or of a supernatural apparition—s/he relishes this dangerous thrill, just as s/he savored contemporary magic shows with their frightening apparitions of spectres, the same visions that made earlier audiences crowd into the Phantasmagoria. One can be taken in by an illusion and, at almost the same time, realize that it is an illusion. What *does* create anxiety in the spectator are the implications attached to experiencing the same dislocations and convulsive agitation, perceptual disturbances (optical illusions, intense afterimages, hallucinations) as an hysteric. The public nonetheless *expects* to have this experience and *derives pleasure* from it. This twofold mechanism has to do with the painful pleasure of receiving shocks to the body through the eyes and brain, and the ever-present need that these thrilling jolts be intensified in order to be exciting. Unfortunately, the effect on the body is very much like the pathological symptoms that spectators had read about. This is why there is a continuing discourse on film reception between 1895 and 1910 that turns on the idea of madness. Maxime Gorky recorded his thoughts on his first film experience, a visit to the "realm of Shadows/Spirits":

> The strangeness of this world . . . devoid of color and sound [doesn't give] the movement of life but a sort of mute spectre. Here I must explain myself before the reader thinks I've become insane. [Spectral apparitions are tantamount to madness.] Everything moves, comes to life, and suddenly, having reached the edge of the screen, disappears who knows where. . . . [N]othing but shadows, spectres, phantoms; one thinks of some evil genie who has put an entire city *in a perpetual sleep*. . . . You end up by being disturbed and depressed by this silent and grey life. . . . You forget where you are. *Strange ideas invade your mind; you are less and less conscious*. (223–27)

Gorky also perceived that "this is a strain on the nerves. . . . Our nerves are getting weaker and weaker, are growing more and more unstrung . . . and thirst more and more eagerly for new, strong, unusual, burning and strange impressions. The cinematograph gives you them" (227–33).[6]

"How will a naive public [recognize] this trickery . . . under pain of inevitable misunderstanding and multiple errors?" (Haugmard 768).[7] The question of early film spectators mistaking representation for reality—whether in films where the viewer was the addressee in an ostentatious manner, or in those where the camera was "invisible" and the staging "natural"—was nuanced by many writers in the 1910s to include reflections on hypnotism and suggestion. In early cinema, film was "a somewhat somnambulistic scientific trick" (Epstein, "Magnification" 240). In addition to psychologists like Toulouse and Mourgue and filmmakers like Jean Epstein in France, Hugo Munsterberg and Frank Woods in America linked the film experience to a hypnotic state, a special "mental attitude"—"an influence akin to hypnotism or magnetism by visual suggestion." This hypnotic spell gives motion pictures an advantage over other forms of illusionist representation (Frank Woods, in Hansen 82–83).

In a two-page-long exposition of how actors motivate actions, Sergei Eisenstein draws an analogy with laboratory experiments where the subject's behavior is motivated by hypnotic suggestion, received in the most primitive levels of the organism, "in the tissues." This source of expression, gesture, and action must have a direct impact on all of the elements in the entire spectacle (*Cinématisme* 180–81). It is, however, a text of the Harvard psychologist Hugo Munsterberg, who was schooled in nineteenth-century psychophysical and psychophysiological research that comes closest to my own formulations about early film spectatorship. After posing analogous relationships between the processes of mind and film[8] (the way that memory works, for example, is perfectly duplicated by the flashback), Munsterberg writes that these analogies are illuminated by the mental process of suggestion, which is "quite nearly related" to memory, attention, and the imagination, already discussed. Hugo Munsterberg finds no better example of the production of emotion through camera work alone than a scene where we "see on the screen a man hypnotized in a doctor's office" (129). A suggested idea is built from the same material as ideas in one's memory or imagination, and the play of association controls the suggested idea too, but there is an important distinction: we *choose* from our memories and fancies, and thus we "do not believe in their objective reality. A suggestion, on the other hand, is forced on us. The outer perception is not only a starting point but a controlling influence, . . . something to which we have to submit. The extreme case is, of course, that of the hypnotist" (108). These suggested ideas, then, have to be accepted as real:

> The spellbound audience in a theater or in a picture house is certainly in a state of heightened suggestibility and is ready to receive suggestions. One great and fundamental suggestion is . . . that this is more than mere play, that it is life which we witness. (108–9)

There is an even more essential similarity between the way that suggestion and film work. "The whole technique of the rapid changes of scene which we have recognized as so characteristic of the photoplay [i.e., film] involves at every end point elements of suggestion which to a certain degree link the separate scenes as the afterimages link the separate pictures" (110–11).[9] Emile Vuillermoz, in an article that appeared a year later, noticed the same parallel processes: "fleeting suggestions analogous to the flashes of mental associations which traverse our imagination and multiply its creative power tenfold"; "the thousands of tiny frames in a moving filmstrip act like the cells of the human brain: the same overwhelming rapidity of perception, the same multiplicity of many-faceted mirrors . . . quick glimpses, memories, hallucinations" (133; translation slightly modified). Munsterberg then considers the all-important role of the emotions in film, underlining that it isn't the emotions in the actor that interest him, but rather those in the spectator. The spectator's emotions, like the "mental activities and excitements [in the act of attention and of memory, are] *projected* into the moving pictures" (122). First, feelings of persons in the film are transmitted to "our own soul"; second, "our imitation of the emotions which we see expressed brings vividness and affective tone into our grasping of the [film's] action" (123). That is how pain, joy, grief, and fear become our own.

> The visual perception of the various forms of expression of these emotions fuses in our mind with the conscious awareness of the emotion expressed; . . . the pain which we observe brings contractions in our muscles; and all the resulting sensations from muscles, joints, tendons, from skin and viscera, from blood circulation and breathing, give the color of living experience to the emotional reflection in our mind. (123–24)

We should remember that this effect on spectators was already noted by Friedrich Schiller at the end of the eighteenth century: "If I am truly moved [by a theatrical representation], I have little need to adjust my body to the tone of the passion, indeed it would be difficult—even impossible—to repress the spontaneous movements of my members" (829). Munsterberg's conclusion is that, since the relation of the images to the character and to the spectator is exactly the same, "we can say that the pain and joy which the spectator feels are really projected to the screen" (124). And they are projected into both the images of the characters and into the decor. "Every shade of feeling and emotion which fills the spectator's mind can mold the scenes in the photoplay until they appear the embodiment of our feelings" (173). The aim of film art can only be achieved through a "far-reaching disregard of reality" in favor of "pictorial suggestions only . . . in order that . . . our inner experiences may be realized on the screen" (209).

In addition to the role of the emotions, imagination, and attention in opening the spectator to suggestion and in causing projective identification, "the mere technical cleverness of the pictures *even today* holds the interest *spellbound*. . . . We are still startled by every original effect, even if the mere showing of movement has today lost its impressiveness" (218; italics mine).

Controlling the Gaze

Glances aimed at the camera, that is, at the spectator, were extremely common into the 1910s, whether by magicians performing illusions, by singers in *phono-scènes*, by contortionists or other performers of attractions, by villains or heroes, by "extras," or by leering, quizzical, or complicitous comics. These looks hardly carry the same intent or produce the same effect as the gaze of the hypnotist when it is directed at the spectator, yet, in 1908, arguing for the prohibition of looking directly into the camera, a journalist wrote that "when an actor looks at the camera, it is like a hypnotist snapping his fingers to bring a subject out of a trance" (in Burch, *In and Out of Synch* 214).[10] The look into the camera can induce trance as well, and this was the usual reason given for the injunction. That is why the actor should not look directly at the camera, which is to say, the spectator. The most striking example of the hypnotic gaze in early cinema is the character of Dr. Mabuse in Fritz Lang's *Dr. Mabuse der Spieler*, Parts 1 and 2 (1922). Note that the very respectable cover identity of Mabuse the gambler, stage hypnotist, and omnipotent head of the *underworld* is that of *psychoanalyst*, a role that takes on greater importance in Part 2. Director of the underworld (or unconscious) thanks to hypnotic suggestion, Mabuse is also he who knows most about hysteria.[11]

Thought-reading and telepathy are staples of stage hypnotists. When Berger invented the electroencephalogram, he believed that he would be able to furnish *visual proof* of the existence of telepathy. Isn't film another invention for making thought visible—like the electron camera invented in the 1930s, which was intended to render visible the actual functioning of thought? And don't spectators of early cinema have to learn to read thought, aided by the expression of emotions through gesture, pose, muscular contractions, and facial expression?

It is of course the filmmaker who controls the magnetizing gaze out into the room. Jean Epstein, who studied medicine and philosophy before becoming a filmmaker, called the film apparatus a "*machine à rêver*" (*Machine* 142).[12] Had cinema followed the path of dream and fantasy rather than realism, it would have reached greater purely cinematic heights. As the director of *The Fall of the House of Usher* and *The Three-Sided Mirror* explained, "the director suggests, then persuades, then hypnotizes. . . . The film is nothing but a relay between the source of nervous energy and the auditorium, which breathes its radiance. *That is why the gestures which work best on screen are nervous gestures*" (Epstein, "Magnification" 240). Let's recall the experiments of Toulouse and Mourgue, mentioned in Chapters 1 and 2. In monitoring spectators' changes in breathing at a screening of Abel Gance's *Mater Dolorosa* (1917) in order to chart emotional response, the doctors wrote that, since the perception of movement gives birth to the beginnings of a corresponding internal movement, "a phenomenon would take place of the same sort as hypnotic suggestion practiced on a subject after he has been placed in a given pose" (in Moussinac 174).[13] The film spectator develops a "hunger for this hypnosis [because] film [greatly] modifies the functioning of the nervous system" (Epstein, "Magnification" 240). In other words, the automatic responses of the spectator's nervous system become dominant (and demand greater and greater physical/visual shocks).[14] These unconscious internal movements triggered in the spectator would supposedly produce the corresponding emotion as well (the James–Lange theory: the *sensation* produced by the unconscious imitation of a gesture, pose, or facial expression itself gives rise to or intensifies the *emotion* represented by those physiological expressions of it, and these sensations are remembered and repeated by the muscles and the nerves). Hugo Munsterberg refers to this theory in *Photoplay*: "It is well known that in the view of modern physiological psychology our consciousness of the emotion itself is shaped and marked by the sensations which arise from our bodily organs" (129). Moreover, according to Gabriel Tarde, muscular memory and habit are even more powerful in somnambulism than in everyday behavior. Unconscious imitation of the onscreen double (and not the psychoanalytic dynamic of projective identification)[15] is the reason that spectators live out the double's emotions so intensely. This is an important (but often overlooked) factor in the "reality-effect" that so many critics of the 1910s and 1920s refer to. What they are talking about is a very corporeal reality, as is made quite clear in a 1927 essay by Antonin Artaud, "Cinema and Reality." At the bottom of every emotion, writes Artaud, is "an affective sensation of a nervous order." "Pure cinema," according to Artaud, would be the recreation of forms and rhythms that capture these vibrations, themselves recollections of known or imagined states. Action in such a cinema "would operate almost intuitively on the brain" (just as the magnetizer's suggestions act on the somnambulist's brain) (411) . And what film genre exemplifies "pure cinema" with its direct access to the brain? The comic genre that *Why the French Love Jerry Lewis* is about to consider.

> It does not detach itself from life but rediscovers the original order of things [like] the early Buster Keatons or the less human Chaplins. A cinema which is studded with dreams, and which gives you the physical sensation of pure life, *finds its triumph in the most excessive sort of humor*. A certain excitement of objects, forms, and expressions, can only be translated into the *convulsions* and surprises of a reality that seems to [ironically] destroy itself. (412; italics mine)

Calling on varying facets of this sense of what film is about, other critics wrote: "Through a particular form of psychism, [the spectator] senses the sentence that *he himself* puts in the mouth of the [mute] character. The spectator in some way hears himself speak" (Ycham 67). "Film acts more powerfully on the affective life of individuals than other modes of experience . . . because the feeling of reality, due to movement in the three dimensions of space, is so intense" (Toulouse and Mourgue 174).[16]

The spectator's sensation of being a physical participant in the action on screen was present from the first projections in 1896. Henri de Parville wrote in *La Nature*, "The Cinematograph [as the film apparatus was originally called] is marvelous. It's unimaginably true. The power of illusion! When you find yourself before these moving pictures, you wonder if you're not hallucinating and if you're a simple spectator or, instead, an actor in these astonishing scenes of realism" (in Jeanne and Ford 20). This is the most prevalent reaction to film screenings in the first decade. The reported fact that 1895 spectators recoiled from the oncoming train in the Lumières's *Arrivée d'un train en gare de la Ciotat* had nothing to do with the intellectual processes of reasoning, judgment, and comprehension; it had everything to do with automatic responses.

In 1910, Ycham, whom I've cited above, underlined that the impression on the film viewer was far more vivid than in the theater. However, he ascribed this to a very different cause from the one studied by Drs. Toulouse and Mourgue: "The spectator's attention is *caught and concentrated on the lu-*

minous projection, without possible distraction" (69). This is why "there is no popular spectacle in which the imagination of the spectator plays a greater role than in the cinema-theater" (ibid.). Is the impact of film in its first decades due to an intense feeling of reality or to an equally intense state of hallucinatory hypnotic trance? The two states, it should now be clear, are in no way contradictory. The *feeling* of reality is in fact the physical stimulus and response of internal bodily movement, and this feeling state is even stronger in somnambulism. "All the inner reality of the crowd trembles on the screen," wrote Jules Romains in 1911 (121).

In 1921, giving lyrical expression to these psychophysiological theories, the poet Blaise Cendrars wrote that film was:

> Automatism. Psychism. And it is the machine that . . . at last uncovers the sources of feeling. . . . The brain is profoundly shaken, overwhelmed (*bouleversé*). . . . Everything is rhythm, word, life. . . . The image lies at the primitive sources of emotion. . . . The spectator is no longer immobile in his armchair; [he is] ripped out of it, done violence to, participates in the action, [and] recognizes himself on the screen among the convulsions of the shouting, protesting, and frantically agitated crowd (qui se demène).[17] (8, 22–23; italics mine)

Cendrars spoke from a privileged vantage point: he was Abel Gance's assistant (scripting, directing, and editing) on *J'accuse* and on *La Roue*, a 1922–1923 Impressionist film in which every movement—within the frame and through montage—is composed with the aim of producing a visceral internal reaction in the spectator. (No French film had a greater impact or influence on filmmaking and criticism in the 1920s than Gance's *La Roue*). Cendrars also wrote his own film scenarios, but is best known as a poet who invented the telegraphic style of simultaneism in poetry (in the 1912 *Prose du Transsiberien*, a year before Apollinaire's *Zone* appeared). A voracious traveler whose nickname was the "*bourlingueur*," it's not surprising that Cendrars writes so perceptively about the possibilities of moving pictures.

Although Cendrars describes the violent (internal) movement of spectators by stating they were "no longer immobile," the fact that they are *initially* immobile in their seats places them in an analogous situation to that of the somnambulist in catalepsy, the stage where the magnetizer and the somnambulist coalesce into one being, a stage which precedes and enables the imitation of movement suggested by the person or entity endowed with hypnotic power (in the hospital, on stage, or on screen).[18] The fascination that fans feel for a film star is perhaps similar to the "attraction exercised by the magnetizer/hypnotist" who first hypnotized the subject and whom the latter feels "a singular need to see again" (Oughourlian 283). This "hunger" is in addition to the primary bodily "hunger for hypnosis" based on film's appeal to the nervous system that Epstein referred to.

However, the same observations could be made from a completely negative point of view. Film's power is "infinitely dangerous [because] it feeds vanity and triggers imitation, for the image is an excitation in naïve souls"; "action, only action, and let it be rapid and brutal"; the "strange combination of intellectual and physical passivity and emotional hyperactivity" in response to cinema's "potent images" produce "silent, hypnotized spectators" (Haugmard 768–70). Reiterating nineteenth-century theories of the dissociation between the higher and lower faculties that causes nervous pathology, Haugmard also wrote:

> Through [the movies], the charmed masses will learn to combat all will to reason and construe, faculties which will atrophy little by little; they will know only how to open their big and empty eyes, and look, look, look. . . . The cinema will be . . . [the only mode of] action for neurasthenics. And we shall little by little reach those menacing days when universal illusion will reign in universal mummery. (771)[19]

Even strong defenders of cinema like Hugo Munsterberg had to admit that the strong sensations that film produces are potentially dangerous.

> The intensity with which [film] takes hold of the audience cannot remain without strong social effects. It has even been reported that *sensory hallucinations and illusions have crept in; neurasthenic persons are especially inclined* to experience touch or temperature or smell or sound impressions from what they see on the screen. The associations become as vivid as realities, because the mind is completely given up to the moving pictures. [Applauding during melodramas, especially in] rural

> communities . . . is another symptom of the strange fascination. But it is evident that such a penetrating influence must be fraught with dangers. The more vividly the impressions force themselves on the mind, the more easily must they *become starting points for imitation and other motor responses*. (221; italics mine)

Normal resistance to crime and vice "breaks down . . . under the pressure of the realistic suggestions" and there is a real possibility of "psychical infection and destruction" in society (222). Fortunately, now that most countries have been alerted to this social danger, "the time when *unsavory French comedies poisoned youth* lies behind us" (ibid.). Strong words, especially from a strong proponent of film like Hugo Munsterberg, and they mesh with everything in these pages on the cabaret, magnetism, and film.

In 1919 a colleague of Freud's, Dr. Viktor Tausk, published "On the Origin of the Influencing Machine in Schizophrenia." His observations in this article correspond closely to case observations cited by G. Gatien de Clérambault in France in roughly the same period, but Tausk's "machine" is directly pertinent to two of the films analyzed in the following pages. Many of Tausk's patients described thoughts and beliefs that were being implanted in the mind against their will. "The machine produces feelings and thoughts that are threatening and alien to the patient, and does so by means of rays or mysterious forces. It creates sensations that . . . in part are sensed as electrical [or] magnetic." Schizophrenics, of course, cannot distinguish between images that emanate from inside their mind and the images that come from without. The influencing machine "often has the ability to project pictures and invisible rays [which are] in some way capable of imprinting [themselves on] the brain." The pictures frequently come out of a "small black box" (Tausk, in Mander 109–11). Keep this little black box in mind when reading the analysis of Cohl's 1910 *The Hypnotic Mirror* below.

Hypnotism as Metaphor for the Cinematograph

Do films that contain the character of a somnambulist or magnetizer support or illustrate the analogy that critics, filmmakers, and psychologists of the 1910s and 1920s drew between film and somnambulism? The continuing French love affair with this analogy is illustrated by the choice of a still photograph from one of Woody Allen's films (*Stardust Memories* [1980]) to serve as the cover for a special issue of *Les Inrockoruptibles* (January 1998) on the filmmaker: in it, the director, played by Allen, is (literally) making a pass at the rigidified body of the actress whom he has levitated in mid-air.

Cinema's most haunting figure of the somnambulist is Cesare in *The Cabinet of Dr. Caligari*. This film drew immediate notice in France: its impact was tremendous, and its detractors were as vehement as its admirers (see Abel, *Film Theory*, vol. 1, for critical articles published at the time).[20] The figures of the psychoanalyst and the magnetizer are fused in this film, and without the frame-story that Robert Wiene tacked on to the original script, the figure is malignant, controlling, and dangerous—not only because it represents absolute authority and criminality, but because it is linked to insanity. Domination and the threat it poses to society is embodied not by a political figure, but by the magnetizer, who causes instinct to surge up from the lower faculties and overwhelm reason. *The Cabinet of Dr. Caligari* was made in 1919, the year that Tausk wrote his article on the Influencing Machine. *Caligari* externalizes the "manifestations of a profoundly agitated soul/mind"; like other Expressionist art, the film is a "shaping of primitive sensations and experiences" (Kracauer 70). Psychotic and hysterical feelings and sensations are expressed through the decor of zigzags that run down streets and up walls, that constitute the contours of the houses and the fairground, that make up many of Caligari's gestures and corporeal poses, and that are especially blatant in the outline of the rooftops over which the somnambulist carries the unconscious heroine.[21] The "primitive sensations and experiences" are shaped by the filmmaker, but they become ours as we watch the film. So when the publicity poster for the film seems to command spectators: "You must become Caligari!," what may really be meant is: "You must become Cesare [the somnambulist]!" The poster is modeled on a shot toward the end of the film where the asylum's chief psychiatrist decides to reenact the experiments of the eighteenth-century magnetizer Caligari. Zigzagging letters across his image spell out "Caligari werden muss!" We first see Caligari not as a psychiatrist, but as a dangerous magician or magnetizer. Knowing that hypnotism played a crucial role in nineteenth-century psychiatry makes the twist in the plot all the more piquant: the research specialization of the asylum director is somnambulism. Caligari exhibits Cesare in fairs as his *Schauobjekt*, at the same time as the fairground attraction and the spectacle of somnambulism become indistinguishable from the film show that we are watching. Showmanship here is clearly mastery over the will of others. Moreover, it is only in the last five minutes of the film that most spectators realize they have been active and unwitting participants in a maniac's world of paranoid delusion. In other words, the spectator has seen the world through the eyes of a madman. Unless, of course, the spectator had attended to the themes and forms discussed here; that viewer would become aware of the manipulation early on. The zigzag is formally linked to the huge "Z" of *Zwang* (obsession) crisscrossed over the frame at one crucial moment.

Frame story or no, the last shot from the film has the psychiatrist—the Director of the Institute—staring into the camera with the gaze of the magnetizer in the framed narrative. With this final gaze addressing the viewer, *we* become Caligari's / Wiene's subjects. The Cabinet is at once a doctors office and the black coffinlike box where the somnambulist sleeps and from which he emerges, and it of course resembles the little black box we've mentioned earlier, the *cinématographe*. Note that the somnambulist, Cesare, has been asleep for twenty-three years. In 1918, the year the script was written, that was precisely the age of cinema. Yes, cinema is a somnambulist trick, as Jean Epstein wrote.

Fairground performances of magnetizers took place, remember, alongside demonstrations of prestidigitators and next to projections of films. Itinerant magnetizers, like filmmakers and exhibitors, need an audience. Somnambulists, with their spectacular display of violent, uninhibited desire, are what draws them in. The somnambulist is a metaphor for the *force* of film's pull on the spectator. It was in fact at the fairground that Hans Janowitz and Carl Mayer found the inspiration for *Caligari*, while watching a sideshow strongman performing feats in what appeared to be an hypnotic trance: the name of the attraction was "*Man or Machine*." It is through the unconscious that the muscular and sensory hyperesthesia of somnambulism and hysteria are linked to mechanical gestures and acts.

In the Méliès film *Le Monstre*, the ghostlike monster, reacting to each gestural suggestion of the Egyptian sorcerer next to him, dances frenetically, waves his arms, and grows taller. The sorcerer, in the manner of a magnetizer or of a psychiatrist at the Salpêtrière, is a figure for the filmmaker, and the ghostly being who copies the gestures commanded by the latter is a figure for the spectator. The somnambulistic double is a monster made visible by the magic of cinema.

A clear example of hypnotism as a model for cinema is the 1922 German film *Schatten: Eine nächtliche Halluzination* (Warning Shadows) by Arthur Robison, in which a magic-lantern show is composed of the acting-out of the spectators' hidden fantasies, conscious and unconscious. An itinerant lanternist and juggler arrives at a castle and asks permission to put on a show for a count, his wife, and her four ardent suitors. Sensing the underlying and mounting passions in his public, he removes the shadows that they are casting and simultaneously puts them under a hypnotic spell, like a magnetizer drawing the magnetic fluid out of the person he is magnetizing. It is thus their own bodies giving way to instinct and desire that they watch in the representation of the magic-lantern show. This is the "nocturnal hallucination" of the subtitle, clearly a metaphor for film spectatorship.

Hypnotism is a specific register for representing film's capacity to unlock the unconscious. In *Warning Shadows*, it also resembles Bergson's idea of the way that the "mechanism of the cinema" merges with the flux like conceptual thought, and descends "toward the *zone of deep-seated instinct*." That is why Marcel L'Herbier finds Bergsonism "precisely analogous to current *cinégraphie*" (149; italics mine). Hypnotism, therefore, should not appear to us as simply one idiosyncratic representation of the film experience; it is integral to the notion of film common to Impressionist, Expressionist, and Surrealist filmmakers and critics of the 1920s and 1930s, just as it had been in the first decade of cinema.

Webber and Watson's *Fall of the House of Usher* (1927–1929) uses double exposure to represent the somnambulistic state and hallucinations. The overriding form in the design of this film (as in *Caligari*) is the zigzag. In the opening shots of the visitor's approach to the house, the form is first composed by the rooftop and gables, then by the floorboards, which zigzag as they expand and are doubled, pulling apart yet superimposed, like the brother and sister who inhabit the house. (Camera angles are also used to create diagonals.) If we apply Poe's analogy between the house and Usher's head to the film, the correlation between the zigzag and the unconscious again appears.[22] The house then splits apart to reveal Madeline preparing for dinner. When the lid of the serving dish is raised at dinner, she has a vision of a coffin, then of several superimposed coffins that expand to fill the screen with diagonals. Madeline's hallucination of her impending death propels her into somnambulism through auto-suggestion, and this has fatal consequences. In the nineteenth century, if one fell into a prolonged state of catalepsy, one risked being taken for dead and, as a result, buried, a very real possibility that obsessed Poe. Suggestion and its subsequent cataleptic state cause Madeline to be buried alive. The difference between the literary and the film narrative is not somnambulism, but the element of *auto-suggestion* through hallucinatory visions, a perfect metaphor for film spectatorship when the figure of a hypnotist is not present. As though to confirm the encouragement and presence of hallucinations in the film's viewers, the next image after Madeline's somnambulistic exit is that of bells pealing, announcing her death. This image is so magnified, rhythmic, and insistent that we *hear* the bells ringing. This is an example of synesthesia, a sought-after effect in films of the 1920s—for example, in L'Herbier's *L'Inhumaine*. (It should be mentioned that from around 1896, psychiatric theory postulated that synesthesia—when it produced the actual hallucination of a second, or "echo," sensory sensation—was pathological. Those who were the most prone to such synesthetic experiences were hysterics.) It is now Roderick who is hallucinating: he sees the coffin and sees his own hands nailing it shut. He approaches the camera and stretches out his hands to *us* (us-her, as Mary Ann Caws cleverly put it in her study of the tale). He mimes the gesture of hammering the coffin shut repeatedly: it has become an automatism and, consequently, we see him doubled, then tripled. There are no intertitles, although letters are painted across the image during the reading of *Ethelred*, quite appropriately, making us read simultaneously with the character in the film, just as we are made to have the same visions as the hallucinating Usher.

Edison's 1899 *Mesmerist and Country Couple* correlates Mélièsian cinematic stop-action substitution shots and epileptic movement with the art of the mesmerist. In the first pass of the mesmerist, the couple's clothes are switched. The man, who is sitting in his chair with his arms folded (like a film spectator), is propelled out of the chair and falls backward with legs up in the air as if he were having an epileptic seizure. The mesmerist is running back and forth in front of him, looking at us. With another pass, the man performs a handstand; another pass, and he is stretched across two chairs in cataleptic rigidity. A final pass from the mesmerist and his own clothes return as he jumps up from the chairs, while his wife reappears as a dummy before resuming her original shape and dress. In *A Visit to the Spiritualist*, another Edison film (1898–1899), a countryman is mesmerized and "sees funny things." For example, a handkerchief "grows larger and larger, dancing up and down and going through funny antics *until before the eye of the spectator* it turns into a ghost of enormous proportions [then] disappears" (description cited in Crafton, *Emile Cohl* 328; italics mine).[23] What's pertinent is that the hypnotized eye in the film becomes the eye of the spectator. This film was modeled on Méliès's *L'Auberge ensorcelée*, Other Méliès films refer explicitly to hypnosis, for example, in *The Magnetizer* (1897), the woman who falls into catalepsy finds herself stretched over two chairs. However, Méliès adds his own touch to this typical feat of magnetism: one trick shot makes the chairs suddenly disappear, and another removes, just as suddenly, the woman's clothes, "leaving her almost naked." Méliès is absolutely right to recognize in the exhibitions of somnambulists a powerful spectacle of the instincts. Similarly, in the film entitled *Le Bacquet de Mesmer* (Mesmer's Basin), immobile statues are transformed into can-can dancers thanks to the fluid of animal magnetism, while the star dancer, a *gommeuse épileptique*, bends over backward in the *arc de cercle* of the hysteric.

A comparison of Du Maurier's novel and the 1931 remake of *Svengali* (directed by Archie Mayo and starring John Barrymore, Marion Marsh, and Donald Crisp) demonstrates the way that cinematic techniques mesh with and intensify the dynamics of suggestion. Each time he deploys it, Svengali's magnetic gaze is directed at the camera. In the first scene of hypnotism, his eyes—shot in extreme close-up—cloud over and become enormous glass marbles staring out at us. The second time, it is late at night as he concentrates all of his force into the gaze that he directs out of the window of his garret (his eyes grow larger and glass over as they stare at us). The camera, in a reverse tracking shot, carrying the gaze and its magnetic power, rushes—flies—out of the room, over the rooftops and, blowing open her windows by its force, into Trilby's room, and into her sleeping (unconscious) mind. She rises and sleepwalks to Svengali's rooms. All of these techniques—the magnification of the close-up, the look into the camera, the tracking shot, the filtered lens—perform the dynamics of magnetism in a way that the novel and the stage could not. When Trilby is about to perform at the end of the film (in Cairo, in the Sphinx Cafe, an exotic addition to the novel, heightening the strange and enigmatic quality of somnambulism),[24] Svengali's reminder to her serves as a reminder of film's grip on the spectator as well: "Tonight I want you to watch me very closely—don't take your eyes off me for an instant—and remember—there is nothing in your heart, in your soul but Svengali, Svengali, Svengali." The association of film viewing with the magnetizer's gaze was so strong in the early decades that a film reviewer endowed himself symbolically with it (an all-powerful gaze containing the ability to penetrate another's body) by naming himself "*le Mauvais Oeil*" (the Evil Eye).[25]

How closely should the techniques of magnetism be related to the magnetism exercised by film stars? In Romeo Bosetti's *The Magnetized Man* (1908), this form of magnetism is portrayed in a very literal way through trick shots. A man buys a coat of mail to protect himself against robbers. The coat becomes magnetized, and all the metal objects on the street, on storefront displays, on houses, and on passersby fly off their rightful place to attach themselves to the man's back as he strolls down the street. The man's helplessness in the face of his newly acquired magnetic personality is very funny, but the truly hilarious scene takes place at the police station (since, now, *he* is accused of robbing others), where the gendarmes' swords, strapped around their hips, spring to an erect position every time that they approach the coat of mail. The quasi-supernatural forces of animal magnetism, including its command of libido and will, have been co-opted by the cinema.

In *The Somnambulist* (1903, American Mutoscope and Biograph), a woman rises from her bed, takes her candle, walks out onto the rooftop, continues walking for two minutes, and then falls off the roof to the street below. A policeman runs to the spot, only to find her dead. With the help of bystanders, he picks her up and carries her off, moving toward the camera until her body is offered out to us in a medium shot. Cut. Precisely the same scene begins again, but within ten seconds we realize that this time, she is awake. She now kneels at the foot of the bed, ostensibly thanking God that it was "just a dream." This is the dream of cinema where the subject is always doubled,

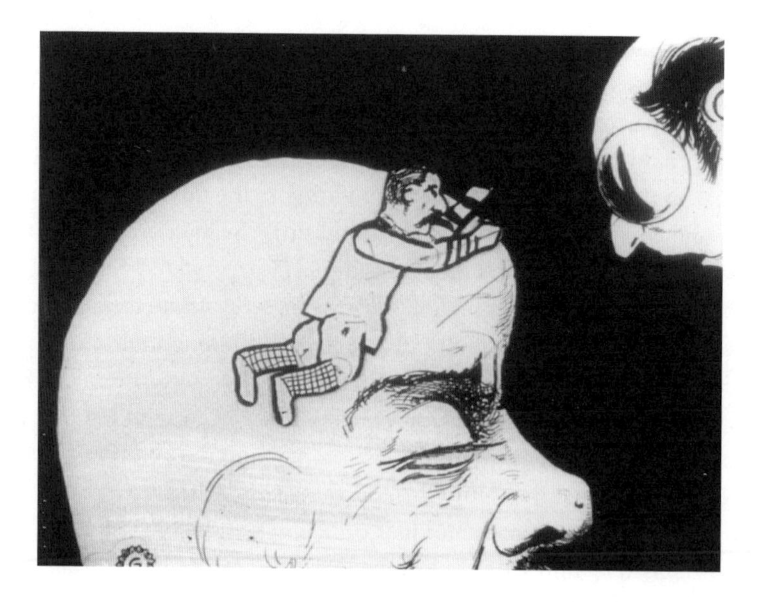

Figure 13. Emile Cohl's "Nothing is Impossible for Man" (Gaumont, 1910). Courtesy Cinémathèque Gaumont.

where the Other can be seen, and where the spectator is doubled in the person of the character watching her unconscious self act as she "sleeps."

In the fourth tableau of Emile Cohl's[26] 1910 mostly animated feature, "Nothing Is Impossible for Man," the eye of a rather diabolical-looking psychiatrist expands until it occupies the entire upper half of his head, at which point magnetic rays emanate from its piercing gaze and penetrate the forehead of the hypnotized subject, whose eyelids flutter, then close as he is put into a magnetic sleep by the psychiatrist. Concealed deep inside the patient's head is an aggressive individual who emerges to clutch an enormous bottle of liquor. As he drinks, the eye of the psychiatrist is transformed into concentric circles which become a vortex and then, again, a huge eye; the bottle falls from the inner-being's hands and the figure sinks down, weeping and desperate. The intertitle reads: "By hypnotism, he scrutinizes hidden thoughts and reads what is buried deep in consciousness" (see Figure 13). That this power resembles that of the film camera is evident from the tableau that follows, "Thanks to the Cinematograph one can stockpile life in order to better dole it out in slices" (a reference to "slice of life" Naturalism in the novel and in the theater). This exceptionally self-reflexive segment shows, on one side, a cartoon cinematographer drawn directly onto the frame and, on the other, the *real people he is filming*, a nurse with a baby carriage and her beau, a policeman. They, of course, *become film images*, which are then projected onto a screen and watched by an audience. The screen appears at a slightly different angle to our point of view, so we are not identified with the audience, but rather with the *camera*, as it produces the curious transformation of "flesh and blood" people into filmic representations. Moreover, the narrative of the film within the film repeats this transformation: behind the backs of the two adults engaged in conversation, a mischievous boy replaces the "real" baby with an inanimate object. Like the psychiatrist who, through hypnotism, sees "behind the scenes" into the unconscious, the film camera sees behind the scenes and captures the antisocial thoughts and acts normally hidden from view. In these early films, the filmmaker is seen to have traits in common with illusionists, magicians, magic lanternists, and in addition—via the exploration of the unconscious—with magnetizers, psychiatrists, and psychoanalysts.

Filming the Unconscious

How often is the anarchic, primitive double in the film meant to reflect the spectator's "double," our double? Jean Epstein sees *all* screen characters as the spectator's "phantom" or "onscreen double" (*Machine* 107). The film historian Georges-Michel Coissac qualified Robertson's Phantasmagoria as "almost cinema" because he "created life . . . by doubling living beings" (29). Ten years earlier, in 1915, Jacques de Baroncelli wrote that the "new actors . . . have sat down in front of the mirror, like the spectator before the screen. . . . A feeling, the deepest of their being . . . take[s] shape in a gesture, a pose. They have rediscovered a primitive source of 'language,' rich, poignant, universal. . . . It is pantomime . . . but how much more deliberate and severe" (126). The screen is a mirror, and its primitive language is a form of pantomime, linked to somnambulism and to the spectacle of freewheeling libido.

In the 1910 *Le Miroir hypnotique*, by Emile Cohl and/or Etienne Arnaud, a black box mounted on a tripod (which looks like a camera but functions like a movie screen) reveals the thoughts of the person placed in front of it

Figure 14. Emile Cohl's "The Hypnotic Mirror," sequence 1: the thief, under trance, is reenacting the crime (Gaumont, 1910). Courtesy Cinémathèque Gaumont.

by causing the subject to fall into a somnambulistic trance and to mime past actions; the "mirror" inside the box reflects the sexual or anarchical acts that the Subject has committed and tried to hide. Acts can be dredged up from the psyche thanks to this invention, which can only be a cinematograph. The films (of the transgressive acts) within the film are a record of the hypnotic state, a state brought on by the apparatus and obviously congenial to cinematic images. Although Ferdinand Zecca had already used the technique of the flashback, here the technical wonders of cinematography are merged with the problematics of hypnosis. Cohl seems to be saying that cinema is a hypnotic mirror: the flickering light of the screen hypnotizes viewers and encourages them to project their fantasies into the on-screen narrative, just as it forces the character to project his libidinous impulses onto it while his body involuntarily mimes the action. Note that this film predates Jean Ep-

Figure 15. "The Hypnotic Mirror," sequence 3: the unfaithful husband. Courtesy Cinémathèque Gaumont.

stein's essays on the camera/screen as self-revelation and mirror of the spectator's psyche by about fifteen years. What scenarios are acted out?: (1) a thief robs and kills a sleeping woman, (2) a schoolboy creates anarchy in the classroom, (3) an unfaithful husband kisses a woman he meets at a dance (see Figures 14 and 15). The cinematograph's mirror contains the projection of the somnambulistic double personality: violence, anarchy, unleashed libido. Cohl's "invention" is even more penetrating than the examples from other early films where photography is shown furnishing evidence of criminal acts and "penetrat[ing] beyond conscious concealment," instances that Tom Gunning studies in "Tracing the Individual Body" (in Charney and Schwartz 37). The first vignette in fact displays the apparatus as a precious invention for the police, but we see that it is far more than that: Cohl's "hypnotic mirror" actually *records the unconscious*.

In almost every film within the film in Cohl's oeuvre (and there are many), the inscribed film is a representation of the psyche or the unconscious (for example: *Brains Repaired*, *Nothing Is Impossible*, *Wondrous Glasses* [Les Lunettes féeriques]). In this last film (1909), every time that a character puts on the magic glasses, a spinning geometric design appears, which transforms itself into an animated cartoon of the character's hidden desire: for alcohol, gambling, love, etc. As Cohl's scenario states, "we see on the curtain [of the magic glasses] all that is passing in the mind of the wearer clearly portrayed in each eye." We are in the position of the psychiatrist (in Cohl's *Nothing Is Impossible*) whose gaze penetrates the other's psyche. Yet, each time a character puts them on, the glasses are framed in extreme close-up; *we* are wearing them and they are controlling *our* vision. Cinema makes it possible for spectators to see inside the character's head, at the same time making those images a part of the spectator's mind.

Cohl's glasses are a "mind-screen,"[27] an ideal metaphor for early cinema, looking backward to the early-nineteenth-century precinematic toy, the kaleidoscope, and forward to the spinning vortex of Ray Dennis Steckler's "hypnowheel." In the 1965 short-lived cinematic, "Hallucinogenic Hypnovision," each time the hypnowheel appeared on the screen, theater ushers in phosphorescent monster masks ran up and down the aisles threatening spectators with cardboard axes. If we consider the structure of the film-within-the-film to be self-reflexive, then, by the recurrent use of this structure, Cohl is saying that film is the equivalent of the unconscious.

Imitation is joined to automatisms and to doubling in *Rigadin's Nightmare* (1913), directed by Georges Monca and starring the cabaret performer Prince. As Rigadin strolls in the park with his fiancée, two passersby begin miming his every gesture. This game causes great hilarity, and Rigadin turns around. Offended, he slaps one of them with his glove, provoking a duel for the following day. The thought fills him with terror, so he promptly goes to a bistro to get drunk, repeating several times the gestures of slapping a face and of thrusting with an imaginary sword, obsessional gestures that have become automatisms, like a nervous tic, inspiring laughter in the viewer. An extraordinary *mise en scène* of doubling now occurs in this otherwise unremarkable film. The hero returns home and goes to sleep, his image reflected in the armoire mirror. As the nightmare begins, we see him doubled, rising to a sitting position in bed and in the mirror. Immediately, a huge image of Rigadin appears in superimposition over the reflected image, as if it were emerging out of it. At the same time, his adversary's ghost image appears on the opposite side of the bed, with a somnambulist Rigadin in the middle, sitting up, eyes closed. Suddenly, there are *four* superimposed figures in addition to the somnambulist and his reflection: each of the adversaries has doubled himself. The doubles' movements, similar but not identical, now grafted, now floating on top of the first figure, create a choreography of spectres lunging, parrying, falling backward: quite beautiful, lasting only a few seconds.

The spectacle of imitation in the beginning of the film is dissected in the *mise en scène* of Rigadin's doubling in the dream sequence. There, the unconscious Rigadin emerges out of the subject as the latter is shown in a somnambulistic trance state, making visible the corporeal manifestation of the unconscious through the figure of the double. The conscious/unconscious duality is enacted literally in the *duel*.[28]

We see the same sort of "mind-screen" in Méliès's 1911 *Les Hallucinations du Baron Munchausen*. Munchausen's reflection in the mirror gives way to a split screen: the dreaming subject can watch his double in the terrifying adventures in the space above, thanks to this cinematic trick. The mirrored double comes from "down below," the body reacting to the hallucinations in the mirror space with great agitation of the feet and arms, or hopping and waddling, or in other varieties of pathological gait. The visions are also pulled down below: radiant visions of women that sink into a well, or devils with pitchforks who force the Baron down onto the ground and then back onto his bed, legs kicking, as though in the midst of an attack of epilepsy; underwater creatures like the octopus dragging the Baron down into the sea, and the man in the moon whose hideously elongated tongue extends out of the mirror, turning into a nose or trunk which douses Munchausen and resembles nothing if not a urinating penis. The hero covers his head (this is an affair of the body and not the mind) and crashes through the mirror, emerging on the other side . . . to find himself outside his house, outside his mirrored self, and necessarily bringing the hallucinations—and the film—to an end. Clowns frame him on either side in the conventional close-up of the character that ends French comedies around 1910. Munchausen is shown with a *splitting headache*: the primitive self engenders nightmares and endangers the mind/head, but it is exactly what makes us laugh, as the presence of the clowns makes clear.

Freud also ties the Double to automatisms, because both arouse the feeling of the uncanny. Dolls, automatons, waxwork figures, catalepsy, dismembered limbs, severed heads, feet that dance by themselves are all forms of the same uncanny perception: an inanimate object that seems to come alive. Epileptic seizures and "manifestations of insanity" also give "the feeling that automatic, mechanical processes are at work, concealed beneath the ordinary appearance of animation" (Freud 132). Freud is drawing from the earlier work of Jentsch, which he uses as a point of departure, interpreting these manifestations in the light of the theory of repression. But we can see how perfectly they mesh with the content of early cinema and nineteenth-century psychiatric theories of the corporeal unconscious. In fact, the uncanny signifies the sensation we have of the "double" in all of us, our corporeal unconscious with its automatic gestures expressing an agenda of which we would prefer to know nothing. As Freud puts it, we see in epilepsy and madness the working of "forces hitherto unexpected" and dimly perceived "in a remote corner of [one's] own being" (151). The last category of the *Unheimlich* is when something we regarded as imaginary suddenly appears in reality. Isn't this what the spectator of Méliès's films experiences? As an afterthought, Freud mentions that the most frequent manifestation of the uncanny, an involuntary recurrence of the same thing, can also "call forth a feeling of the comic" (154).

The split between the first and second personality of the somnambulist is represented in a great many films where the character is mirrored, or where the head is separated from the body, or where the head or the entire body is multiplied. The extremely frequent presence of the double in early cinema functions as a paradigm for somnambulism, automatisms, and the "lower order" and, as critics from 1912 to 1930 intimated, for the film experience itself. Jean Epstein writes of our need to "imagine ourselves . . . and our refusal to accept ourselves, as soon as the deeper level of personality is uncovered. . . . In his on-screen double, what the spectator notices first is the vulgarity of a pose, the awkwardness of a gesture, that shame of being seen, that . . . he had thought he'd succeeded in hiding" (*Machine* 106–7).

In the film *Onésime contre Onésime: "Allégorie"* (ca. 1912–1914), starring

Ernest Bourbon and directed by Jean Durand, doubling, joined to dismemberment and incorporation, is clearly designated as the division between the higher and lower faculties. The first intertitle reads: "The good Onésime knew how to conduct himself in society, but the second one behaved like a hoodlum." Under the civilized being lurks the personality ruled by instinct and desire. And, in this film, the second personality is clearly all libido, equipped with an insatiable appetite. The second Onésime always emerges, through double exposure, from the body of the first. With the grotesque figure of the clown, knees bent, and buttocks high in the air, the Double grimaces to the camera. His pranks include creeping up behind the cook and grabbing her buttocks in one scene, and stealing the silverware in a restaurant in another. In this last instance, the good Onésime orders his double to leave, and pushing him, causes him to fall against some other patrons, upon which a general melée, anarchy, and destruction ensue. That is to say, the "good" Onésime is drawn into the ways of his troublemaking double. Disgusted by his alter ego, Onésime, "angry, separates himself from the other"; he does this by rolling out of bed and leaving the other (somnambulistic) self behind. But the "bad Onésime took advantage of the new situation by behaving even worse yet." Imitating his "better self's" gestures, he becomes indistinguishable from him. Conversely, the good Onésime, in extreme close-up, now grimaces at the camera and jumps into a river to escape. His double, following close behind, somersaults into the river. Division and incorporation, up until now staged through superimpositions, are again enacted in the film's final scene, but here incorporation is literal. Driven to distraction, the once-civilized, "good" Onésime dismembers the bad Onésime and *eats him*. (The intertitle reads: "As he couldn't win the upper hand over his adversary, the good Onésime tore him into pieces and ate him.") The double falls asleep in an armchair, and the enraged Onésime grabs him, tears off an arm, the legs, the torso, and throws them up in the air. Suddenly, an idea occurs to him: he smiles at us and salutes with his hat. The actual moment of incorporation by devouring is missing from the print (held at the Centre National de la Cinématographie), but the look into the camera at the penultimate moment is telling: it is the spectator who is implicated in the act of incorporation.

Incorporation is a common theme in early cinema, beginning in 1901 with Williamson's *The Big Swallow*, where the actor, in extreme close-up, swallows the motion picture camera filming him. In *Calino Ate Horsemeat* (Gaumont), Calino (Paul Bertho) gorges himself with horsemeat and by ingesting the meat, *becomes* a horse who bolts out of the house and gallops uncontrollably down the street, wreaking havoc. Like the spectator, he has incorporated the movements and identity of a foreign being. Finally, he is captured and carried into a hospital, where a surgeon cuts open his abdomen to remove a toy horse! In *Boireau, Gingerbread Man* (1913), the hero falls into a vat of dough, is baked, bought, and devoured by two schoolgirls in close-up, facing the camera. Immediately after Boireau has been incorporated into the bodies of the two little girls, we cut to the close-up of the grimacing actor, a convention for ending comic films in the teens, a remnant of grimace films and of cabaret performance. Here, Boireau sticks out *his tongue* in a gesture of oral incorporation, hands wildly gesticulating. These images serve as metaphor for the dynamic described in these pages as the spectator's incorporation of the filmic image by virtue of internal mimicry. Film's excessiveness penetrates spectators and becomes part of them.

Do You Want to Dance?

The Hypnotist's Revenge (American Mutoscope and Biograph 1907),[29] consists of several sequences, all of which have considerable pertinence to the themes discussed in the previous chapters. First sequence: Regression. Professor *Still*man (an allusion to cataleptic trance?) invites four volunteers up from the audience. The hypnotist makes passes, and one man regresses to the level of a child and gets into a fight over a game of marbles, whereupon the woman volunteer spanks him. A member of the audience protests, and Stillman puts him into a trance; he is then made to dance with a broom, chase the "child," and become a waiter hallucinating dishes, silver, and so on. There is sudden immobilization after each suggestion. Finally, the now helpless participant is made to leap onto a dinner table as though it were a horse. When he is made to snap out of the trance, he becomes enraged and attacks the hypnotist who has subjected him to public ridicule. Second sequence: Devolution and Dance. The intertitle reads: "Professor disguised as musician, makes a monkey out of society chappy at a dance." The guests' bodies move to the rhythms that the hypnotist's violin dictates. His gaze is directed suddenly at "Chappy" (the irate spectator from the first sequence), who falls to the floor, jumps up and down like a monkey, lies on his back and rises kicking in an epileptic version of a Russian cossack dance, leaps and jumps like a caf'conc' performer, grabs a woman, then a valet, whom he spins around wildly by the waist, their feet off the ground, finally dragging a man onto the floor, until the horrified spectators are turned into "wild people." Third sequence: Alcohol, Acrobatics, Anarchy. Professor Stillman disguises himself as a waiter and "gets Chappy crazy drunk." The latter climbs onto the dinner table, grabs and kisses a woman, hangs merrily from a chandelier, and then repeats the same acts upside down. The scene is one of total anarchy and destruction. Fourth sequence: Shifting Identities. "Chappy is made to believe he is Bridegroom at Wedding." The last sequence is missing, but here is its description from Niver's *Early Motion Pictures: The Paper Print Collection in the Library of Congress*: "The police are called and the skeptic [Chappy] is taken off to an insane asylum where he is cured of his hallucinations and convinced of the efficacy of hypnotism." Note that this ending is a confirmation of the fear that severe psychological consequences often resulted from public shows of magnetizers. Note too that it took the talents of a psychiatrist (using hypnotism?) to cure the poor man. The message of this film is that in stage hypnotism, it is the spectators who become the actors, and that there is no denying hypnotism's power to affect us.

The unconscious tendency—not to say, irresistible urge—to imitate another's gestures or movements is often used to comic effect in French cinema, from early Pathé comedies to Jacques Tati's *Les Vacances de Monsieur Hulot*. Compelling demonstrations of imitation and viewer contamination are found in a 1909 Gaumont film, *La Bous-Bous Mie* (probably directed by Etienne Arnaud and written by Emile Cohl) and in a 1907 Pathé comedy, *The Yawner*. Like Méliès's *Cake-Walk Infernal*, analyzed in the following chapter, *La Bous-Bous Mie* illustrates the irresistible suggestion exercised by popular spectacle and, specifically, the contagion of extravagant dance movements.

A stout Parisian concierge goes to the music-hall (the "Casino des Tourelles," one of the venues where Maurice Chevalier supposedly made his professional debut in 1901) to applaud the new dance, the "Bous-Bous Mie" —a mixture of the undulations of Arabian belly-dance and African jerking of

Figure 16. Etienne Arnaud/Emile Cohl's *La Bous-Bous Mie* (Gaumont, 1909): Mme Ducordon is imitating the cabaret dancer. Courtesy Cinémathèque Gaumont.

the hips and buttocks, with arms raised akimbo waving from side to side. After the dancer leaves the stage to enthusiastic applause, a comic takes her place, only to be upstaged by Mme Ducordon, the concierge, who has risen from her seat and is dancing the Bous-Bous Mie (Figure 16). The gendarmes have to forcibly put her back into her seat but, seconds later, she uncontrollably begins dancing again. This time, she's firmly escorted out onto the sidewalk, where she starts to dance again—but now the gendarmes are irresistibly caught up in the movement.[30] Suddenly, they realize what has happened to them, and turning on their heels, they march back into the music-hall (these rigidly controlled steps are in sharp contrast to the erotic and anarchic abandon of the body in the dance). We then see Mme Ducordon back in her *loge* (a word denoting a concierge's lodgings, a theater dressing room, and box), where the dance has gotten such a hold on her that—

Figure 17. La Bous-Bous Mie: Mme. Ducordon's performance. Courtesy Cinémathèque Gaumont.

ignoring the calls of the occupants of the building—she stands on a stool in front of the mirror gyrating to the Bous-Bous Mie. (She is now both spectator and entertainer.) The intertitle underlines the terrific pull of the dance and its power over the will: "The Bous-Bous mie had done its work" (*avait fait son oeuvre*). When a resident comes in to complain, he too is caught up in the movements. In the last scene, there is a reception for friends in the *loge*. Here, Mme Ducordon's transformation from the role of spectator to performer is fully realized. Her husband, acting as master of ceremonies, taps three times as Mme D. makes her entrance (in oriental costume); soon everyone present is imitating the movements of the Bous-Bous Mie, faces ecstatic or convulsed with laughter (see Figure 17). In the meantime, unheard in the uproar, some very proper bourgeois are impatiently pulling on the cord outside the front door. They finally break in, and they too are disarmed by the erotic, anarchic, and highly contagious movements of the dance.

In the last sequence, we see the concierge (the half-involuntary performer, submitting to suggestion) clearly using these suggestive movements to fascinate, entrance, and disarm others; her audience is put into a state resembling hypnotic trance and they are helpless to resist imitating the movements they see before them. If one is not a performer exercising this power over others, then one is in the position of the spectator, in whose body these "uncivilized" movements take root, one who is clearly *not* in control of him/herself, whose body—like a second personality or an unconscious—is an expression of explosive sexuality and anarchy.[31] (For example, the initial confrontation with the police is superceded by their conversion, since a policeman who figures among the friends at the party takes center stage at one point, imitating the bumps and grinds in a totally lewd, uninhibited fashion; and there is a collapse of class distinctions between the concierge and the bourgeoisie at the end of the film). Arnaud and Cohl's film, for all its gaiety and hilarity, is an illustration of the dangers of popular entertainment's propagation of frenetic movement.[32]

If it is true, as Charles Keil believes, that "reflexive films . . . can indicate how the nature of the actual reception situation in this period might inflect our understanding of the operation of psychic mechanisms traditionally held to be transhistorical" (65), then we should look very carefully at films where spectatorship is represented in relation to unconscious imitation, and where somnambulists, doubles, automatons, and popular entertainment are juxtaposed.

Hypnotism is an important component of the power struggle between rival criminal bands in Feuillade's serial *Les Vampires*.[33] The only other character capable of vying with those played by Musidora is the handsome hypnotist, Juan-José Moreno (played by Fernand Hermann), who demonstrates his power in the episode "Les Yeux qui fascinent," hypnotizing a young servant and thereby producing a somnambulist, whom he later carries in a coffinlike trunk to a hotel, where she is used as Musidora's double, allowing him to capture Musidora and put her into a magnetic sleep. And it is in this way that he also captures her heart. Needless to say, when he hypnotizes the servant, and then Musidora, he looks directly into the camera. With *Les Vampires*, a clear analogy is made between anarchy and the cabaret, since the cabaret is the site where the lower classes and the anarchist band of thieves, "the Vampires," gather. Of Musidora's endless disguises in the serial, that of the firebrand cabaret singer Irma Vep is the most memorable. Her name itself, like a prestidigitator's magic trick, challenges the spectator's perceptual and intellectual faculties to grasp or produce Méliėsian *vues à transformations*, in this case, juggling the letters to reveal the anagram "Vampire." (This talent for deciphering is, in fact, one of the chief attributes of the serial's hero.) The ability of the cabaret singer to affect the audience and stir the crowd to action offers a *mise en abyme* of the film actor's ability to do so. The sequence of her performance on stage is followed by the spectators' exit and the descent of the *habitués* into the cellar. The planning for the next raid is combined with an apache dance. At the end of Cendrars's *ABC du cinéma*, previously cited, the automatisms and hysterical movement (the lower orders) poeticized are linked to social uprising, just as they had been in dire prophesies of the 1870s and 1880s: "The crowd who leaves the cinema, who flows out into the street like black blood, who *like a powerful beast* extends its thousand tentacles and . . . smashes the palaces and prisons" (23).

Sneezing, Itching, Yawning

The suggestive power of the film image for unconscious imitation via physiological response can be seen in its most basic form in films whose sole premise is a single involuntary physiological act. The first example in cinema history dates from 1894, with Edison's Kinetoscope film of his assistant Fred Ott sneezing (*Kinetoscopic Record of a Sneeze*). Grimace films and films of itching produce an even stronger impulse to reproduce the movement seen.

Yawning was known to be the *most* contagious of all acts among hysterics, the first studies being published in 1888 by Charcot and by Féré. A "Contribution to the Study of Hysterical Yawning," written by Drs Gilles de la Tourette, Huet, and Guinon appeared in volume 3 (1890) of the *Nouvelle Iconographie de la Salpêtrière*. The much-photographed Augustine was an athlete of the yawn: she "continues non-stop throughout the entire day" (100). A photograph documents an attack of yawning of another hysteric, Rosalie Gay . . . , where the "exaggeration is not only in the frequent repetition of the yawns, but in the extraordinary intensity and the length of time each one

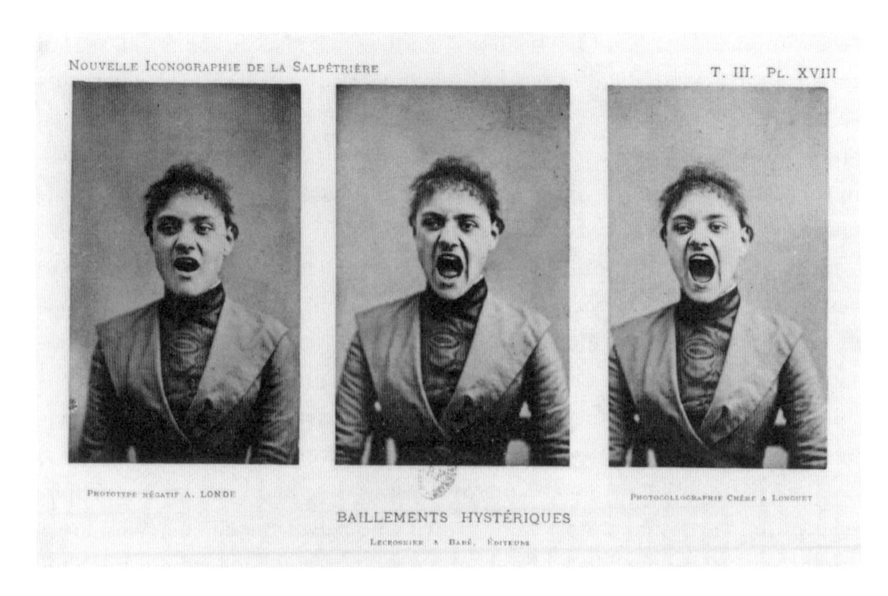

Figure 18. Hysterical Yawning, from *Nouvelle Iconographie de la Saltpêtrière*, vol. 3 (1890), plate 18. Photo Bibliothèque nationale de France, Paris.

lasts. . . . [Her] yawns seem powerful enough to disconnect her jawbone from the rest of her face" (*bon à décrocher la mâchoire*) (see Figure 18).

This photograph from the *Iconographie* looks a lot like the last close-up from the 1909 Pathé comedy, *The Yawner*. As the first scene of the film opens, the main character yawns as his wife is helping him on with his coat. She yawns. Once outside, he goes past four soldiers at attention in front of their captain. He yawns. They yawn, then break up laughing: order is defeated by this loss of control. The Yawner is himself subject to contagion: as he passes a stone fountain with a grotesque's head spewing water out of its wide-open mouth, he is impelled to yawn, and the fountain squirts him as onlookers laugh. Yawning provokes hilarity because loss of control and involuntary automatisms are, as Bergson underlined, funny. The Yawner goes to a society gathering, and of course ignores the laws of social etiquette by yawning: the act is so contagious that all the heads in the framed family portraits on the wall begin yawning. The characters' yawning in the cinematic frame are clearly marked as artistic representations. At the sight of this uncanny repetition where the irresistible impulse to imitate transcends the boundary between reality and representation, the hero leaves screaming, then buys a strap to tie around his jaw to prevent himself from wreaking imitative havoc on the world. The last image is of the Yawner in extreme close-up wearing the exaggerated makeup of a clown (in French: *grimé*, thus the enhancement of the grimace), and yawning while looking directly out at us as the strap breaks. Conclusion: there is no possible means to control contagion, neither within nor outside the film.

Public Shows of Magnetizers, Early Cinema, Cabaret, and the Circus

In Chapter 2, we saw Dr Simon assimilate the dangers of magnetizers' shows with prestidigitators' shows, making both responsible for the onset of hallucinations. In the same period, Dr Azam wrote that there were "those for whom the marvelous is a spectacle that bears some analogy with the agile tricks of a clown" (353). Magnetism—prestidigitation—the agility of clowns: is there a thread that ties these spectacles together? It is hypnotism that links them. One of the greatest prestidigitators of the late nineteenth century was, of course, Méliès, one of early cinema's greatest artists, and with him, we will see how easily the skills of the prestidigitator, the clown, and the filmmaker fold into one another and are at times indistinguishable from one another. When Alfred Binet wasn't making vital contributions to the study of animal magnetism, double consciousness, and hysterical sensory pathologies, he was writing plays for the Grand Guignol theater (see Chapter 3) and publishing articles on prestidigitation. His article, "The Psychology of Prestidigitation" (for which he consulted Méliès), was published in the *Revue des Deux-Mondes* in 1894.[34] In it, he consistently calls on hypnosis to explain the illusions produced by prestidigitation. Seeing what doesn't exist (negative illusions), for example, is "the result of the influence of one mind over the other" (558). It is very interesting to note that the two questions which the 1889 Congress of Physiological Psychology (of which Binet was of course a founding member) addressed were public spectacles of hypnotism and negative illusions. "Negative illusions . . . have been [best] made known to us through hypnotic experiments. The subject is commanded not to see this person [or object], and the command is sufficient to cause the disappearance of the person—of his becoming invisible, as it were. . . . How a person perfectly sane . . . is prevented from seeing objects placed immediately before his eyes [is difficult to comprehend]" (563). This is accomplished by the prestidigitator's *hold* on the attention of the audience "in order that their mind enter into relation with his"; "Robert Houdin says that [he] must have a frank, bright, penetrating glance, which he must concentrate boldly on the eyes of the spectators [so that] their eyes become riveted on his and a feeling of mutual sympathy arises" (559). Binet, writing only a short time before Méliès made his first films, made verbally explicit what Méliès had learned from his mentor, the magician Robert Houdin, and was about to stage in films where magnetizer and prestidigitator were fused into one person.

The overlap of Méliès the magician and Méliès the filmmaker has often been pointed out, and their relation to the spectator is indeed comparable. It should be remembered that Satan was called the Great Prestidigitator because he commanded illusion and hallucinations in the minds of his prey; the roles of Mephisto and of the magician that Méliès played in his films were not so different, and the latter is often transformed into the former, as in *The King of Makeup*. A parallel with the magnetizer begs to be made as well.[35] The filmmaker's illusionistic techniques inspired one critic to exclaim: "This apparition-maker . . . knows how to pronounce the terrifying phrase of magnetizers: 'I want it thus!'" (Paul Gilson, in Sadoul, *Méliès* 156). Moreover, for Méliès, the magnetizer appears to be perfectly interchangeable with the magician, as the beginning of a scenario of *The Magnetizer's Revenge* (1909) suggests: "a magician—a renowned magnetizer" (Malthête et al.).[36] In another lost film, *Cabalistic Doubling* (1898), a magician transforms commonplace objects into a young woman. "The magician hypnotizes her; two airy forms leave the young beauty's body and remain at her side." Here is a precise concretization of somnambulistic doubling realized by the "magic" of cinema. Put another way, somnambulistic doubling effected by the magnetizer is identical to the doubling effected by film magic. Thus, the most troubling and amusing hallucinations can be produced by the magnetizer, by the psychiatrist, by the magician/prestidigitator, or by the filmmaker—all of whom operate through suggestion. With this difference: the suggestions of the magnetizer, the prestidigitator, and the psychiatrist provoke hallucinations and illusions that are the products of the subject's brain, whereas the *vues fantastiques* of the filmmaker create hallucinatory visions in the external world and place them before the spectator's eyes.

In *The Magician* (1898), the magician changes himself into a gesticulating clown, and then into Mephistopheles. The supernatural takes a back seat to the magic of stop-action camera work; Mephisto is subordinated to the magician, and magic is to art; in a final transformation, he becomes a sculptor whose art consists of making statues come to life; in other words, his talent consists in turning immobile representations into moving ones. In this it resembles the art of the filmmaker. (We remember that the spectators present at the first screening of the Lumières' *L'Arrivée d'un train en gare de la Ciotat* reportedly exclaimed "Ça bouge!" when the projector cranked into motion the image of the train.) In order to dominate others, Mephisto is obliged to call on the medical technique of hypnosis, as in the 1906 *Alchimiste Parafaragamus*, where he hypnotizes the alchemist.

The demonstrations in *The Magnetizer* and *Cabalistic Doubling* assimilated the talents of the magnetizer and those of the filmmaker, while showing how much more the latter could astonish his spectators. Seated in the darkened room, their eyes fixed on the luminous screen, the spectators of early cinema are in a vulnerable position, exactly as they were at public shows of magnetizers, astonished and subjugated. And this is the hypnosis-effect shared by magnetism, prestidigitation, circus, and film.

The sense of marvel and surprise experienced at the first film projections closely resembled "that which arises in a music-hall audience watching the exercises, more or less mysterious, more or less in contradiction to the apparent laws of nature, of a prestidigitator or an illusionist" (Jeanne and Ford 21). It wasn't even necessary to include the person in control of the spectators' perceptual and psychological functions in the film (in the figure of a magnetizer or a magician); film, by its very nature, had the same identificatory hold, commanded the same form of attention, by the power of illusion, as the magnetizers and prestidigitators whose shows resembled it but could not match it. Here is the reaction of a guest present on 28 December 1895 for the Lumières' dress rehearsal of the first film screening: "At this spectacle [of a suddenly animated street scene] we remained speechless, struck with stupor, surprised beyond all expression" (Sadoul, *Histoire générale* 1:271). The spectator was none other than the master of surprise and stupefying magic tricks, Georges Méliès.

Louis Haugmard's fears seem far more credible once we perceive these resemblances. The pathologically narrow focus of attention and fascination with one sensation dominating, to the detriment of all others, signaled to psychiatrists of the late nineteenth century a failure in mental synthesis. Haugmard claimed that it is this type of experience that is not only encouraged, but fostered, by film viewing.

The suggestive power of gesture and movement in popular entertainment takes on a dimension perhaps previously unsuspected by readers at the end of the twentieth century. It is to the specific forms of movement and gesture in early French film comedies that I turn to in the next chapter.

CHAPTER SIX

Hysterical Gesture and Movement in Early Film Comedy

"The gesture creates the decor as well as everything else."

—JEAN EPSTEIN, "For a New Avant-Garde"

"The cinematograph . . . is in the process of turning into, like an appendicitis, the national malady."

—*Le Cri de Paris*, 1907

Cabaret Meets Cinema

Charlie Chaplin began his career performing in London music-halls in the mime troupe of Fred Karno, and the earliest posters show him grimacing angrily. The caf'conc' stars Dranem, Little Moritz, Louis-Jacques Boucot, Chevalier, and Mistinguett became film stars, while Ferdinand Zecca (singer and monologuist in the cabaret) became an actor and director in films and was Pathé's artistic director in charge of production; his popularity, according to G.-M. Coissac, was equal in France to Chaplin's. Zecca is particularly remembered as the initiator of narrative realism, or "scènes dramatiques et réalistes," as they were called (*L'Histoire d'un crime* [1901] and *The Victims of Alcoholism* [1902], for example), but also made a number of comedies and grimace films, films composed solely of close-ups of people grimacing for the camera.[1] France's biggest film star, Max Linder, began in the music-hall, as did numerous others. The company actors of Pathé's branch in Nice, *La Comica* (known for its politically radical scenarios as well as for the chaotic anarchy of its comic invention) came from the caf'conc', the circus, and fairs. Many actors were acrobats, like Buster Keaton and W. C. Fields in America and André Deed, né André de Chapais, in France, ensuring that dislocations and contortions of the body would continue to occupy a central place in popular entertainment. Like commentators on the cabaret before them, some film historians were repulsed by the predominance of the Low in the style and themes of early cinema, pointing to their origin in the caf'conc'. "The level of the majority of Pathé-Zecca's comic productions are of a surprisingly low, base nature [and] plunge into the mire. . . . Nonetheless, . . . the unforgettable sidekicks of Charlot are the direct descendants of the types that Zecca and his followers went looking for in the residus of the caf'conc'" (Sadoul, *Histoire générale* 2:192–93). (Examples of film scatology include Dranem's *The Enema* [1904], Zecca's *Wrong Door* [1904]—where a telephone booth is mistaken for a W.C.—, Chomon's *Effects of Melon* [1906], and Gasnier's *Pull the Chain, Please* [1908]. Even Max Linder didn't turn his nose up at the chance to appear in *It's Papa Who's Taking an Enema* [1907].) Cabaret and music-hall performers—mimes as well as comics—first moved to film because they were better paid there, and around 1905 the popularity of cabarets and music-halls was being overshadowed by that of film. Paulus, accordingly, tried to win back audiences by combining film and live stage performance. His magnified image was projected onto a screen hung from the ceiling of his cabaret, the Ba-Ta-Clan, while he sang in the wings, only appearing on stage to sing the last couplet (Paulus 172; Malthête-Méliès, *L'enchanteur* 229). These were the first films made with artificial light, and it was Georges Méliès who filmed Paulus's act, later doing the same for the singers Fragson, Polaire, Polin, and Paul Delmet. The great majority of early film comics came from these entertainments, and that is why the first comic films owe so much to the themes and especially to the rhythms of cabaret comedy style.[2] This fact ensures that the performance codes of the cabaret are carried over into the new art, and that the "messages" conveyed by gesture (certain movements and tics of the face and body are read as mental pathology) are transmitted to the spectator as before. In fact, the two forms of entertainment often existed side by side in the same venues. In fairs, where cinema first found the majority of its audience, music-hall stars performed between films. The same stars also made films that were screened in these fairs. René Jeanne points out that this humble origin weighed against the idea of film as art: in certain milieux, cinema was not taken seriously because it was a fairground attraction. Jeanne also argues that the fairground public was responsible for "a good part of . . . [film's] vulgarity" (67). Nevertheless, these were the spectators that Méliès appreciated so much: "the true public . . . , the only one who laughs at a gag without restraint" (in Jeanne 65). Certainly, it was logical that new forms of entertainment should begin where audiences for spectacle already existed. It is nevertheless true that the coexistence of these genres could not help but create a specific climate for the reception of the newer art form. The Folies-Bergère incorporated films in its program beginning in 1898, the same year that pantomime suddenly reemerged as a major attraction on stage as well as on screen (Pathé released a "Pierrot" film every year between 1896 and 1901). The popularity of pantomime undoubtedly prepared the way for that of silent film, not only because the stylization of gesture replaces the spoken word, but also because of the oneiric quality of both genres. Similarly, the Shadow Theater of the Chat Noir, like Emile Reynaud's Théâtre Optique and Pantomimes Lumineuses at the Musée Grevin in the 1880s,[3] paved the way for film's popularity. Méliès, we remember, worked for the Théâtre d'Ombres in 1890.

By 1910, the various pathologies of the body that had been exploited by café-concert singers such as Paulus, Dranem, and Mlle Bécat could now be seen in film comedies; tics and bizarre gaits would become the "signature" of film comics (see Figure 19). Chaplin, whose film debut was in 1913, typifies this trend, but no more so than his predecessors in France. It is important to note that Mack Sennett became a director by "stealing his first ideas from Pathé [Films]" (Goudet 4). The Keystone Kops are the progeny of Boireau and Bosetti. The original gait of Jacques Tati's Monsieur Hulot belongs to this tradition.[4] An advertisement for a 1911 Pathé film attributed to Cohl, *L'Automate acrobatique*, poses the question: "This curious attraction. . . . Is it an acrobat? Is it a dummy?" (Another lost film by Cohl, made for Gaumont in 1908, is entitled *L'Automate*.) The body's fantastic exploits continued to be associated with the phantasy of being a mechanical being, just as they had in the cabaret.

Comics were "mostly wild, inhuman creatures, animated comic strips," David Robinson notes as he compares these performers to Max Linder, who

Figure 19. André Deed in *Boireau Cuirassier* (Pathé, 1912). Photo, Bibliothèque du Film, Paris.

"had the gift of naturalness [and] recognized that films need not be invaryingly frenetic from beginning to end . . . while his contemporaries traded on their own grotesque appearance" (Robinson 199). This of course is precisely my point: the year 1912 already marks the beginning of the refutation of this explicit and crude mirror of the corporeal unconscious in all of its "wild" (in other words, instinctual, primitive, savage) and "inhuman" (mechanical, automatic, puppet-like) barbaric splendor. What critics refer to as "dehumanized" in these comic figures, I see as the corporeal unconscious. The dominance of the comic genre in French cinema up until 1912, which some (like Georges Sadoul) believed was a function of a largely proletarian and petit-bourgeois public, is also a barometer of how magnetic these expressions of the corporeal unconscious were for spectators.

Robert Desnos shares my regret at the sophistication, or "humanization," of French comedy: "From its invention, cinema knew perfection in the comic genre. *L'Arroseur arrosé*, *Boireau épicier* (Lumières' 'The Sprinkler Sprinkled,' or 'Watering the Garden,' and 'Boireau the Grocer') are already perfect films. It took the intervention of the pathetic (*lamentable*) Max Linder and Rigadin to rob cinema of all interest in France; the ridiculous rules of theater then replaced spontaneous fantasy" (119). Another Surrealist, Paul Eluard, wrote in 1945 that the actors and directors of the first period of French comedy had a "sense of burlesque plasticity all their own, burlesque comedy in motion that had its raison d'être only in the cinema. . . . They move about in an impossible extra dimension and make the walls around them crumble" (10). A letter sent in 1917 to Emile Cohl from his collaborator, Benjamin Rabier, states that "the public likes things that are a little less incoherent." The general public was far from embracing Dada two years later. The tolerance for *zizanie* was diminishing, and the era of "primitive comedy," mourned by Desnos, was definitively over. "The public demanded that the comic hero be humanized. They wanted realism. . . . The second generation will deliberately distance themselves from burlesque and from a degenerated comic register" (Eluard 10).

Faster, Faster

René Doumic wrote in 1913 that "movement is the triumph and the essence [of the filmmaker]. [His] dramatic art must therefore be an art of using movement in order to obtain effects of surprise, terror or comedy (*drôlerie*). . . . The perfect cinema-drama, if we're given it someday, will achieve perpetual motion" (927). The velocity of kicks, leaps, sudden arm and leg movements, were already what constituted novelty, astonishment, and laughs for spectators of English pantomimes in Paris; the gestural frenzy of singers and eccentric dancers in cabaret and café-concerts was equally stupefying. I have already traced the incursion of pathology in the character of Pierrot in the

1880s and, simultaneously, the appearance of the zigzag in his movements. This Pierrot, called for by Jean Richepin, also emphasized velocity: "Zig! zag! paf! . . . speeding by like an express train." Added to the velocity and jolts of mimes and eccentric dancers like the Clodoches were the jerky, zigzag movements of epileptic comics and *gommeuses*, and of singers in the style of Paulus and Ouvrard. Like the perceptual shock of trains hurtling through space that often comprised the sole subject of a film in cinema's first decade and that continued to be a privileged object in mise en scène,[5] hysterical movement provided spectators with a novel perceptual experience in cinema. Hysterical movement, like the train, is an idiosyncratic but important part of modernity's essential paradigm—movement—of which cinema is the crowning achievement. Movement—the faster and the more extreme the better—and hysterical movement is movement at its most extreme and intense. The more pronounced the movement, the more intense the spectator's internal repetition of it. As concerns early film *comedy* in particular, hysterical movement, gesture, and vision constitute the very basis of comic effect.

The shocks to the spectator's body were transmitted all the more effectively by the jerky cadence of cinema exhibition and projection (16/18 frames per minute). "The screen danced, fluttered. The image advanced by little spurts/jolts (*secousses*)," wrote the journalist Louis Forest, describing the first projection of the Lumière brothers (in Jeanne 12). The accelerated, jerky movements of early cinema are naturalized by our perceptual processes; we compensate for the breaks by "seeing" it as continuous, but underneath the *illusion* of normal movement is the subliminal perception of what may very well have reminded viewers of hysteria.[6] The effect of accelerated movement on audiences was explicitly linked to the onset of mental illness in an article by the American comedian Sidney Drew, who warned in 1917 of "mental upheaval due to [the] rapidity of comic action, incidents [and] ill-timed facts" in some films (in Jenkins 56).[7] Here is what Leon Moussinac had to say about movement and the film spectator: "Movement devours him, absorbs him [and the spectator] abandons himself to this joyfully" (7). Ricciotto Canudo, another film critic of the first decades, also names "velocity" as the symbolic essence of film. The series of visions and images are tied together "in a vibrant agglomeration," thanks to "the excess of movement to be found in film." Canudo is talking about the rapidity with which the reels of celluloid unroll and the "vertiginous rapidity" of changes of set and location. Nonetheless, for him as for Doumic, "what is truly symbolic in relation to velocity are the *actions* of the characters. We see the most tumultuous, the most unlikely scenes unfolding with a speed that seems impossible in real life." Moreover, the instructive function of cinema takes one to the "farthest countries [where the] most unknown peoples [are shown] moving, shaking, throbbing" before the spectator, transported by the extreme rapidity of representation. The "excess of movement" in cinema seems to draw forth a parallel excess in the shaking bodies of "unknown" or "primitive" peoples. And it isn't long before Canudo draws an analogy between the educational exhibition of "unknown peoples" and "the display of 'freaks' at the old fairgrounds" (59–60, translation modified, italics mine). We will shortly have the occasion to analyze this convergence. One of the attractions that film comedy will borrow from fairs and cabarets in this period is the display of deformity and accompanying pathologies of movement. The "distance" between the highly evolved French spectator and the representations of "unknown peoples" is supposedly immense, just as is the distance between the physically normal spectator and the 'freaks' that moved from fairs to early French comedy (in, for example, Pathé's *Grotesque dwarf*). Film comedies take advantage of this "difference" and then point up how easily it evaporates.

From the beginning, movement was the essence of cinema. The excess of movement of bodies within the frame is mirrored by what is happening inside the spectator's body: frenetic movement perceived produces nervous and muscular activity. In the same essay in which Jean Epstein explained that the job of the director was to suggest, persuade, and then hypnotize, and that the film was "nothing but a relay between the source of nervous energy and the auditorium," he went on to explain why "the gestures that work best on screen are nervous gestures." He admires the "little, short, rapid, spare, one might say, involuntary gestures of Lillian Gish." Nervousness, which often exaggerates reactions, is photogenic:[8]

> Chaplin has created the overwrought hero. His entire performance consists of the reflex actions of a nervous, tired person. A bell or an automobile horn makes him jump, forces him to stand anxiously . . . a synopsis of his photogenic neurasthenia. The first time that I saw

> Nazimova agitated and exothermic . . . I guessed that she was Russian, that she came from one of the most nervous peoples on earth. (238)

The nature of film, in its broadest yet most essential conception, is velocity and perpetual movement. In this context, the rapidity of movement and the "nervousness" of gestures (this term includes the automatic gestures of hysteria, epilepsy, and other nervous disorders) is an intensified, specific form of film's essence. The intensely felt *reality* of the film image is due, as I've said, to the automatic reactions of the muscles and nervous system in response to the movements seen on screen. I came to this understanding of spectatorship in early cinema through the study of nineteenth-century psychophysiology, psychophysics, and psychiatry. Filmmakers who were familiar with theory in these disciplines (Epstein studied medicine, Eisenstein was familiar with biomechanics) immediately saw their relevance to cinema. Observing spectators of his films "rocking side to side at an increasing rate of speed as the shots on the screen . . . accelerated," Eisenstein writes that the perception of motion pictures is "physiological in its essence" and therefore "psychic in its nature" (in Petric 7).[9] Epstein claims that the cinematic feeling is "particularly intense" because of the "hunger for hypnosis" and modification of the nervous system that it fosters. Because of this modification of the nervous system and "hypnosis-effect," "to attract customers, the circus showman must improve his acts and *speed up* his carousel from fair to fair. *Being an artist means to astonish and excite*." It is the *cinema* that is above all capable of producing "the habit of strong sensations" (240; italics mine). Moreover, velocity is one of the primary motors of comedy. Think of the comic chase (and remember that the French comedies discussed here predate the Keystone Kops, which debuted in 1912). Along with the chase, there is the rapid-fire response, the acceleration of the domino effect of chaos and demolition in anarchic comedy (examples are Pathé's Boireau series with André Deed, as well as the Clémentine and the Onésime series), the trick of speeded-up movement, and finally, hysterical or epileptic movement. The dynamic of physical comedy's effect on the spectator is one of muscular tension and shocks in the body giving way to sudden release of tension through the explosion of laughter; velocity adds considerably to this dynamic.

Cohl's *Le Retapeur de cervelles* (Brains Repaired) (1909, Pathé) "cures" the disturbed patient by removing his mind-boggling phantasies (in the scenario, "l'enchaînement de ses idées folles") and by putting them into our eyes and head. An older couple enters the doctor's office; the man is biting the tip of his cane and is besieged by tics and trembling, which are traits of the male hysteric: the character is meant to be, at the very least, a neurasthenic. Dr Trépanoff (*trépaner* means to cut open the cranium) puts a megaphone to the man's head and, as the film switches from live action to animation, the fun begins. The inside of the head is first seen as an insect, then a brain, then five different heads (angry, happy, etc.), then a dancing cossack, among several other transformations. Yet this changing tableau of the patient's psyche is only the beginning of a truly dizzying metamorphosis. The doctor drills a hole and pulls a very long white worm out of the man's head. As he puts this worm up onto a blackboard, we watch the white line of the "brain lesion" go through astonishingly rapid transformations, constantly mutating into different objects. For example: the head swallows itself (incorporation), a man looks through a telescope (the gaze that transforms reality), doubles repeatedly shake hands, detachable body parts move about, figure and ground switch places with each other. The velocity and the forms taken by the line's metamorphoses are clearly due to the animator/filmmaker, but in the scenario they belong to the neurotic or hysteric. Who is it that exposes them to view? The neurosurgeon, Dr Trépanoff, alias Emile Cohl. Most hallucinations are indeed characterized by mobility: "one image substitutes itself for another . . . at times hallucinatory phantoms [shift] in a veritable metamorphosis of images" (Simon, *Sur l'hallucination visuelle* 15). Thus, our experience watching this film is tantamount to an hallucination. As Don Crafton writes, "Cohl, throughout his career, was preoccupied with the theme of insanity and its relation to laughter" (*Emile Cohl* 272). This sort of vertiginous movement in relation to an abnormal mind or mind-state also appears in other Cohl films. A lost film of Emile Cohl is recounted by a spectator of the period: in this "genial, fantastical film where animation and live action are combined, . . . an errand boy is charged with transporting a little box, no bigger than a fist, in which, out of curiosity, he had cut out a little hole." What the errand boy saw inside the box "made a very strong impression" on this spectator. "A little man, drawn almost as a stick figure, was jumping around, executing all sorts of capers and somersaults, breaking up into separate parts and reassembling himself. . . . [When] the box was delivered, the little man, no longer imprisoned, suddenly grew to the size of a little monkey and set about tormenting his involuntary host and destroying his office" (Chessex).[10] Corporeal agitation is linked to devolution and regression in the mind of this spectator, whose first thought was to compare the character to a monkey. What *is* this box that unleashes the destructive and agitated creature: the unconscious or the film apparatus? Cohl's genial technical accomplishment of combining animation with a realistic decor and live actor appeared as early as 1908.

Metamorphosis is not only characteristic of hallucination but is also an aspect of hysterical personality disorders. Dr Charles Richet treated the hysterical personality disorders of a somnambulist, who in turn "became" a peasant, actress, general, priest, nun, sailor, old woman, and little girl (the case is reported in Richet, "La Personnalité" 228–31). Shifting identities are a staple of music-hall comedy, and the speed of costume changes increased dramatically with the advent of film stop-action photography and substitution. Film made it possible to visually realize the hysteric's phantasies of the body. The psychiatric lore of the period could easily be called upon to describe Mélièsian *vues fantastiques*: Dr. Galopin writes that "one meets people every day who . . . believe themselves changed into lions, bears, fountains, fish ...*neurotics*!" (137). In *Illusions extraordinaires* (1903), Méliès takes the separate parts of a dummy —legs, torso, head—out of a box and tosses them onto the floor where they form a living woman. As he demonstrates, her head is still detachable. She is then transformed into confetti, only to become a monkey dressed as a cook, and a dummy again, whose dismembered body is thrown up into the air by the magician who gleefully cavorts on a table top as the film ends.[11]

On 16 December 1929 Méliès emphasized the effect on the viewer of "this enormous accumulation of unexpected trick shots that struck the spectator of the time with stupor. . . . Incomprehensible images where I executed the wildest cavorting and pirouettes to amuse [them]" (Sadoul, *Méliès* 136). The filmmaker called these trick shots "the whole arsenal of fantastic and mystifying compositions capable of driving the most fearless spectator insane" (Méliès, "Les Vues cinématographiques" 370). Méliès referred to his films as his "crazy productions" in a letter to Maurice Druhot (reprinted in *Ciné-Journal*, 17 January 1930). Should we take these allusions to madness seriously? Was the filmmaker consciously drawing on medical science for his images of dismemberment, multiplication of the self, and convulsive movement? His first persona in the cabaret was as Dr. Melius, and the wacky scientist in his films is named Professor Maboul (*maboul* means nutty in French). I do not mean to suggest that it was the filmmaker's invariable intention to represent attacks of hysteria or epilepsy, simply that he was not unaware that these cinematic images might well remind spectators of those pathologies and thus produce in them the same *secousse* or thrill. After all, they had been well prepared by their attendance at cabaret performances and at fairground attractions. Reactions that might have been dulled by habit (as in the well-worn tricks of the stage *féerie*) were compensated for by the surprising newness of film technology.

Comical or fantastic invention is often equated with the inventions of the wildly gesticulating mad scientist in the films of Georges Méliès and Emile Cohl (for example, in *Brains Repaired*). "In joining together the mirage of science and speed, Méliès discovered new forms of the comic" (Bardèche and Brasillach 28). Indeed, the combining of fantasy with science corresponded to the zaniest images in the Mélièsien imagination.

Before he made *Mater Dolorosa* and *Napoleon*, Abel Gance made a short film, *La Folie du Dr. Tube* (1915), a grotesque tour de force illustrating the parallelisms between madness, science, and filmmaking. Among the first in the mad-scientist genre, *Dr. Tube* is devoid of the terrifying elements that the genre would take on with *Caligari* only four years later. Yet the power of this grimacing, white-jacketed, cross-eyed clown with a pointed head is no less menacing. He possesses the ability to deform one's perception and to transform those who enter his laboratory into physically deformed beings. The effect (produced by convex and concave mirrors, lenses, and split screen) is akin to the fairground attractions of the funhouse mirror and, to a lesser degree, of the freak show. The characters who fall under Tube's sway are doubled, like the Siamese twin attraction. The film stages the impact of the cinematic image on the body of the spectator; it creates doubles who repeat each other's gestures in comic, automatic, and imitative fashion, and the tendency to imitate is shown to be the fissure that opens the way to potential pathologies of vision and of the neuromuscular system. The scientist himself is not immune to these disturbances: at the sight of the effect his experiments have on people, his arms and legs gesticulate wildly, flailing like an epileptic's, while his jaw works mechanically more and more rapidly. The close-ups that open and end the film are significant for the filmmaker / mad scientist's power to create disturbing perceptual illusions that change the viewer physically. In the first frames, Dr. Tube is staring out at us, eyes wide open. In the final sequence, he is reading a scientific treatise with a magnifying glass and, in the other hand, holding up a white ladle that looks like a camera—as though he were photographing us according to his scientific theories. He waves his magnifying glass like a baton, now directing the spectators. The image becomes "normal" again. *He* is mad (as the title of the film indicates), not us, and consequently he puts his head into a cage, capturing/framing himself as he had done to others in the experiments. The hysterical symptoms of his madness—outrageous grimacing and the jaw automatically moving up and down—return in the magnification of this final close-up, which purports, in the intertitle, to be the "Explanation of Tube's Madness." Emile Cohl said that the film animator's craft would cause one to "end up in the Charenton asylum," and Méliès said that his trick shots would drive the spectator crazy. Gance's film appears to be saying both of these things.

Moving, Shaking, Throbbing

Not only velocity, but the *type* of movement filmed excites and astonishes. In the chapters on cabaret, I pointed out the agitating effect on the spectator of automatic and mechanical rhythms, citing contemporary journalistic and literary remarks on the "shocks," "shaking," and "magnetic" pull felt by the audience: these are the qualities that make an act an *attraction*. The comical and uncanny effect of these movements and rhythms was enhanced by trick shots and other purely cinematic techniques in early film comedy.

As I stated earlier, the more pronounced the movement, the more intense the spectator's internal repetition of it. Like Cohl's *Bous-Bous Mie*, Méliès's *Cake-Walk infernal* (1903) stages both the performer and the spectators who *become* performers of an exotic dance. The adjective "infernal" is double-edged: it refers to Hell and also to the unstoppable contagion of frenzied movement. In a 1905 song performed by Strit, it is the music itself that alone merits the adjective: "The thing that makes me craziest is when an infernal orchestra furiously attacks an original cake-walk." Satan returns from a visit to the world above where he had enjoyed himself at the music-hall. The new dance craze in turn-of-the-century Paris was, as we saw in Chapter 3, the cake-walk and was prominently featured in music-hall programs contemporary with this 1903 film. Jean Cocteau described the 1902 musical review *Les Heureux Nègres*, where "Mr. and Mrs. Elks" first performed the cake-walk in Paris, and we can note the striking similarities with the aspects of angularity and dislocation that I emphasized in cabaret performance. "They danced: skinny, crooked, . . . their ears, knees higher than their thrust-out chins, . . . wrenching their gestures from themselves. . . . They reared, they kicked, they broke themselves in two, three, four." The public "vented its 'delirium' by 'stamping its feet'" (Cocteau, *Portraits* 74).[12] In the years 1903–1906, in addition to cake-walk reviews and songs—"La Cake-walkomanie," "Professeur de cake-walk," "American Noir," "Mr. Loufok," "Turbulent," "Uncle Tom" and many, many others—the dance was featured in films. *Cake-Walk* and *Kickapoo* featured the Elks in 1903, and another film, *The Dwarfs' Cake-Walk*, was made the same year. (A description and analysis of this last film appears in Gaudreault 106–8.) Méliès's *Cake-Walk infernal* opens with the acrobatic exploits of little devils who hop-frog wildly over each other; in other words, it opens with a typical music-hall number. Mephisto appears and, like a magnetizer, orders his little devils to somersault, to perform other feats, then to dance the cake-walk in the flames, thus visually superimposing music-hall frenzy over the supernatural. Then Satan dances the cake-walk with inspired abandon, but a vaudeville couple (the man in blackface) suddenly appears, who perform the dance in a truly breathtaking manner. Their more angular, authentic style exactly reproduces the movements of the hystero-epileptic attack (including the repeated arm movements up and down and the *arc de cercle* where the body arches over backward) *and* of the *chanteuses épileptiques* who had been performing in cabarets from 1875 on. Loss of bodily control is spectacular: it rivets the gaze, and it is an exceedingly popular music-hall and film attraction. Not to be outdone, Mephisto bursts out of a huge *cake* in the guise of a grotesque, deformed rag doll dancing the cake-walk, and manages to surpass the extravagant agitation and contortions of the couple. In an even more spectacular exhibition than theirs, the Prince of Darkness's arms and legs wave, twist, and shake in all directions with such force that they are pulled apart from his body, as the detached members continue to dance independently, testimony to the furiousness of the rhythm and movement. It is the apotheosis of nervous reflex and the body as pure autonomy from the head. At the end, "they all begin to dance like *madmen* (Star Film scenario)." Tiring of the festivities, Satan makes everyone disappear, as he too is swallowed up into the ground. "But the infernal flames, themselves taken over by the fever of the dance, start to dance the cake-walk" (Star Film scenario). Certainly, accelerated movement like this is "diabolical," and the recurrent presence of little devils and of Mephisto is a sign of this component of frenetic movement in Méliès. Alexandre Arnoux wrote that, in film, "acceleration belongs to the Devil, slow-motion to the domain of God" (in Bizet 179). Yet, the scenario is telling: it is madness, hysteria, that must be read in these infernal dance rhythms; the modern preoccupation with hysteria clearly covers over and supercedes the spectre of the supernatural. What is satanic is the talent for elevating the Low (the Underworld of the instincts and automatisms) to an art form; what is diabolical is the contagiousness of the "Low."

Like the African Bous-Bous Mie, the abandon of the body in the cake-walk ("moving, shaking, throbbing" like the "unknown peoples" in the documentaries of "the farthest countries" that Canudo referred to)—with all its implications of the domination of the "lower orders," sexuality, and regression—is imported into France from an "uncivilized" place, America, and more specifically, black America. Joined to the regressionary pull of uncivilized locales in *Cake-Walk infernal* is the degenerative stigma of epileptic movement. Epilepsy and barbaric peoples meet again in Willy's novel, *La Môme Picrate*: as the title character gets more and more carried away dancing the cake-walk, the male spectators remark that she "must have an unstable character. . . . She snorts [and is] geometry in spasms" with her "devilish, high-stepping legs, saluting with the fury of a barbaric chieftain" (16–17).

I said in Chapter 3 that I would return to Willy's assimilation of epilepsy, savages, and the cake-walk, whose violent, jerky movements were fairly captured by Cocteau's description. Willy called it "a dance of epileptic savages." Because it is raced, all of the fantasies (sexual and other) attached to blackness in the French turn-of-the-century colonialist mind are brought to bear on the dance. What produces a fascinating overlap with this already heavily charged perception is the fact that the movements of the dance replicate many of those found in an epileptic fit. And they do so just as strikingly as the performances of the *gommeuses épileptiques* who had created such a sensation in the caf'conc' for over two decades. A Parisian would naturally think of epilepsy in seeing the cake-walk because s/he had been to the caf'conc' and had seen the performances of *gommeuses épileptiques*. Remember that you were "not Parisian for two cents if you [had not] seen Naya, the eccentric, hyperbolic *gommeuse*." In fact, after the appearance of black Americans or of Europeans in blackface, it was the *gommeuses épileptiques* who popularized the dance. (See Eugénie Fougère on the book jacket: photographs of her show that the medallion she is wearing on her dress is of a black cake-walk dancer.) The cake-walk, moreover, is earmarked as pathology in Paul Marinier's 1903 song "The Conservatory of Mimi Pinson." The young ladies in the dance class "take fantastic poses, throwing their legs in the air. . . . It's the cake-walk. . . . Why are they shaking themselves about like that, the poor girls! But this dance isn't new. It used to be called the Dance of St. Guy" (St. Vitus's Dance, the name the Goncourts used to qualify the epileptic comic at the Eldorado). The wild abandon of limbs flailing about, if it isn't the mark of a savage, must be the symptom of epilepsy/hysteria. The extraordinary attraction (with an underlying apprehension) for the Parisian public is the same in both cases. Was the cake-walk as popular in America? Yes. Was it compared to epilepsy? I can't answer that question in the present volume, but my guess would be no. The hold that hysteria had on the imagination in France had its equal in no other country.

In Charcot's *Leçons sur les maladies du système nerveux faites à la Salpêtrière*, a patient (celebrated in the annals of hystero-epilepsy) suffers from *tarentisme* (she is compelled to continually dance the tarentella). "She is a *démoniaque*, a possessed woman [taking] the most frightening poses" (323). The distance between Charcot's patient and the characters in Cohl's and Méliès's films is small indeed.

Dismemberment

Going deeper into the realm of pathology than cabaret comics could, film was able to make visually concrete the hysterical feeling of "dismemberment of the self" (Binet's description, in which he is referring to doubling and multiple personalities) (see Figure 20), as well as the sensation of anatomical dismemberment or partial anesthesia. As Otto Rank stated in his psychoanalytic study of the Double, "representation in the movies . . . expresses in clear and sensual picture language certain pathological conditions and connections that the poet cannot always grasp with words" (in Kittler, 7 n). The nineteenth-century obsession with the Double is an expression of the division between consciousness and the corporeal unconscious, as I've already suggested, and it is an extremely frequent figure in early cinema, as are the automatisms that also make up a large part of nineteenth-century spectacle. The multiplication of the self and dismemberment (the body in pieces) are frequent in Méliès's films. The character is doubled in *Dédoublement cabalistique* (1898), in *L'Illusioniste double* (1900), in *Un peu de feu, s.v.p.* (1903), in *La Lanterne magique* (1903), and in *Les Hallucinations du Baron Munchausen* (1911), among many other examples. In the first two films, the power to double oneself is attributed to the supernatural[13] or to the talent of the prestidigitator; in the last two, to hallucination or to proto-cinematic magic. Méliès triples himself in *Un Homme de têtes* (1898) and in *Un Match de prestidigitation* (1903), splits up into four selves in *Equilibre impossible* (1902), into six in *Le Chimiste repopulateur* (1901), and into seven in *L'Homme orchestre* (1900). Here, seven identical musicians, playing seven different instruments emerge out of one man (Méliès). When they play, "their grimaces and contortions are most amusing to see," as the publicity blurb in the Star Film catalogue puts it. There are extraordinary stagings of Méliès's detachable head in *Une Bonne farce avec ma tête* (Tit for Tat [1904]), *L'Homme à la tête de caoutchouc* (Man with the Rubber Head [1902]), and in *Le Mélomane* (The Music Lover [1903]). In the last film, the bandleader Méliès tosses his head up onto a suspended musical staff several times, each time producing a note in the melody that the female chorus sings until they all cavort gaily off screen. *L'Illusioniste double et la tête vivante* (1900) combines the two themes. This mania for detachable heads is pertinent to the nineteenth-century theories surrounding hysteria already discussed here, since it is precisely because of the split between reason (and the other higher faculties) and the body (the lower faculties) that hysterical phenomena such as hallucinations and automatisms occur. What is more, the obsessional theme of dismemberment and decapitation is filtered through a

Figure 20. Clowning and split personality: "The Man with Three Faces," drawings by Emile Cohl (11 in. x 3½ in.). Courtesy Pierre Courtet-Cohl.

parodic view of medical science: *Le Malade hydrophobe qui a des roues dans la tête* (The Hydrophobic Patient with Wheels in his Head [1900]), *Le Système du Docteur Souflamort* (1905), *Les Echappés de Charenton* (The Escapees from Charenton [the Paris Asylum], or The Bus of Madmen [1901]), *Le Secret du docteur* (1909), and *Une Indigestion*. In the last film, made in 1902, a man suffering from indigestion goes to the doctor. The doctor proceeds to cut off his arms and legs with a large saw, to cut open his stomach and to insert a keg; then, using a spatula, the surgeon pulls out various objects (including two rabbits); when the patient protests by shaking his head, the surgeon cuts it off. Finally the body is sewn back together and the man leaves the office, cured. In addition to the production of surprise or shock, the visual interest of multiple selves and detachable body parts is undeniable. It furthers the tendency toward an excess of movement in early cinema: the more parts, the more elements there are to set into motion. Detachable body parts were a part of magic shows, puppet shows, and Grand Guignol too. Indeed, images of dismemberment were as widespread in popular entertainment of the turn of the twentieth century as they are in the horror films of the present day.

Three Méliès films that clearly demonstrate the consequences of the split between the body and the head are *Une Bonne farce avec ma tête* (Tit for Tat [1904]), *Le Bourreau turc* (The Terrible Turkish Executioner [1904]), and *Tom Tight et Dum Dum* (American title: *Jack Jaggs and Dum Dum* [1903]). Decapitation is definitely an affair of High and Low in *Turkish Executioner*, with the body representing automatic movement and loss of control: the executioner's body is chopped in two at the waist, and even when he fits himself back together, his legs are shown still kicking on the floor before rising.

Tit for Tat is a wonderful illustration of the war for dominance between the higher and lower faculties. Méliès comes on stage, entering the frame from the left, removes his head, puts it in a transparent box and, putting on a new head that exactly matches the first, lights up a cigarette and blows a considerable quantity of smoke into the face of the imprisoned head. He repeats this act of provocation four times until, beside itself with anger, the head escapes from its box, floats upward, and spits onto the head of its tormentor (see figure 21). At this, the owner of the head becomes extremely agitated, frantically waving his arms, running back and forth and shaking his fist. Finally, he jumps up to catch the rebellious head and applies a tremendous punch to it. These

Figure 21. Méliès's "Tit for tat": the spitting image of the lower faculties. Library of Congress.

infantile, uncontrolled reactions illustrate the disappearance of reason and the inability of the will to govern instinct and the body. The failure of the will to triumph over the body is disquieting because, at the same time as it gives the spectator a momentary thrill of liberation, for turn-of-the-century viewers this failure implies neurosis, degeneration, and even madness.

An even more violent depiction of this bellicose division appears in *Tom Tight et Dum Dum*, surely modeled on a music-hall act. This film is a veritable compendium of hysterical traits: constant agitation, aggression, anesthesia, and the phantasy of dismemberment. A pot-bellied "eccentric comic" enters stage left with a life-sized stuffed doll in three parts—head, torso, legs—which he assembles on a chair at the rear of the stage. As he exits momentarily, a singer enters stage right and begins performing with exaggerated gestures. The comic returns and executes some very rapid dance steps, when he suddenly notices the other performer. He taps him on the shoulder, hits him, but nothing fazes the singer, who continues his act. The comic stamps, jumps, throws his arms up in the air, gesticulates wildly, and runs to the left, where he grabs a stool, sits and watches for one second, then hits the singer over the head with a large stick (no effect), squirts him with seltzer (still no effect), hits him over the head with a huge mallet until the other is buried up to the waist beneath the stage, and *still singing*. Again, the comic strikes with the mallet and the singer is now completely buried except for the head—which keeps on singing! Furious, he *stomps* the head into the stage, kicks the mallet aside, and sits down in an exaggerated pose, legs extended, removing his coat and kicking the left leg outward. Two female assistants now appear who toss him the head of the doll, which he kisses and then hurls to the ground. It bounces like a rubber ball and he catches it, then tosses and catches it again, balancing it on a paddle. (As before, he is agitated in a way that defies description, throwing himself from one place to another and kicking in all directions.) The head is tossed up and lands on the comic's head like a top hat. His assistants toss him the other parts of the doll, and all are placed on a stool and covered with a sheet. It is obvious by now that this epileptic comic is also an illusionist; indeed, the doll has turned into a live woman: a ballerina who pirouettes and leaps into the air. The pot-bellied illusionist imitates her, leaps around her, and then catches her—at which she reverts to separate body parts. Astonished and dismayed, he leaps up and turns around to grab the two assistants, whom he transforms into two flags. Meanwhile, the singer has risen from the trap. In a flash, the comic/illusionist tosses him up into the air in little bits—which fall onto the pile of ballerina parts. The comic stomps furiously on all of them and then sits on them for good measure. The singer rises from the heap, now half-ballerina and half-man with the head and clothing of the comic!

Other filmmakers build scenarios around dismemberment: in Etienne Arnaud's *Le Bon Invalide et les enfants* (Gaumont, 1908), a kind-hearted war veteran feels sorry for a group of children in a public garden who have lost their ball. So, removing his head without the slightest difficulty, he loans it to them to use as a substitute for the ball. He continues to gesticulate while the children throw his head back and forth on the ground. Unfortunately, it doesn't bounce, so the children return to ask for one of the old man's legs, and then the other, to use as wickets. He cheerfully unscrews his legs for them. When they tire of rolling the head between the two legs, they go back—this time without even asking(!)—to take off his arms to make additional "wickets." They thoughtfully put the head and members back before leaving the garden. He rises, gives himself a shake, and limps off.

Dr Pierre Janet used a form of semantic dismemberment in the treatment of hysterical patients suffering from an idée fixe. A patient's obsession with the word "cholera" (and the attendant images of the disease, which cause terror in her) is dismantled by Janet's transforming the word into a "Chinese" name, cho-ler-a, which then becomes "chocolat." Janet proceeded by several forms of suggestion (which, as we now know, constitutes a vital element of early cinema): first, the naked and putrefying blue and green cadavers in the hallucination are "dressed" in costumes that the patient, Justine, had seen at the World Fair. The principal cadaver becomes a Chinese general, and the hallucination of him rising to his feet and marching around—instead of producing terror and cries—is so comical that the cries become bursts of laughter. Then, under hypnosis, Justine begins to write out "cholera," but Janet interrupts the act of automatic writing to suggest a different ending to the word, which will be imposed as the name of the Chinese general: cho-colat (Ey 2:885–87). The idée fixe of decomposing cadavers is rendered comic in exactly the same way that Méliès transforms frightening figures into comical ones, dressing them and undressing them with stop-action photography and reverse editing, transforming them from devils into clowns, and so forth.

The universe of cinematic trick shots, where people and objects appear and disappear before our eyes in hallucinatory visions, where the body is cut up into pieces or multiplies uncannily, gains force from the general public's familiarity with hysteria. Some of the films that depend on these bizarre images refer explicitly to mental alienation, such as Romeo Bosetti's *Le Tic* (1908) and *Le Matelas épileptique* (The Epileptic Mattress [1906]). In the 20 December 1929 issue of the newspaper *L'Ami du peuple du soir*, Jean Mauclair (the founder of Studio 28 in Paris) categorized a large number of films from around 1900 as "the spectacle of funny automatisms . . . [and] sentimentalo-epileptic dramas."

Méliès's *Escapees from Charenton* (1901) gives us dismemberment and more. The black passengers of a bus become aggressive white clowns who, after fusing together into one personality, "break apart into a thousand pieces"

(Malthête et al. 45). The scenario and images of this film were only possible through the substitution trick. In other words, Méliès's cinematic inventions made it possible to represent the phantasies of hysterics (as the title of this film implies), and the spectator could see and feel what it was like to be an hysteric. Cinematic metamorphoses are obtained by double exposure, dissolves, masking, stop-action substitutions (or, instead, the glueing together of different frames)—"tricks" that Méliès said were capable, remember, of "driving the most fearless spectator crazy."

In these films the dizzying rapidity of the metamorphoses is matched by the incredible furor of movement in the person of Méliès himself, as actor. Méliès described the "stupefaction" of an American fair impresario who came to Paris to buy the films in which he'd seen the filmmaker perform as a "gesticulating acrobat." The American was stupefied when he found that Méliès was like anyone else: "He had probably imagined that I was, offstage, *demented*, a *madman*, *completely crazy*, a *devil or a sorceror* that he'd seen on screen. [On the contrary], one has to remain completely calm . . . in order to flawlessly execute this funambulesque clowning!" (Malthête-Méliès, *L'enchanteur* 251; italics mine).[14]

Undoubtedly, the frenetic gestures and contortions of certain Mélièsian roles *did* remind spectators of epileptics, hysterics, "demented" and "completely crazy" people afflicted with tics, limps, and other pathologies of movement. The invention of cinema exactly coincides with the widespread circulation of the *Nouvelle iconographie de la Salpêtrière* and with the publication of a considerable number of articles on hysteria and hypnotism in the popular press. Even Curnonsky, Willy's great friend and a contributor to *Paris qui chante*, is able to casually use medical terminology linked to hysteria with the certainty that the readership of this popular magazine will understand: the original style of [the epileptic comic] Darius M. "consists of a jovial epilepsy and a methodical ataxia" (vol. 4, no. 182 [1906]). In film, characters "come and go, just as we do ourselves, when we are very agitated. . . . [They] have a stiff walk, as though they were afflicted with ankylosis, with the gestures of automatons" (Doumic 921). The invention of cinema also coincides with the invention of X-rays (Méliès's *Rayons X* dates from 1898);[15] the public of 1895 was fascinated by the body and all of its phenomenal pathologies, beginning with Siamese twins and including dwarfs, giants, somnambulists, and *disloqués* (people exhibiting disjointed members), all of whom were guaranteed success in fairs, circuses, and cabarets. As one star of the caf'conc', the "comic trooper" Polin, sang (in the song "The ballade of the Conscript"): "Je suis atteint d'anatomie" (I'm afflicted with anatomy).

Laughing Hysterically

Fascination with epileptic or hysterical movement is great enough to furnish the sole pretext and interest of a film, as Romeo Bosetti's *Epileptic Mattress* proves.[16] (Bosetti was an acrobat before directing films, and he demanded that his actors be capable of the same corporeal exploits as he.) A mattress maker in the countryside is stitching together a mattress to be delivered to a young couple. She goes to a café, and while she is there, a drunk staggers by, falls to the ground, and curls up in the mattress. On her return, she finishes the sewing and has a devil of a time transporting the object, which seems to have a mind of its own. After being run over and falling off a bridge, the mattress's movements become epileptic. Finally transported to the couple's apartment, its convulsive movements propel the pair up into the air. The effect on bystanders of this crazily agitated mattress is fear and astonishment, as though they were in the presence of a supernatural event. Bosetti, however, did *not* entitle his film *The Bewitched Mattress*, preferring to lay emphasis on medical science and pathology rather than the supernatural. Nonetheless, the fear and astonishment on the part of the spectators in the film reminds us that the sight of an attack of epilepsy in 1900 was met with just as much superstition as if it were a supernatural event. The deliberate ambiguity between medicine and the occult can be seen in numerous Méliès films, where the feats of magicians and magnetizers are interchangeable with those of doctors and psychiatrists.

In Méliès's *Déshabillage impossible* (Impossible Undressing [1900]), a man tries to undress, but his clothes have a mind of their own and keep flying back onto his body.[17] He becomes enraged and has what the scenario explicitly names an epileptic fit, arms waving and feet jerking on the floor. The first part of Cohl's *Chambre ensorcellée* (The Bewitched Room [1911]) resembles the Méliès film: a man who rents a room finds it impossible to remove his hat (the series of reappearing hats was, of course, a staple of cabaret comics), and then has the same problem with his jacket and vest. At each attempt to rid himself of them, a different style of hat or clothing fastens itself to his body. Despite leaps into the air, pirouettes, furious spinning around, and falling to his knees, the uncanny and infuriating renewal of clothing continues. Here indeed is the perpetual movement that Canudo called for, and it is as funny as it is terrifying. He somersaults, then falls on the floor looking for his gloves, which have disappeared. And now the supernatural power of the room (or, rather, of the witch/hotelkeeper who has cast a spell over it) manifests itself in a new way: all the furniture is swallowed up by a hole that has opened up in the floor. The poor man throws himself down on the floor in a fit, rolling about wildly in the pile of clothes. Finally, he is irresistibly drawn, head first, into a large mouth in the wall, which swallows him up and spews him and the pile of clothes out onto the street. The perpetual and involuntary movement in this film is as troubling as is the magnetic pull of the screen: both exercise an incomprehensible force of attraction that is out of our control, reminding us of the supernatural and of pathology. In support of the latter, note that Cohl's scenario calls the events "hallucinating obsessions." Like the character in the film, we are incorporated into the void of the screen's open mouth. At the same time, film is an *excess*: an excess of movement, internal and external, an excess of images rapidly flitting by or superimposed, an excess of emotions experienced and overlaid with those of our own life. We cannot *divest* ourselves of its images: it is, in other words, *Déshabillage impossible*.

Other Méliès films where one can observe epileptic movements (some of which end in what the scenario explicitly names "an epileptic fit") are: *Maestro Do-Mi-Sol-Do*, *Le Compositeur toqué*, *Une Indigestion*, *Jack and Jim*, *His First Job*, *Munchausen*, *Le Bourreau Turc*, *L'Eclipse du soleil en pleine lune*, and *L'Agent gelé*. Take, for example, the last sequence of *L'Eclipse du soleil en pleine lune* (1907), where Méliès (as the gesticulating astronomer) falls from a second story head-first into a barrel of water (only the bottom half of his body is visible, with legs convulsively kicking); he is pulled out and, held on either side by his assistants as his legs continue to kick automatically to each side, the group advances toward the camera. One can observe precisely the same image in a series of films shot two years earlier in a New York hospital by

Walter Greenough Chase (the "epilepsy biographs," American Mutoscope & Biograph, 1905) when the epileptic, kicking to each side, approaches the camera, but there the group consists of a patient held on either side by hospital interns. Cut to the observatory, where the astronomer is placed, shivering and teeth chattering, into an armchair, but then (in response to his students' attempts to help... by smothering him with blankets), he falls to the floor, legs kicking wildly as in an epileptic seizure. His students lift him up onto the chair, where he becomes rigidly cataleptic. The astronomer's fall and subsequent corporeal contortions were due to the visual fascination of Mélièsian trick shots, for it was while viewing the unbelievable escapades of the "wandering stars" and the very risqué rendezvous of the sun and the moon that he leaned too far out of the window.

In *Le Baquet de Mesmer* (A Mesmerian Experiment [1904]), Mesmer magically draws nine dresses out of his tub of magnetic water, throwing them onto statues, who then break into a music-hall number. They are identifiable as *gommeuses* by their awkward, angular, and silly leg movements as well as by their costumes. The lead dancer performs an eccentric, acrobatic dance, bending over backward in the *arc de cercle*.

One of the dozens of films in which Méliès performs a magic act is *Mystical Flame* (1903). The performance begins gracefully enough, with every gesture elegant and controlled, but ends with the same jumps and frenetic kicks seen in *L'Eclipse*. These are very clearly in reaction to the hallucinatory disappearances and transformations that the magician/filmmaker has himself created. In *L'Agent gelé* (The Frozen Policeman [1908]), on the other hand, the epileptic fit ensues when the policeman is put on top of a stove to defrost, then on the floor (see Figures 22 and 23), then onto a chair where alcohol is poured into his mouth, after which he becomes a raving maniac, jumping on the desk, running in circles on all fours like a monkey, and attacking the other officers.

Hysterical movement and behavior also appear in *Tom Tight et Dum Dum* (analyzed above) and in *Le Mariage de Thomas Poirot* (Woes of Roller Skates [1908]). The latter opens with a depiction of spectatorship: in the foreground, can-can dancers are followed by a roller-skating couple who perform in a restaurant for a wedding party that is facing us in the background. One member of the party jumps and gestures with his hands in rhythm to

Figure 22. Méliès's "The Frozen Policeman" (1908): the epileptic fit. Library of Congress.

the music, throwing his hands and head backward at the finale of the cancan. When the group, thrilled and overwhelmed with enthusiasm by the roller-skating display, learns that they can rent skates themselves, the legs of the same enthusiastic spectator become wildly agitated in imitation of what he has just been seen. The group hastens out to rent skates and bring them home, using the dining room for their essays, upon which total mayhem ensues, none of them ever having roller-skated before. Thomas Poirot, in particular, an extremely large clown with a stomach the size of a dirigible, cuts a hilarious figure on his back on the dining room floor with his roller-skate-clad feet kicking in the air. The police intervene and bring the party to the station, where, in front of the prefect, they mime the movements of the would-be skaters. This gives the prefect a bright idea: the police will *in fact imitate* this collection of clowns and use skates to catch criminals (a scheme that is obviously doomed to failure since none of them knows how to skate).

Figure 23. Epileptic Fit, from Chase, "The Epilepsy Biographs" (1905). Library of Congress.

The last sequence of mad movements superimposes the anarchy of the body and the annihilation of law and order.

If there were a competition for the most grotesque, most outrageous and side-splittingly funny film of the period that incorporates epileptic and hysterical movement, the film that would win hands down is *La Dent de Margottin* (Margottin's Tooth [Pathé, Nizza 1912; directed by Alfred Machin]). It opens and closes with close-ups of the character, Margottin, grimacing in pain at the beginning, and then in relief at the end. His toothache is so excruciating that, in the first scene, he is hurling himself against the bedroom wall, and then attaching his tooth to a rope on the ceiling in an attempt to pull it out. As he falls to the floor in an epileptic convulsion, two women—one, extraordinarily tall and in blackface with a sort of carnival mask, the other made up (*grimé*) as well—come to drag his now-rigid body to the dentist. Once in the street, he begins kicking and screaming; it is impossible to describe the extreme agitation and utter abandon with which the characters cavort in this five-minute-long film. The tall woman performs with as much mad energy as Margottin, truly more a wild creature than a human being. In the dentist's office, the patient jumps up out of the chair and crashes through the stone wall of the waiting room with total destruction of the premises as the result. He then runs madly down the street to the "swing the mallet and hit the bell" attraction at a fairground, where he pays the men who operate it to allow him to lie down on the base of the machine and to hit his head (and, by extension, his tooth) with the mallet. They do so, thereby ringing the bell, but his tooth still aches! With ever-increasing frenzy, he runs to a construction site, where he pays the operator of the steamroller to roll over his head with the machine; the man does so, and Margottin's head disappears into the ground, his legs twitching and kicking. Still to no avail. Finally, the two friends put a firecracker in his mouth, and the last frame shows Margottin grimacing happily in close-up, spitting out all of his teeth. Agitation was a new phenomenon among neurasthenics, as opposed to hysterics, Pierre Janet wrote in 1903. I believe that the previous seven years of cinema viewing contributed to the appearance of this new symptom in neurasthenia.

Camera movement could also be "pathological," as this quotation from Louis Delluc demonstrates: "Even if . . . the cameraman is an hysteric . . . all is saved if the actors are photogenic" (34). The disconcerting rhythms of an hysterical camera were unwelcome in Delluc's view, but certainly not in René Clair's. The angles, jolts, and syncopated rhythms of the camera (and editing) in *Entr'acte* (Intermission [1924]) or *The Magic Ray* (also 1924) are, in their way, a continuation of the mechanical and epileptic rhythms of the caf'conc' and of movement in the first comic films. We can place this citation of Delluc alongside Méliès's words describing the production of movement in his films, not by the *movement* of the camera—for Méliès's camera was immobile—but by the creation of vertiginous movement through the techniques of substitution, multiple exposure, and collage that he proudly stated could drive the spectator mad.[18]

Emile Cohl often repeated the following observation in regard to film animation: "For the artist . . . this path leads nowhere. No, I'm wrong. It will lead him to Charenton if he doesn't watch out" (in Crafton, *Emile Cohl* 200). An American periodical, *The Nickelodeon*, reported in 1909 that "trick pictures . . . especially those pictures of inanimate objects in motion, require a great deal of time. . . . One French manufacturer consumed seven months in working out a single trick picture and then was overcome with a mental malady due to the continued close application" (in Crafton 171). Was it close application alone or, more precisely, sustained involvement in the optical tricks themselves, here resembling the continually shifting perpetual movement of the hallucinations of hysterical vision.

Epilepsy and the Eye of the Viewer

In Cohl's *Peintre Néo-Impressioniste* (1910), it is a common disturbance of vision in hysteria, monochromia, that is imposed on the viewer, which then produces an "epileptic" attack. The viewer is represented here by the art collector who is introduced into the painter's studio in the beginning of the film. The painter produces monochromatic canvasses with titles like "A Cardinal Eating a Lobster and Tomatoes by the Red Sea" (the images are drawn before our eyes on a totally red field—a vibrating rectangle of color representing the canvas—that fills the whole frame). As the cardinal begins to eat, the lobster bites him and flips over into the sea, at which point tables, chairs, and cardinal all disappear. The painter brings out other canvasses to show the prospective buyer: *A Chinese Man Transporting Corn on the Yellow Sea on a Sunny Summer Day*, *Clown and Flour Producer Drinking Cream*, and so on.[19] In the meantime, as the paintings are shown to him—and as they fill our field of vision—the painter's client, trembling, walks brusquely back and forth with a noticeably jerky step. His movements become more and more uncontrollable and spasmatic until, upon seeing *The Green Devil Playing Billiards with Apples on the Grass while Drinking Absinthe*, the collector falls to the floor, his arms and hands gesticulating convulsively (see Figure 24). Stunned, he continues to stare at the contractions of his fingers. The film ends with the devil disappearing into the absinthe as a bush metamorphoses into Cohl, the perpetrator of this Incoherent art (see Figure 25). The collector's convulsions are responsible for our laughter, yet, by virtue of the fact that these "paintings" occupy the entire screen, Cohl has put the spectator in exactly the same position as this poor devil. Naturally, we are not as susceptible as he because the titles have already elevated us to the status of participants who savor incoherent humor and are "in on the joke." In addition,

Figure 24. Emile Cohl's 1910 "The Neo-Impressionist Painter": the epileptic fit; courtesy Cinémathèque Gaumont.

the modern viewer understands the "trick" of animation and thus is not mystified by the images "tracing themselves." But that was not the case for the film spectator of 1910. For this public, these were "enchanted drawings," and people were "astounded when the drawings began to move." One account explains: "Suddenly, the figure becomes animated with life, the umbrella is . . . deftly caught again by the sketch. After this astonishing occurrence . . . several of these mysterious and fantastic sketches appear" (in Crafton, *Emile Cohl* 131). For several years after the first animated films appeared, newspaper and film magazines continued to marvel at them, claiming it was "impossible" to uncover the secret of how the films were made, how the drawings "spring to life": "How all this is done, we do not know." Viewers were also "baffled" by the way that objects moved, appeared, and disappeared by themselves: "food which is consumed noone knows how, by

Figure 25. Exhibit of Incoherent Art: drawing of Jules Lévy by Emile Cohl (10 in. x 7 1/4 in.); courtesy Pierre Courtet-Cohl.

some invisible being, something like a [Spirit manifestation in a seance]. . . . So many strange marvels" (136, 138, 326 n. 44). The illusion was apparently complete, and it lay in the eye of the spectator, unmediated by a magnetizer, a magician, or a psychiatrist. It is even possible that animations where one perceived a figure being drawn without the artist's hand visible reminded viewers of automatic writing, a phenomenon that was perceived as either a manifestation of the spirit world through the hand of a medium, or as one of the strange examples of the hysteric's double personality, guided by the suggestions of the psychiatrist standing behind him or her. Once again, cinema would evoke both the supernatural and the pathological.

Were spectators *really* baffled? Or did they simply want to remain prey to illusion? Visual fascination is a *need* at the end of the nineteenth century when cinema came into being; there is a palpable craving for optical illusion in particular, and this can be seen in the proliferation of toys like the kaleidoscope (from the first quarter of the century), the stereoscope (from the middle of the century), and the trompe-l'oeil designs that were so popular at the end of the century in humorous drawings, in Art Nouveau, and in the art of the Nabis. This "hunger" is perhaps related to the "hunger for hypnosis" that Jean Epstein referred to when trying to analyze the public's attraction to film. The ambiguous or shifting object one focuses on is a source of visual fascination in the same way that the metamorphosing, luminous moving images are on the screen. And while the vocabulary of amazement used to describe the film techniques continues to draw on the supernatural, the marvels of technology have in fact supplanted the marvels of the supernatural. Séances of spiritism have been replaced by motion picture séances: *séance* is still the French term for film screening. The "magic" comes from the mind and body of the spectator as much as it does from the filmmaker. As Cocteau wrote, the motion-picture audience makes the tables turn "and speak by secret means, since the words [attributed to tables at seances] come from the darkness within us" (Cocteau, *Art of Cinema* 41).

The shift from what the character sees to the eye of the spectator is especially dramatic in films like Cohl's which incorporate animation sequences into a narrative with live actors. The switch to animation takes place when the camera focuses on what is in the character's mind, or on what s/he is seeing when s/he looks through optical devices like the "wondrous glasses" or the microscope. For example, as a patient looks through the microscope in a doctor's office (in *Les Joyeux Microbes* [1909]), the images of the germs in his body fill the frame to become the spectator's vision. What happens to the patient when he has this privileged look into the pathology at work inside his body? He becomes, according to the scenario, "a raving lunatic." One might well object that spectators have no reason to fear, since the pathology is not in *their* bodies. But we've seen that the mere act of *looking* at pathological movement (in epilepsy, for example) was thought to produce the pathology in the viewer. In Cohl's *Le Binettoscope* an eccentric comic shows the audience an optical device (which looks very much like a television). With a pulling gesture of the hands, he demonstrates how he will *put* the spectators *into* the apparatus and project their caricatures onto the screen. And vision itself can wound. A decade later, Antonin Artaud wanted to create films "with purely visual situations whose drama would come from a shock designed for the eyes, a shock drawn, so to speak, from the very substance of our vision" ("Cinema and Reality" 411). Cohl's *Génération spontanée* (1909) seems to illustrate the shock or wound of cinema. In it one sees a scientist pouring liquid into a beaker, which explodes into a question mark and jack-in-the-box. This shape becomes an eye. After undergoing a series of metamorphoses, two round white eyes return and are immediately transformed into pliers that grab and pinch, at the same time as the face containing the two eyes develops a very long arm that reaches into the left side of the image as though to grab hold of something. The scientist returns as a clownlike figure, laughing as he looks through a magnifying glass at a kitchen pot.

The question mark at the film's outset asks: "What am I going to see?" And as the question mark becomes an eye, it answers its own query by assuming a variety of shapes and objects. There is a perfect overlap between the screen and the eye of the spectator: there is no possible distinction between the two. The scientist who has concocted this new system of seeing is the filmmaker-cartoonist. Thanks to the animated cartoon, the eye can become a pair of pliers and aggressively pull things out of the screen image. At the end of the film, the scientist-clown brandishes a device for improved seeing. What is he cooking up with this new invention? Laughter. But let's not forget the aggressivity of the eye that is so much a part of this laughter.

Monkey Business

> "What a humiliating parody of man the monkey is! That, nonetheless, is what we were or what we will be. Is the monkey . . . a principle or a decadence? That is a problem that future science will no doubt decide."
>
> —THÉOPHILE GAUTIER, *1865 review of a circus act*

I've laid a great deal of emphasis in this book on the nineteenth-century notion of a radical division between the higher and the lower faculties, indicating its importance in psychiatric theory and noting the inflection given it by Darwinian and Spencerian theories of evolution. The vision of continual evolutionary progress will be called into question by studies of degeneration in the very period that cinema was emerging. Early film comedy is implicated within the questions surrounding evolution by its foregrounding of all that is Low. Psychiatry and evolution meet in Pathé's Boireau series, where André Deed, as a monkey-man, is put in an insane asylum (*L'Homme-singe*). Return of the Primitive, regression to an animality represented by the body in anarchy abandoning itself to automatic gestures, the sort of body one could also see at the Salpêtrière and in fairground shows, a vision of the body liberated from its head or, on the contrary, looking into the recesses inside the head, thanks, in both cases, to techniques that only film could perfect. This is *cinéma primitif* with a vengeance, a term that valorizes the extraordinary emphasis in this cinema on movement, sensation, shock, and pathologies of vision and of the body.

It is precisely an invention like cinema, *La Photographie électrique à distance* (1908), that enables one to see the hidden personality of the person posing for the camera. The new technology of moving pictures—here conflated with medical and magnetic cures at a distance, which had the approval of part of the scientific community—reveals what is hidden in the unconscious: when the camera focuses on a subject, the "second personality," dominated by sexuality, appetite, instinct—the "low"—emerges from the body of the seated, immobile subject, and begins to move. The husband in an old couple becomes a monkey, and his wife a grimacing maniac. The Low is often figured in Méliès by devils, clowns, or by monkeys. And in several films, little devils turn into monkeys. In a chase sequence of *Les 400 Farces du diable* (1906), the little devils running on all fours chasing three cooks become monkeys whose gait and movements are exactly the same as the devils' until, finally, the cooks take on the same movements and gestures too. In Méliès's *Le Savant et le chimpanzé* (1900), an evolutionary fable, an agitated monkey, kept in the home of a scientist, demolishes his cage when the scientist leaves the room. Running back and forth, jumping up onto the curtains and furniture, the hairy creature wreaks havoc on the house. Coming back into the room, the scientist is aghast at this sight of total destruction. His attempts to dominate the animal who has taken over his house soon demonstrate that he has been contaminated by the object of research: he becomes just as agitated as the monkey and his movements are those of an hysteric. In fact, as though to symbolize this contagion, the chimpanzee's tail, which the enraged man of science has ripped off, remains very much alive and flies onto the scientist's nose, where it becomes an appendage. (This is a cautionary tail.) The maid arrives and detaches the tail from the *savant*'s nose, but in the meantime, the monkey *sans* tail is on the second floor (we see both floors simultaneously), where the fury of his movements causes the ceiling to give way and he falls to the first floor between the two, ripping the maid's clothes off as he does so.

The presence of these monkeys (*singes*) in Méliès's films is perhaps not innocent: *singer* is a French verb meaning "to imitate." They are there to remind us of *our tendency to imitate what we see on the screen*. These are the automatic gestures expressing the instincts and impules of a being who resembles all too closely our simian cousins. As I stated in Chapter 1, the alienated part of one is invariably a representation of the corporeal unconscious with its automatisms, always so visible in the hysteric. This is our double, and laughter is the attempt to exorcise that double.

Shaking, corporeal agitation, convulsive laughter: all are signs of the lower faculties, the body dominating reason, hysteria—loss of control. The link to primitive societies, degeneration, anarchy, and the masses was not difficult to establish in the minds of those whose fears surrounding these "threats" to civilized society allowed them to see demons in darkened rooms where people sat transfixed and where their bodies, unbeknownst to them, mimed the spectral and convulsive images before them. But then again, perhaps this is a peculiarly French problem: why do between *seven and eight million* people in France suffer from a disorder called *la spasmophilie*? In its featured cover story, the December 1997 issue of the magazine *Top Santé* (Top Health) discussed the symptoms of spasmophilia, an illness that was first described by French doctors in the 1980s: spasms and other forms of neuromuscular hyperexcitability, like tingling sensations and trembling, headaches, vertigo, palpitations, tics, fainting spells, contractions in the legs and spine, irritability, emotivity, digestive problems, and a lump in the throat! This is the very catalogue of ailments that, among others, made up nineteenth-century hysteria.[20] And why was a French law enacted on 3 August 1993 (in response to thirty reported cases) requiring that, on certain video games, there be a label warning of the danger that prolonged focusing on them could cause epilepsy? Is the visual triggering of epilepsy more to be feared in France? Are the French an inherently "nervous" people, as degeneration theory held? Not only the vogue of hysteria and neurasthenia would have one think so, but so, too, the parallel performance styles of idiot comics, epileptic singers and comics, and of hysterical movement in early film comedy. The spirit of this aesthetic, which first emerged in the café-concert, imbues the work of Jarry and is carried over into Dada after its "wild, inhuman" representatives in early film have lost favor with the public. A half century later, a new generation will rediscover this vein of humor pushed to painful and idiotic corporeal extremes in the person of Jerry Lewis.

Epilogue: Shock Waves in the New Wave and in the Films of Jerry Lewis

J. L. and J.-L. G.

To indicate how very strong a hold the notions of automatic gesture and unconscious imitation have on cinema—and not only in early cinema—I want to propose an example from what is perhaps the most famous film of the Nouvelle Vague, Jean-Luc Godard's *A Bout de souffle* (1959). In it, the *source* of the automatism is clearly depicted as film viewing itself. As the title implies, *A Bout de souffle* is about velocity and perpetual movement, both in the action and in the montage, emphasized in its jump cuts. It is at once completely new and an homage to the cinema of the past, carrying on the earliest idea of cinema as velocity. The most evident homage is to Bogart, with Michel's repeated gesture of running his thumb across his lower lip in imitation of "Bogey"—an example of Godardian self-reflexivity that points to itself in an obvious way when it is staged in front of a movie theater with a poster from a Bogart film. It may well be Michel's tribute to the Hollywood tough-guy roles played by Bogart, just as it is Godard's tribute to film noir, but to the extent that it has become a tic, it stands an example of unconscious imitation of what one has seen on screen. Yet, even more involuntary and telling is *Patricia's* repetition of Michel's gesture, as though her efforts to rid herself of the "bad influence" which she rightly fears as the pull of the "lower faculties" we've analyzed here—instinct, libido, violence, anarchy, automatisms—were useless. Even with Michel dead, he is now an indelible part of Patricia in the film's next-to-final frames, as she runs her thumb across her lip. These instances of imitated gesture, both the copy and the copy of the copy, in *A Bout de souffle* offer a perfect allegory of film spectatorship.

With the exception of the critic and fanatical Jerry Lewis admirer Robert Benayoun, there is no bigger Lewis fan in French cinematic circles than Jean-Luc Godard.

Jerry Lewis and the French

12 MARCH 1984: JERRY LEWIS IS AWARDED THE LÉGION D'HONNEUR

The descriptions of hysteria, epilepsy, and the comique idiot in cabaret and early cinema may have already brought to mind the comic style of Jerry Lewis. In fact, it is in that comic tradition that Lewis belongs, and that is why the French appreciate him so much ... although they may very well be unaware of the reason. Does it strike the reader as strange that Lewis's best-known role of the last thirty years should be as the host for the Muscular Dystrophy Association Telethon? In fact, his on-screen spastic movements made some of those with MD very uncomfortable. Despite his phenomenal fundraising abilities (over $100 million each telethon) protesters in the early 1990s tried to convince the organization that he had painted "the worst [possible] picture of disability" (in Levy 466) with his "patronizing" image of "Jerry's Kids." The "picture of disability" with its attendant spectatorial response is very much at issue in the present study, as the reader is well aware. This response has changed considerably since the age of "primitive" comedy ended around 1912.

In 1956–1957 the French critic Gilbert Salachas exclaimed that he "never understood the fascination of the masses (and of certain critics) for the laborious idiocies of Jerry Lewis" (in Labarthe 3). Similarly, Jean-Pierre Coursodon thought that "Lewis represent[ed] the lowest degree of physical, moral, and intellectual debasement that a comic actor can reach. The majority of his films are physically close to intolerable" (in Polan 44). Coursodon, in 1960, had not seen the early comedies of André Deed, Roméo Bossetti, and some others discussed here: most were still unrepertoried and unrestored reels in cans in attics or at the Cinémathèque Française. Nonetheless, the memory of these primitive, "mostly wild, inhuman creatures, animated comic strips" as we saw them called, remained ingrained in the collective memory, for the French public was apparently delighted with this American comic who was not afraid to take on the outrageous, grotesque traits of the first strain of French film comics. Before turning to the reasons for Lewis's critical success, not very long after these two articles appeared—reasons that are closely tied to the themes analyzed in this book—let us consider the amplitude of the French public's love for Jerry Lewis. An entire generation of French children and teenagers grew up watching Martin and Lewis films, then films directed by Lewis, on a weekly French Sunday afternoon television series devoted to Hollywood films. When Martin and Lewis split up in 1956 and Jerry began working closely with Frank Tashlin, "enthusiasm for their films among French audiences was extremely high" (Levy 332). *Artists and Models* (1955) had sold forty-six thousand tickets in its first week, and the Lewis and Tashlin combo continued to be excellent box-office draws. A decade later, in 1965, Jerry arrived at Orly airport in Paris "to a rock star's" reception by "a swarm of wild-eyed fans, a phalanx of reporters, a rout of photographers and a small but select group of France's leading film critics" (*New York Times*, cited in Levy 328). Planned were a retrospective of his work at the Cinémathèque Française and a Jerry Lewis festival at the cinema Le Passy. As Shawn Levy writes, "He was both genuinely popular *and* critically respected in France" (ibid.). In 1980, Lewis came to Paris to present a César award to Louis de Funès for "typically indigenous French comedy." It was a completely appropriate choice on the part of the programmers, since Jerry Lewis perpetuates this comic tradition as faithfully as de Funès does. The audience was delirious with laughter at the mere sight of Lewis (see Polan 43). His stock was still high when he returned to France in 1983; this was the year that his performance in Scorcese's *The King of Comedy* was called sublime in Cannes, and that a television series entitled "Bonjour Monsieur Lewis," produced by Robert Benayoun, ran through the summer. But the fact that the French love for Jerry Lewis had been listed by the *Village Voice* as one of the "101 Reasons to Hate the French" did not concern only the comic's appeal to the Gallic masses; the critical praise heaped on his films was far more galling.

When Salachas and Coursodon wrote the articles cited above, the team of Martin and Lewis had just split up and the first film directed by Lewis, *The Bellboy*, had not yet opened in Paris. Lewis the director was to win over some of Lewis the comedian's sternest critics. In 1983, Salachas published (at his own expense) a book of sketches of Jerry Lewis by Pierre Etaix. Coursodon wrote that, in the films directed by Lewis, the actor had "metamorphosed while remaining the same, and this phenomenon has become the theme of his films, obliging us to transform our own vision" (in Polan 44). Indeed, it is this theme of the Double, running through all of Lewis's films, that seized attention and has been most seductive for French critics. It is also, as I'm certain the reader has noticed, a primary theme in the present book, crucial as it is both in theories of hysteria and in theories of film spectatorship. I have also argued here that the Double in early cinema (from grimace films to Surrealism) is a figure for double consciousness, with one gesticulating half—the corporeal unconscious—presenting to spectators the triumphant emergence of the lower faculties, replete with the automatisms of idiocy, epilepsy, and hysteria. This is the portrait of the characters portrayed by Jerry Lewis in his films. François Truffaut found the portrait repulsive: "It goes without saying that he is also overpowered by all the known signs of degeneracy . . . [including] an extremely acute sense of smell" (in Levy 329). As we can see, the discourse of degeneracy was not dead in France; in fact, the vestiges of nineteenth-century psychology were still very present in the French Imaginary in the 1950s and in the 1960s when the *Cahiers* critics elevated Lewis to the rank of genius. The aspect of devolution did not escape these writers. Jean-Louis Comolli devoted a rubric to "Darwin" in his Lewisien cinematic alphabet: "Lewis' regressive tendencies take him back, on the level of the individual, to childhood, and on the level of the species, to the monkey" (Comolli, "Petit lexique" 59).[1] Jerry said himself that the team of Martin and Lewis was made up "of the handsomest guy in the world and a monkey" (in Bukatman 190).[2]

Truffaut, too, would change his critical stance regarding the comic. Before looking at the critical analyses of Lewis's films in the 1960s, however, consider the important place that the Double and degeneration play in Truffaut's *Shoot the Piano Player* (1960). The main character, Charlie Kohler, is a two-bit piano-player in a bar with a tiny stage where the trio's numbers are interspersed with songs by the master of wordplay—linguistic *zizanie*—Bobby Lapointe. Both the bar and the performer would be perfectly at home in a nineteenth-century cabaret. But Charlie isn't Charlie. He is leading a double life: he is really Edouard Saroyan, an acclaimed concert pianist. Indeed, he is leading a triple life, since every movie-goer in France recognized him to be Charles Aznavour, the actor and musician. Edouard/Charlie/Charles: very like the doubles doubled by the real Jerry Lewis in the films we're going to look at next. The off-screen, disembodied voice that Charlie hears in his head (thought and reason detached from the body) is only one instance of the alienation that exists between the split-off parts of the pianist/piano-player. Parts that his name, Kohler (the French verb *coller* means "to glue") can't glue back together. The character is paralyzed and can't take action; in a flashback we discover that there is a trauma that has caused this inability to act. Yet, before the traumatic event of his wife's leap to her death from a fifth-story window, there is a deeper reason for his fear. Fear of what the double represents. This is figured by Edouard's flight from his family, a family of criminals. In the climactic sequences of the film, when Edouard returns home, having killed a man, he gazes at himself in the cracked mirror of the tumble-down mountain home, now a hideout for his brothers. Truffaut wrote the following piece of dialogue for him: "It skips a generation . . . the Saroyans . . . until the time that this species of madness, hysterical, frenetic . . . of wild beasts [returns]." This is the discourse of evolution, degeneration, and hysteria. And this, in 1960. Truffaut, we should remember, was also the director of *The Wild Child* and of the *L'Histoire d'Adèle H.*, the story of Victor Hugo's hysterical daughter. But *Shoot the Piano Player* is not set in the historical context of the nineteenth century, as are the other two films. Its explanation for the roots of the double personality, though, is contemporary with Truffaut's conversion from stern critic to fan of Jerry Lewis.

As I've already noted, what French critics appreciate most in Lewis's films is the theme of doubling. In his important article, "Chacun son soi," J.-L. Comolli writes that the theme of the Double engenders "vertiginous variations on the notion of resemblance and difference, identity and alterity." On the level of narrative, Lewis multiplies himself by playing a character who then plays another character and causes others to act "in an endless relay between author, actor and creatures of both. It is then that, more subtly, the notion of the Double contaminates the form of the films and that the spectacle constituted by the film reveals itself as that which constitutes the trajectory and the body of the film (*The Patsy*, *Three on a Couch*)" (51). Comolli is impressed by the number of characters played by Lewis in a single film: "two for *The Nutty Professor*, seven for *The Family Jewels*, four for *Three on a Couch*. Had he never seen a film by Georges Méliès, then? "The notion of the double induces the very functioning of the films" (52). One might easily say the same for many films of Méliès: for example, *L'Homme-orchestre*, where the whole point of the film is to revel in the capabilities of cinematic multiple exposure to create the multiple personalities of seven Georges Mélièses. In other films, moreover, Méliès, as the magician in the film, foregrounds himself as the creator of this proliferation of selves. Lewis, too, creates a "disproportionate overproduction of creatures compared to their creator. . . . One character (Professor Kelp) manufactures another in the body of the fictional work, reconstituting in the film the operation responsible for making the film" (53–54) (again, this dynamic describes what not only Méliès but Emile Cohl excelled in doing, while at the same time underlining the self-reflexive nature of cinema). Self-reflexivity is the second characteristic of Lewis's films that Comolli singles out for praise.

We have noted how frequently early films include a metanarrative or self-reflexive element in the plot that doubles back on itself in order to underline the art of filmmaking or the experience of watching a film, be it by focusing on a hypnotizer who reproduces the hypnosis-effect, by including an apparatus that stands in for the film apparatus, by reproducing the defining characteristics of film, velocity and perpetual movement, in the filmic action, or, indeed, by foregrounding the Double and replicating the couple actor/spectator. There are further parallels to be drawn between early cinema and the aspects of Lewis's films that critics so admired.

Comolli vaunts "the modernity of these films without any law, place, or time other than those that the characters feverishly drags along and deposits" (54). He is referring to the proliferation of characters, the "spontaneous generation of faces, bodies, and movements . . . which is one of the springs of Lewisien comedy" where the narration is passed on from one character to the other. The result is "the apparent disorder of all of Lewis' films, their disconnectedness (*le décousu*)" (ibid.). Here again, one can hardly come closer to a description of the animated films of Emile Cohl, and—only at a slightly less feverish pitch—to the transformations and spewing forth of faces, bodies, and movements in Méliès's, Bosetti's, and Durand's films.[3] The "modernity" of Jerry Lewis is also the modernity of French comedies made between 1896 and 1912.

Benayoun also notes the disconnected quality of Lewis's films, their "nauseatingly scabrous scenes," the regressive nature of Lewis's comic character, and the "gags based on physical pain" (24, 108). He makes the comment that Lewis's comic style is thematically "torturous" and that Jerry takes up comedy where Langdon or Stan Laurel left off, flying into the "Never-Never Land of the absurd" (24). Is it necessary to point out that the entire corpus of "Incoherent" comedy in French cinema before World War I is ignored or unknown to this critic?

The Films

Of all the films directed by Lewis, the one that must be discussed first here is *The Nutty Professor*, his 1962 version of *Dr. Jekyll and Mr. Hyde* (its French title is *Dr. Jerry and Mr. Love*), where—as good luck would have it—Hyde takes on the personality of a cabaret singer. Was this a backhanded homage to his ex-partner, Dean Martin, the seducer and sex symbol of the team? Yet, the roles are reversed: the disarticulation, deformity, tics, and grimaces belong to the professor, the scientist Julius Kelp, and the immoral, unscrupulous, dangerous personality belongs to the handsome crooner who possesses the charisma of a magnetizer and of a performer. Kelp's quest to transform himself into a desirable man lets loose an aggressive, alcoholic, and sadistic character whose appropriate milieu appears to be the nightclub/cabaret.

There were twenty-two silent versions of Stevenson's story, including satiric versions, and as J.-L. Leutrat writes, the extraordinary number of adaptations "shows how much early cinema recognized itself in this theme" (123).

Of the twenty-two films, there is only one other that I know of where Hyde is figured as a cabaret performer. It is a 1959 version made for French television by Jean Renoir, *Le Testament du Dr Cordelier*. The first view of Hyde (rebaptized Opale in Renoir's film) shows him as a creature of devolution afflicted with the tics and deformities of a degenerate or a male hysteric: facial and corporeal asymmetry, little hops in the gait, and tics of the head and shoulders. What stroke of genius possessed Renoir (or Jean-Louis Barrault, who plays the double role) to translate Hyde's pathological gait into that of a performer in a music-hall number? Jekyll's transformation into Hyde takes place in front of a full-length mirror in the lab (as it does in the novel). It is a true caf'conc' number with tap dancing and cane: a perfect mesh of music-hall, hysteria, degeneration, and the vital energy that infuses the doctor's body as he rejoins Hyde. In the flashback that retraces the different stages of Jekyll's experiments, Jekyll's voice on tape tells us that "this completely changed body was the transparent reflection of my instincts." It is then that we are treated to this troubling but exhilarating music-hall number. And, whereas the Dr. Jekyll of the 1931 version, directed by Rouben Mamoulian, gives a talk on evolution to a public gathering, here the character tells us that his medical practice was composed primarily of neurotic female patients on whom he practiced hypnosis.

Leutrat compares the dynamic of doubling in Renoir's film with that in Jerry Lewis's: in the former, the doubles (Cordelier's friend, Joly; his rival, the psychiatrist Séverin; and his alter-ego, Opale) all refer back to Dr. Cordelier. In *The Nutty Professor*, the other characters "fall under the sway of the contagion of doubling. Even Kelp's parents invert their personalities at the end of the film" (75). Contagion is the key word here: it has been ever present in our discussion of hysteria and of spectatorship, and it is a primary motor of comic effects in early French cinema as well as in the films of Jerry Lewis. Without naming the theme of degeneration, Leutrat notes that Kelp's problem is hereditary: his mother claims that the father is descended from a family of pigs and once refers to him as a toad's egg. That is why Kelp sends the formula to his parents. Lewis updates the medical context for Stevenson's story by having Kelp explain: "A headshrinker told me I had a dual personality."

Turning to the Martin and Lewis films, one sees the same themes of physical deformity, hypnosis, and devolution. The mere mental image of the contracture of the hands in *My Friend Irma Goes West* (1950), directed by Hal Wallis, is enough to make me laugh (evidence of its effectiveness: I saw this film a half-century ago!). Granted, these are not hysterical contractures, but the result of squeezing grapefruit and oranges all day long (Jerry works in a sidewalk juice stand); nonetheless, the visual effect is the same. There is a grimace contest in this film: Jerry competes with a chimpanzee, "Pierre," causing the former to exclaim, "This guy Darwin was really on to something!" The ads for the film featured the two. Another highlight of the film is Jerry's can-can number. In *The Caddy* (1953), directed by Norman Taurog, a flashback shows us a young Harvey Miller (Lewis) trying to follow in the footsteps of his father, a world-champion golfer. But he is paralyzed by panic when a crowd surrounds him on the green. He tosses his putter away and runs into the woods with his legs at right angles from the knees. The film is speeded up as he runs in zigzags, finally becoming an ape (or chimpanzee, if one prefers), screeching and making the gestures of a monkey. The explanation: "People make him very nervous: he's high-strung." The flashback ends. We then see Harvey in his room asleep with a truly idiotic expression on his face, making idiotic noises. Joe (Dean Martin) tries to wake him up, and we discover that Harvey is a somnambulist. Later, when he has had too much to drink, the Lewis grimace, lips protruding and eyes crossed, also creates a strong simian resemblance. The other examples of the Lewis dislocated body in *The Caddy* occur in the song-and-dance numbers. From ape to cabaret performer without a blink, just as in *My Friend Irma Goes West*. At the end of the film, after the last routine performed by Joe and Harvey, Martin and Lewis come on to follow their act. The resemblance between the four is so perfect that their own wives don't recognize them, and in this early example of Lewisian doubles and reflexivity of the fictional world and the real world, the two Dean Martins and the two Jerry Lewises stand facing each other in disbelief. In another 1953 film, Hal Wallis's *Scared Stiff*, Jerry's character, Myron, plays the role of wooden dummy to Dean's ventriloquist. He has a chance to perform on his own as well: lip-synching to a Carmen Miranda recording of "Yo Quiero." The Double is present here as well: Myron confronts his conscience in a full-length mirror, a division that is underlined by a split screen.

The uncomfortable feeling one gets watching Lewis, the truly painful awkwardness in the gait and gestures of this body, expressed in the angularity of the gestures and of the skinny frame itself—its a-rhythmic cadences, and its simian characteristics—will not change when the comic becomes the director as well. The discomfort is, if anything, even more intense in the films he directed, for there is no partner to offer "relief" from this dislocated body with its spastic twitches and grimaces.

The first film written, directed, and produced by Lewis was *The Bellboy* (1960). It is an overt homage to silent film comedy: throughout the film, Stanley the bellboy (Jerry Lewis) doesn't speak. Expressive grimaces suffice. As was the convention in early film comedy, a half-dozen totally different grimaces in one short scene (the scene where Stanley is waiting for the elevator) are all made directly to the camera. The character utters his first word for the first time only in the last minute of the film. The homage is rendered explicit when an actor playing Stan Laurel approaches Stanley in the hotel lobby. Stan/Stanley. Laurel/Lewis. There the resemblance ends, for Stan Laurel's gait cannot compete with Jerry Lewis's. In the first post-credit sequence, the comic executes a repetitive, aimless series of false starts, turning from one direction to the other, very much like the pathological gait and aimless dance steps of the hysterical male patient at the Salpêtrière (see Figures 10 and 11). His walk also resembles the typical posture of Boireau with the buttocks thrust out. When Stanley walks up an escalator, legs akimbo, arrives at the top and can't get off, his hands grip the sides and his body is further contorted by the force of being pulled backward.

In a pre-credit sequence that parodies a convention of Hollywood films of the period, the film is introduced by the Studio Head, who informs us that what we are about to see is "a picture without any story." Modern, yes: a modernity that reminds us of Cohl's Incoherent films. The theme of the Double is present here as well: Stanley is doubled in this film by Jerry Lewis (as himself), who makes a celebrity appearance at the hotel. The hysterical tendency to imitate what one sees, is represented here too, as it will be in *The Errand Boy*. Stanley visits an art exhibit in the hotel. Seeing a small abstract clay bust, he sucks in his mouth in unconscious imitation of the sculpture. As his face contorts, he tries to rearrange the clay mouth, and discovering that the clay is wet, remodels it. The vignette ends with Stanley's horrified look at the resulting monstrous, chinless, one-eyed creation. A metaphor for Lewis's comic creations? Isn't physical comedy, as it has been analyzed here, itself monstrous? In any case, *The Bellboy* is a very funny, inventive, anarchic,[4] and at times inspired homage to early film comedy.

The *Errand Boy* (1961), written by Jerry Lewis and Bill Richmond and directed by Lewis, also begins with a parody of the Hollywood convention I've referred to: here, it takes the form of a pseudo-documentary on cinematic illusion. The film proper is also set in the Hollywood studio, continuing the thread of self-reflexive commentary on cinema. The studio bosses are looking for "someone really stupid," and Marty Tashman (Lewis) is hired as the new errand boy. Pathological gait is interestingly recreated by a zigzag trajectory with an odd cadence: the errand boy's first delivery produces hesitating steps to the side, at the same time as one leg juts forward extending the stride in a 1-2, 1-2 rhythm. In the realm of language disturbances, trying to pronounce the Eastern European names of the studio bosses gives Lewis the opportunity to string together nonsense syllables, as caf'conc' *comiques idiots* like Dranem did. There is a cabaret scene in the film: the errand boy turns up on the set of a 1920s cabaret and is made an extra in the scene. Seated at one of the front tables, he sings along with the other extras, repeating the lyrics of the song that the performer has just sung. "Whack, whack-a-do." Naturally, Lewis sings in his famously high-pitched, strident voice. Worse, he can't *stop* singing "Whack, whack-a-do," and what is more, rises from his table and executes a few dance steps to accompany the tune. The reader may remember the case observation of another male hysteric at the Salpêtrière who unceasingly repeats the same song lyrics. Obviously, he has ruined the take and finally ceases, coming out of the state of unconscious imitation; the tune "made me" do it, he stammers apologetically, hastily exiting.

The Family Jewels (1965), also written by the team of Lewis and Richmond, and directed and produced by Lewis, is more ambitious but comes off as strained. Jerry Lewis plays the roles of six uncles and the chauffeur, Willard. The elements that are pertinent to our discussion and which reappear in this film are self-reflexivity, doubling, and the tip of the hat to silent film comedy. In the visit to the photographer uncle, Julius, we are treated to Julius's mugging and grimacing into the aperture of his camera in close-up (cf. the grimacing close-ups in the final frame of French comedies around 1910). We are in the position of the camera. There is a film within the film in the sequence where Uncle Eddie pilots a plane filled with motorcycle-riding matrons. In the in-flight film, the characters are shaken by the extreme turbulence visible in the cockpit where Uncle Eddie sits, while the contagion of sensation leaves the passengers paradoxically unaffected. Two of the uncles, Julius and Bugsy (the gangster), rival the nutty professor, Julius Kelp, in their hideous ugliness. In the final scene, Willard is made up as the uncle who works as a clown. A painter puts a "Wet Paint" sign on his nose, which Willard has to turn upward to read. As he does so, the audience is able to read the message on the reverse side: "The End." The film ends as Willard walks into the camera, mouth open, thus recalling Williamson's *The Big Swallow*.

Funny Bones

The only other country that spawned a very similar tradition of physical comedy, England, is also the other country that was most preoccupied with nervous illness in the nineteenth century. (In the Appendix, I look briefly at two recent British contributions to automatisms and grotesque corporeal contortions in physical comedy: "Mr. Bean" and "Wallace and Gromit.") This last section of our consideration of Jerry Lewis's work and its relationship to the aspects of the comic tradition studied here ends with a British film.

Was Jerry Lewis conscious of the extent to which he was the perfect choice for the 1995 film *Funny Bones*? It situates the origins of his comic style squarely in the music-hall tradition of physical comedy. Peter Chelsom's lovely and original film is about the relation of comedy to pain and to death, and it develops this relationship with brio. Jerry Lewis plays George Fawkes, a hugely successful American comic whose career is totally indebted to the gags and routines that he stole from his first partners in England. While he enjoys fame and fortune, they are still in a dilapidated English seaside resort, destitute and forced to earn a few bob in a funhouse ride where, as the car rolls around the bend in a tunnel, they pop out, faces tinted green, at the side of a coffin with a decomposing body and a decapitated head rolling by. Pure cinema of attractions material. The spectators are petrified and thrilled. Across the Atlantic and most of the United States, the Great Comic's son, Tommy, wails, "I'm gonna die! I'm gonna die out there." He is about to go on stage in his Las Vegas debut and his father is in the audience. He does "die" on stage; his angry and morbid jokes are met by the audience with frozen silence. In addition, he *is* going to die: he has a fatal disease and one month to live. That month, he decides, will be spent at the English seaside resort where he was a little boy; there, he will hold auditions for a variety show, and there he will discover his father's secret. The auditions are a compendium of zany and grotesque music-hall acts which clearly show how much Jerry Lewis is a part of this tradition. The acts are filmed frontally by an immobile camera in the style of "primitive cinema" with direct address to the spectator. Tommy discovers that he has an illegitimate brother (Jack), a born comic genius, extraordinarily gifted acrobat, and a bit insane: "The kid is a known, bona fide maniac." Bona fide (maniac) echoes Funny Bones, and bones, of course, signifies death as well. The show will be spectacular, superimposing Jack's death-defying acrobatics onto the spectators' terror and laughter. *Funny Bones* lovingly recreates the comic tradition I've described in this book, and restores it in all of its madness, crudity, shocks, and daring.

"Beware of Film Images"

This is the title of the last chapter in Alexandre Arnoux's *Du muet au parlant* (1946) and a passage from it will provide the last word here, not only because Arnoux's warning echoes the one Louis Haugmard trumpeted in 1913, but because it demonstrates the continuity of the belief in what has been a guiding notion in *Why the French Love Jerry Lewis*: the corporeal unconscious and the direct link between the cinematic image and nervous reflex.

> The film image, the moving image . . . works silently, mingles with the unconscious. . . . It directs us invisibly; it winds up directing our reflexes, our opinions, even our ideas insidiously. . . . It creates a state against which we have no protection [will and judgment have no place here]. The only thing that counts in cinema is visual rhythm. . . . images where cadence dominates take root in the heart, in the brain, and continue to ferment there, preparing their delayed explosion. . . . Beware of the moving image! (207)

APPENDIX: CLOWNS, SPIES, AND AUTOMATONS IN LANG AND LUBITSCH[1]

What was the fate of this population of nitrate automatons, somnambulists, hysterics, and idiots after 1912? These primitive figures of the unconscious did not disappear along with what has been called "primitive" cinema, as we've seen in the example of Jerry Lewis's films. The silent comedies of Ernst Lubitsch are also built around these figures and have a great deal in common with the cabaret tradition discussed in this book. Yet, neither were these figures consigned to comedy, as some of the examples in Chapter 5 indicated. They occupy a privileged place in German Expressionism. Their presence there and in Lubitsch's silent films warrant a brief excursion into German cinema. Finally, Rowan Atkinson's creation Mr. Bean suggests that the themes and figures studied in this book remain very much alive throughout the first one hundred years of film history.

In 1908 Ernst Lubitsch was performing in cabarets and music halls, putting his body through the same sorts of painful contortions, dislocations, and pratfalls that Berlin audiences, like those in Paris, found hilarious. In 1913 he became a film comic, playing a Jewish character named Meyer, and when he began directing the following year, he made slapstick comedies. The years 1918 and 1919, however, saw Lubitsch inventing a style of his own, one that I believe was strongly influenced by the cabaret aesthetic. In *Die Puppe* (The Doll [1919]) "extraordinary gestural stylization" (Domarchi 34) accompanies the theme of the automaton. The film opens with a prologue: Lubitsch assembling a miniature set—a dollhouse and grounds that will become "real." The visual design of this prologue is one of boxes within boxes: like a magician pulling a rabbit from a hat, Lubitsch pulls the square dollhouse out of a wooden box and then pulls the two puppet-characters out of the dollhouse. Is Lubitsch tipping his hat to Méliès? or to Cohl? He is certainly placing his art squarely in the domain of the illusionist, and foregrounding this play as a self-reflexive statement on filmmaking.[2] The hero of the film, Lancelot, is being forced by his wealthy father to marry, but he is terrified of women. Monks from the nearby monastery suggest that he fool his father by substituting a doll for a living bride. His terror of women is represented visually by the zigzag pattern traced by Lancelot as he flees an entire village of "maidens" in his pursuit. The zigzag pattern appears again in the shop, the costume, and the hairstyle of the heroine's father, Hilarius. The zigzag expresses danger, anxiety, and the angularity of the mechanical, as it had in the cabaret. Hilarius makes lifesize mechanical dolls, and his daughter is posing for a new model, playfully contorting her face into ugly grimaces when he's not looking. When he leaves the room, his apprentice dances with the new doll, whose arm unfortunately breaks off (as in French comedies, the theme of corporeal dismemberment accompanies mechanical movement). The daughter poses as the doll to save the apprentice from her father's wrath, and is purchased by the young and wealthy Lancelot. The heroine, Ossi (played by Ossi Oswalda), plays along, continuing to exhibit mechanical-looking gestures and gait (her dance style and angular, piston-like handshake are especially laughter-inducing), and comically concealing from her groom that she is real. Thus, although she is not an hysteric, she is made to act like one. After the wedding ceremony, Lancelot brings her to the monastery where the monks are to be presented with the gold given to him by his father. Lancelot speaks to the doll tenderly and is dumbfounded when she repeats what he says, but then he assumes it must have been an echo. He falls asleep and the doll comes to life in his dreams, coming in through the window in double exposure. Of course, what he takes to be a dream of a real woman is in fact real. Although not quite. The doll who appears to him as real is a cinematic trick. The "real" nitrate heroine is on the other side of the frame, in a doubling that speaks volumes on males who have difficulty loving a "real" woman. Distinguishing between illusion and reality isn't easy, but Lubitsch's male hero makes the leap (after all, he too began as a doll in the prologue): they kiss and the film ends.[3] The switching between illusion and a "reality" that is foregrounded as illusion, or cinematic "magic," and the inclusion of hysterical gesture are accompanied and enhanced by the use of an enormous number of trick shots: split screen, superimposition, high-speed photography, and multiple exposure. As we saw in the films of Méliès, these techniques foreground illusionism at the same time as they offer a means of reproducing the automatic movements of the corporeal unconscious.[4]

Die Austernprinzessin (The Oyster Princess), made the same year as *Die Puppe*, opens with the heroine (again played by Ossi Oswalda) in the midst of an hysterical rage of destruction, hurling and smashing every object within reach. She is an hysteric, and the frenetic action in the film is "in the spirit of Alfred Jarry" (Ollier 33). The "cure" for her hysteria is to marry (it was thought in the nineteenth century that hysteria could result from the absence of sexual relations, hence its appellation as "the malady of virgins"). At the wedding celebration, the foxtrot is depicted as "an epidemic," with the frenetic gesticulations of the orchestra conductor whipping the guests into a St. Vitus Dance–like frenzy, as one musician repeatedly slaps another as part of the score.

Hysterical gesture and gait also dominate *Die Bergkatze* (The Cat of the Mountains [1921]), where anarchy is represented thematically by a band of robbers led by Rischka (Pola Negri). Their chaotic movements are a counterpoint to the mechanically regulated, repetitive movements of the army garrisoned at the fortress. Both are "relics" of the nineteenth-century pathology of hysteria. Lubitsch will often have recourse to the military for automatic gestures used to comic effect, for example, in *The Smiling Lieutenant* with Maurice Chevalier. As the film ends, a dream sequence involving erotic desire and distortions of the body is cut with the image of the heroine tossing and turning in bed more and more violently until she appears to be having hysterical convulsions. She then stands bolt upright, hallucinating. Her father, seeing this, exclaims: "You must wed!"

Along with their emphasis on hysterical movement and their use of trick photography, these three early Lubitsch films privilege decor as expression in the way that Méliès's films did. There are Rococo sets and repetitive patterns formed by soldiers in *Die Bergkatze*; highly stylized geometric patterns formed by servants, and floor mosaics whose paths are mechanically retraced by the film's characters (in *Die Austernprinzessin*); and the zigzag pattern of the floor of Hilarius's display room, which is repeated in the zigzags of the dollmaker's hair and collar: this emphasis on repetition and on mechanical movement mirrored by the decor is the perfect foil to the explosion of anarchic abandon of control in the actions of the characters in these films.

Even after the 1927 advent of sound, Lubitsch continued to prize gestural and visual language over verbal language. A critic from the *New York Sun* wrote in 1931 that *The Smiling Lieutenant* was a great talking-picture because it was "refreshingly mute" (Weinberg 130). This can be seen as a continuation of the cabaret and music-hall aesthetic, and it is not merely coincidental that the male lead in five of the musical comedies made between 1929 and 1934 was Maurice Chevalier, whose career also began in the cabaret.

ILLUSIONISTS AND PSYCHOANALYSTS

The same concatenation of elements I pointed out in early French cinema and in Lubitsch's early comedies underlies the powerful and frightening effect on the viewer in Fritz Lang's *Spies* and *Mabuse the Gambler*. But here, these elements produce anxiety, fascination, and fear instead of laughter. In the climactic scene of *Spies* (1928), the music, aggression, and hysterical gesture that Lubitsch plays with are again joined together, and they are even presented in the context of the cabaret, but Lang has stripped them of anarchic joyfulness to reveal the ominous nature of destruction that is never really very distant. The master-spy Haghi's last (and from our standpoint, most interesting) disguise is as Nemo the Clown, a performer in a music-hall. He is singing, and we see gigantic notes drop from the ceiling; some of them are flat, so he shoots them down with a revolver. The violence of cabaret/music-hall performance is underscored by the decor of zigzags that frames the clown. Hopping around the stage and playing a horn, he then begins to scratch himself frantically, the horn and his body forming sharp angles. After much bodily contortion, he reaches into his pants and pulls out a tarantula, which he throws into the air and shoots. He then rapidly fires at a government agent in the audience. He misses, and with a laugh that contorts his features insanely, he shoots himself in the head, calling for the curtain. The camera places our point of view as though we were seated in the audience, but not so forcefully as Lang does in *Mabuse, Part 2* (The Inferno of Crime), where the camera is actually *in* the audience among the filmed spectators, not simply in front of the stage.

Like Haghi in *Spies*, Mabuse is a master of disguise, of acting a part, like the actors of early cinema, who were able to magically transform themselves. Play-acting is coupled with card-playing, both in the service of achieving power and domination over the minds of others. The first images in Part 1, which focus on the intensity of Mabuse's gaze as he stares out at us directly are intercut with shots of his lover, Cara Carozza, who stars as a dancer at the world's best-known music-hall, the Folies-Bergère. Her can-can kicks are aimed at the gigantic phallic noses of Guignolesque heads. Shots of Mabuse hypnotizing his adversaries and robbing them of their will while playing cards are then superimposed over this playful, erotic aggression set in the music-hall. The guignols are puppets in love, seduced by the cabaret star who pulls the strings. This is a nice foil for Mabuse, who turns others into puppets devoid of will. Card-playing recalls the art of the prestidigitator "master of illusion." For Mabuse, there is no such thing as love, "only the will to power," which stands in contrast to the character Carozza, who loves him. He is "the unknown man towering over the city." His other principle identity, doubling that of the gambler and criminal mastermind, allows him to earn a respectable living and enjoy considerable social status: Mabuse is *Doctor Mabuse*, a *psychoanalyst*.

In Part 2, Count Told, whose wife Mabuse has kidnapped and imprisoned in his home in order to seduce her, is hypnotized into cheating at cards by Mabuse and goes mad as a result, hallucinating multiple selves, "nocturnal spectres" of the unconscious that Lang produces by multiple exposure. The Count seeks psychiatric help and, of course, seeks it from Dr. Mabuse. Thanks to the gaze and the hypnotic suggestions of Dr. Mabuse, Told becomes more and more ill, until he is about to be placed in an asylum. His madness is echoed by the decor of zigzags, the sharp, cutting angles that also presage his suicide with a razor. I want to pick up a comment made by Noël Burch in his notes on *Mabuse* in *Out of Synch*. He notices how Hull "becomes a stick figure" and assumes "a farcical quality." I believe that these characteristics derive from the automatisms that rise to the surface under the influence of a hypnotist. Von Wenck, too, moves like an automaton, although he manages to triumph over this lack of will.

In one of the last scenes of the film, Mabuse as Dr. Weltmann (Worldman), a psychic on stage in a large hall, performs mass suggestion on his audience—us. Through the use of dissolves, Lang makes Mabuse's detached head enter the audience, at the same time as the expanding mysterious "Chinese" words Mabuse's gaze is projecting: "Tsi Nan Fu." The Psy (the psychoanalyst) isn't *fou* (the French word having already been introduced in the film in the music-hall scene with Folies-Bergère?). But in fact the "psy" himself will soon become mad. In the last scene of Part 2, Mabuse is trapped in the room of blind men at the bottom level of his crime ring; the power of the hypnotic gaze, no longer able to operate on others, boomerangs to exert its pernicious power on the doctor. And of course this power to manipulate and distort perception belongs to the filmmaker and is achieved through the techniques we saw in Méliès's and Cohl's films: in a series of superimpositions, Mabuse is made to hallucinate cards, money, machinery, and hypnotic eyes, the accessories of madness in the film. Until the end of the nineteenth century, the magnetizer or illusionist was in control of the illusions and hallucinations he produced. By the end of the century, even psychiatrists—not to mention artists—are prone to the same visions and maladies.[5]

In *Mabuse*, hypnosis is clearly represented as a dangerous power in the hands of the unscrupulous, be they gamblers or psychoanalysts. Does mind-control replace illusionism? Not really: there is no clear transition from one to the other. Illusionism is still part and parcel of mind control (superimpositions here represent spectres, hallucination, insanity), and the card tricks of Méliès the magician are now the card tricks of Mabuse the psychoanalyst.

THE RETURN OF HIGH AND LOW

The symbolism of High and Low in Lang's *Metropolis*, organized spatially, could not be more clear in terms of social commentary on class structure. The world of this film can also be looked at as a division between the bodies who live underground—worker-robots whose automatic, mechanical movements represent the human transformed into machine—and the intellect-executive power that rules them from the city above. The split between mind and body is conceived in accordance with the psychiatric theories of High and Low analyzed in this book, and this is corroborated by the presence of the Double. The doubles are Freder (son of the owner), who changes places with Georgy, a worker, and, more importantly, the robot Maria, who is substituted for the evangelist-prophet Maria (daughter of the Proletariat). The false Maria enacts her will on the machine-bodies (as she does on the male spectators at the nightclub, Oshiwara) through magnetism, sexual and otherwise. The power of magnetism penetrates the underground world of the unconscious—in other words, of the body and its automatisms.

A very recent example of the mechanical workings of the corporeal unconscious in relation to the forces of instinct, anarchy, and crime is *The Wrong Trousers*, a British claymation feature with the characters Wallace and Gromit. And, in the domain of antisocial, anarchical behavior, Rowan Atkinson as Mr. Bean in the British television series brilliantly carries on the tradition of "primitive" comedy. When Bean makes himself the double of an elegant young vacationer (in "Mr. Bean was in Room 426") by imitating his every movement in a hotel restaurant, he brings things down to the lowest possible level. He takes everything on the buffet that the object of his envy chooses, but his uncontrolled gluttony impels him to devour two sausages at a time, two chicken drumsticks, and two celery stalks, the leaves protruding from his mouth and, as a finale, a dozen (rotten) oysters in the space of ten seconds. At midnight, in a profuse sweat with a case of food poisoning and completely naked, he locks himself out of his hotel room, horrifying the other guests.

As the film *Funny Bones* showed, the tradition of primitive comedy anchored in the British music-hall tradition is very much akin to the one studied in *Why the French Love Jerry Lewis*. The question posed in the Epilogue remains to be answered: Is that because in the nineteenth century England is the only other country with an equally impressive array of nervous disorders and their sufferers? That question, along with a more sustained look at our themes in German silent film, must be left to future studies.

Reference Matter

NOTES

PREFACE

1. I proposed the analogy in papers read at the 1985 Colloquium in Nineteenth-Century French Studies at Vanderbilt University; at the 1988 symposium, *Representing Hysteria*, organized by Dianne Hunter at Trinity College, Hartford; and in my essay entitled "Le Caf'conc' et l 'hystérie."

2. Recent studies look at the diversity of classes in attendance in the first decades (see, e.g., Abel, "Blank Screen"), and the cultural phenomenon I discuss in this book cuts across class boundaries.

3. To my knowledge, there have only been three other studies that link a form of popular entertainment to hysteria: Elin Diamond's "Realism and Hysteria," which compares acting in melodrama to hysteria; Felicia McCarren's *Dance Pathologies*, particularly in the section of chapter 3 entitled "The 'Symptomatic Act,'" which brings together hysteria, hypnosis, electricity, and dance in the extraordinarily popular performances of Loïe Fuller; and Lynne Kirby in her article, "Male Hysteria," in which she discusses train films (metaphorically aligned with early cinema itself) and hysterical symptoms caused by shell shock. McCarren very rightly remarks that in nineteenth-century France the cultural authority of the body's somatic meanings can be seen even in dance receptions. "Medicine [becomes] a major cultural index by which the body's meanings are measured" (16). Elaine Showalter synthesizes and interprets the importance of studies like these in *Hystories*.

4. The bulk of the research in primary sources on psychiatry, psychophysiology, and psychophysics accomplished between 1983 and 1993 will appear in my *Sensation and Soul*, under advance contract at Stanford University Press. Some of this work appeared earlier in the form of articles, as well as in "Ornament and Hysteria," the last chapter of my book *Ornament, Fantasy, and Desire*. The work of Drs. Paul-Max Simon, Augustin Galopin, Lucien Grellety, and Jules and Henri Dagonet will probably be new to readers. When sources are al-

ready well known to scholars familiar with recent work on hysteria, I have tried to uncover and work with less familiar aspects or with previously disregarded studies of well-known psychologists and physiologists (such as Alfred Binet's study of prestidigitation).

CHAPTER ONE

1. See, for example, Vanessa Schwartz on the wax museum, the morgue, and the popular press, Jonathan Crary on the stereoscope, and Laurent Mannoni on the magic lantern. In *The Ciné Goes to Town*, Richard Abel writes that "the least examined area" in the history of early cinema, a history that he and others are now reconstructing, is the "historical reception of films . . . in France before the Great War." This space, "left open for further research" (xviii), is the one I am exploring here.

2. Charles Richet was a psychologist, physiologist, and novelist. In addition to his experimental work in physiology, he wrote extensively on animal magnetism. Under the pseudonym Charles Epheyre, he also published novels featuring somnambulists and hysterics. He told his public in 1887 that, since writers had begun combining art and pathology, "there have been numerous portraits of hysterical attacks or of hysterical figures" in literature ("Les Démoniaques d'aujourd'hui" 346). One hundred years later, scholars in larger and larger numbers have begun to study this convergence.

3. Gilles de la Tourette (1891), Glafira Abricossoff (1897), Gaston Amselle (1907), and Henri Cesbron (1909) (see Micale, *Approaching Hysteria* 35–37, for summaries of these histories).

4. Briquet described hysteria as a *neurosis*, a psychological malfunctioning of the part of the encephalon that receives emotional and sensory impressions.

5. See, for example, Thornton.

6. Neurasthenia, similar to hysteria but less marked in the way that the symptoms manifested themselves, became "the malady of the century" in the first decade of the twentieth century. The term "neurasthenia" was coined by Dr. George Beard in America. Several works on neurasthenia appeared in France in the 1890s; the symptoms of the disease consisted of suggestibility, an exaggerated exaltation of the nervous system, and lack of will (the latter being the primary symptom of degeneration and, indeed, the illness was thought to lead to degeneration). The correlation between neurasthenia and modern life was made again and again. The shocks of the modern urban environment had a greater impact on the neurasthenic's nerves than on his unaffected contemporaries, and these stimuli contributed to a further deterioration of mental and nervous functioning. One of the hit caf'conc' songs at the turn of the century was Dranem's "I'm a Neurasthenic" (see Chapter 3).

7. Singer's discussion of sensationalism in newspapers and posters that formed a background for early film draws from turn-of-the-century observers like George Simmel, who pointed to the "intensification of nervous stimulation" in modern urban life (in Singer 74). Cinema emerged, as scholars such as Ben Singer and Vanessa Schwartz have shown, in a cultural context—from newspapers to the morgue and the wax museum—that was rife with sensationalism. The observers I draw on in the present volume continually reiterate the fears and fascination connected to this atmosphere of hyperstimulation, but in the present case the cultural observers in question are medical practitioners and reviewers of the cabaret and café-concert.

8. See Ey 2:1010–11.

9. In a wonderful book on vaudeville and film, Henry Jenkins goes so far as to say that the "pseudoscience of affective 'mechanics' dominates the discourse of early-twentieth-century show business [in America]" (34). Social scientists used quantitative surveys (just as psychologists did in France in the 1880s and 1890s) to measure reactions to jokes, for example. Jenkins's citations from George M. Cohan's and George Jean Nathan's 1913 article, "The Mechanics of Emotion," are very interesting, and should be juxtaposed to Eisenstein's formulations ten years later. However, it is important to note that this idea, which originated in the 1870s with Gustav Fechner and drew heavily on the study of nervous reflex already in full swing in the last quarter of the nineteenth century, was exploited scientifically and artistically primarily in France—by psychiatrists of the school of "scientific psychology" and by poets, actors, and painters. Psychophysiological mechanics of emotion were widely accepted in the decade that cinema was emerging and continued to be accepted into the 1920s. I devote a chapter to Fechner, Henry, and psychophysics in relation to aesthetics in my manuscript-in-progress *Sensation and Soul.*

10. Here, in a letter to the editor, Henry is responding to criticism of his work ("Correspondence," *La Revue philosophique* 29 [March 1890]: 334). This is only one instance among several where data garnered from experiments on hysterical patients become part of aesthetic theory. All translations in this book are mine except for the citations from Richard Abel's *French Film Theory and Criticism.*

11. Ribot, named Professor of Experimental Psychology at the Sorbonne in 1885, then at the Collège de France in 1888, was one of the most important French scientific thinkers of the end of the nineteenth century. He was also the founder and editor-in-chief of the most important French organ for debates in psychology, psychiatry, physiology, evolutionary science, and philosophy per se, *La Revue philosophique de la France et de l'étranger*. Articles on Darwin and translations of Spencer, for example, appeared in almost every volume of *La Revue philosophique*, testimony to the extraordinary impact their theories had in France.

Issues of this journal also provide evidence of the continuing French interest in Fechnerian psychophysics and aesthetics up to the end of the century.

12. All of these notions are examined in Henri Bergson's *Essai sur les données immédiates de la conscience* (in particular, 13–28).

13. I draw heavily on Souriau's work, in particular *La Suggestion dans l'art*, in my *Ornament, Fantasy, and Desire*.

14. Edouard Toulouse was director of a laboratory in experimental psychology in Paris and founded the state organization for mental hygiene. Raoul Mourgue was a Belgian doctor who specialized in the study of diseases of the nervous system, for example, Huntington's chorea. Theory based on physiological response in film spectators continued to be important in France until the focus shifted to a Metzian semiotics of film language. See, for example, Séat-Cohen.

15. Antonin Artaud also believed that every movement of the body (including breathing) corresponds to an idea and an emotion, and that this corporeal language is universally comprehensible. In the theater, the rhythmic repetition of certain syllables and the timbre of the voice, "bypassing the processes of judgment involved in attaching meaning to words, act directly on the nervous system, creating a more or less hallucinatory state, and forcing the sensibility and the mind to undergo a kind of organic alteration" (Artaud, *Oeuvres* 145).

16. Jean Epstein is particularly remembered for two brilliant Impressionist films, *La Chute de la Maison Usher* and *La Glace à trois faces* (restored in 1996 by the Cinémathèque française).

17. Examples of deformity range from comic chases involving legless men in carts to films like *Grotesque Dwarf*, an 1897 Georges Méliès work, which is also the title of a 1902 Pathé film. These attractions were not confined to sideshows, but were featured in the music-hall, the most famous midget comic of the period being Little Tich.

18. Bergson dispenses with acknowledgments of previous theories of laughter in the introduction, but the convergences with Baudelaire's essay are impossible to miss.

19. Shaviro's understanding of film reception is similar to my own: film images are first received as sensation before the spectator is conscious of them (45), and the power of contagion is inherent in film through mimeticism (52).

20. Medical science was of course not a unified intellectual endeavor. The doctors I refer to whose work bears a direct relationship to the pathologies of movement studied here, however, were (with the exception of Pierre Janet) strict adherents of the new physiological psychology of the 1880s. Binet became head of the Sorbonne laboratory of physiological psychology in 1891.

21. The doctor-patient relation in hypnosis and in other experimental and treatment contexts within hysteria has been discussed in a great many studies published over the last fifteen years. The mastery of doctors and magnetizers

over their patients often had grave results (see chapter 2). See Beizer, Carroy, and Didi-Huberman for discussions of this relationship.

22. This is the case in either spontaneous somnambulism or under hypnosis in hysteria. Binet had already devoted a considerable amount of research to somnambulism (see *Le Magnétisme Animal*).

23. This was not yet a generalized concept of the unconscious, since the "unconscious personality which exists in the case of hysterical patients, even in their waking state" and the "secondary ego . . . [, which] is identical with the somnambulistic ego" do not yet extend to include non-hysterical subjects (Binet, *Altérations* 150–51).

24. Optical illusions are another example of commonplace experience that became stigmatized as symptoms of hysteria. I consider these in "Pathologies de la vue."

25. I can suggest no better source than Harrington to readers who want to further familiarize themselves with the broad scientific context for the culture of late-nineteenth-century France.

26. This posture runs parallel, of course, to the flaunting of sexuality (seminudity, nudity, "perversions," and "illicit" pleasures) that was apparent in posters for the milieu of the cabaret, in music-hall reviews, in street prostitution, and in the Decadent novels of Rachilde, Jean Lorrain, Octave Mirbeau, or Catulle Mendès.

CHAPTER TWO

1. The principal difference between magnetism and hypnotism is that the former operates through the transmission of the universal "magnetic fluid," which supposedly traverses all bodies, animate and inanimate. Hypnotism, on the other hand, is an artificial sleep, induced by the hypnotist or the psychiatrist, that produces muscular rigidity, along with various suggested gestures and acts. R. de La Ville de Rigné offers a further distinction: in magnetism the spirit remains free and lucid even while undergoing the suggestions of the magnetizer. The brain is passive. In hypnotism, the spirit doesn't come into play; it's the brain that receives the suggestion; it becomes like a machine, registers the hypnotist's will and thoughts, and no longer acts by itself (20). A more concise definition was arrived at in the 1889 Congress of Physiological Psychology: hypnotism is all of the phenomena produced by suggestion; magnetism is all the phenomena that derive from the direct action of the magnetizer outside of suggestion.

2. For a complete understanding of the vicissitudes of hypnotism's acceptance, as well as of the important differences between Bernheim and Liébault in Nancy, and Charcot in Paris, see Dominique Barrucand's *Histoire de l'hypnose en France* (Paris: Presses Universitaires de France, 1967). For a broader understanding of hypnotism that extends beyond France or beyond the time period that concerns

us here, see Maria Tatar's *Spellbound*, Robert Darnton's *Mesmerism and the End of the Enlightenment in France* (Cambridge, Mass.: Harvard University Press, 1968), and Adam Crabtree's *From Mesmer to Freud: Magnetic Sleep and the Roots of Healing* (New Haven, Conn.: Yale University Press, 1994).

3. Delboeuf also spoke out at the 1889 Congress of Hypnosis against the adoption of the following resolution:

> Given the dangers of public representations of magnetism and hypnotism; considering that . . . the applications of hypnotism belong in the domain of psychiatry, we declare that
>
> 1. Public shows of hypnotists and magnetists should be forbidden. . . .
>
> 2. The practice of hypnotism as curative method should be regulated by the laws of the medical profession.
>
> 3. The teaching of hypnosis . . . should be officially introduced in the program of psychiatric clinics. (Delboeuf 52)

4. Mesmer did not propose that magnetism and electricity were one and the same thing, but he *did* borrow the existing scientific terminology of electricity for his definition of magnetic fluid. Hence, the confusion between the two in popular parlance and—as we see here—in medical and parascientific treatises one hundred years later.

5. Some of the "prodigious effects of personal magnetism" listed in the table of contents of this manual are: "making oneself loved, easy conquests, advantageous wills and testaments, borrowing money, power over judges, becoming a senator, a member of the Académie française, always winning in duels, in cards, being adulated and invited everywhere, dominating one's fellows" (Roche 1). Many similar books were published around 1900; see, for example, St.-Jean's *Guide du magnétiseur*, *La Force pensée* by G. A. Mann, and *Volonté magnétique dominatrice: Guide secret du succés* by Louis Boyer-Rebiab. Serious scientific literature on hypnosis abounded in the same period.

6. Strohl was a pharmacist as well as a contributor to this newspaper. He himself had hypnotized numerous subjects.

7. See Jacqueline Carroy's important and groundbreaking article, "Hystérie, Théâtre, et Littérature au XIXe siècle," for descriptions of the last two novels, as well as other texts.

8. The representation of violence, anarchy, and sexual perversions is dangerous, since all tendencies are present or virtually present in each of us. Ribot makes a case for the belief that one can move from the extreme case to the normal by degrees. The example he gives is the following: from the pleasure of killing to the imperious desire to kill, to the pleasure of witnessing a murder, to the pleasure due to the representation of violent and bloody melodramas. "The property of regression is to act in the direction of the strongest attraction or of

the least resistance, which is a characteristic of reflex activity and the opposite of inhibitions set up by the will" (*Psychologie des sentiments*, in Delay 102).

9. The Congrès de Psychologie Physiologique was reported on in the *Revue philosophique de la France et de l'etranger* 28 (1889). The summary of Danilewsky's paper is on page 545.

10. "Je suis comme dédoublé, je me donne en spectacle à moi-même" (patient quoted in Janet, *Les Obsessions* 312).

11. Moreover, the unconscious thoughts of hysterics could supposedly be read in their highly expressive gestures.

12. Joseph Roach analyzes the import of Diderot's *Eléments de physiologie*, published in truncated version in 1875, for his acting theory. In these texts, Diderot foresaw nineteenth-century "evolutionary biology, nerve physiology, and the emergence of psychology as an independent science" (Roach 157). Roach's summary of Martersteig's acting theory, in the year 1900, shows the degree to which it represents a marked departure from Diderot's *Paradoxe*, where the actor is not totally immersed or abandoned emotionally in the role. There are, nonetheless, convergences, for example, the "double personality" or dual consciousness of the actor, which allows "his mind to coldly direct his body through sequences of passion without mentally experiencing the same emotions" (147). William Archer's 1888 psychology of acting, *Masks or Faces?*, returns to this unusual quality that actors possess. Joseph Roach discusses the celebrated French actor Talma's *Lekain*, a text that borrows from Diderot: acting is a psychophysical process and the actor's nervous system must be particularly responsive. "Lekain has attained apparent spontaneity by conditioning his nervous system into certain regular patterns of action and response. . . . [He] has become an acting machine. . . . In Talma's view, much of this construction of a character happens unconsciously . . . speaking directly to the point of affective memory [cf. Ribot]" (170–71). Stanislavsky used this text "as a springboard into the System" (ibid.).

13. Diderot mentions the historic persecution and ostracism of actors and "also seems to recognize . . . that society has a self-defensive need to degrade the actor whose transformations it desires to witness" (Roach 137).

14. Gabriel Tarde devotes a long article in the November 1889 issue of the *Revue Philosophique* to debunking Lombroso's thesis that "every true criminal is a more or less disguised epileptic; in every criminal type there are traces of epileptic or epileptoid temperament" ("Le Crime et l'épilepsie" 450). Tarde easily reveals the flaws in Lombroso's notions and holds them up to ridicule, but the Italian psychiatrist's reputation in criminology was not so easily dismantled. His theories enjoyed wide currency in France, and not only through his disciple Max Nordau.

15. "The subject's brain belongs to you; it is yours; it is as though it were inside your head" (124).

16. Méliès contributed several original illusions to Dorville's cabaret.

17. Galopin wrote his thesis on scrofulus and tuberculosis in 1894 (Paris Ecole de Médecine). In the same year he wrote the eccentric work I cite here, he also published a psychophysical study of women's perfume and its effects on love.

18. I consider this blurred border in greater detail in my work in progress, *Sensation and Soul.* Tarde's social theory of imitation is founded on nineteenth-century physiology and neuroscience: repetition from cell to cell in the cortical stratum of the brain is largely based on habit; in the subcortical region, imitation is a reaction of the nerves reproducing a stimulus. Like the repetition from cell to cell in the brain, imitation is suggestion from person to person in the Social Body.

19. The actor would be comparable to both magnetizer and magnetized.

20. Fear of contagion is described long before the hypnotist, Mario, enters the narrative; the family staying at the seaside resort next to the narrator's family, terrified that their children will contract whooping cough merely from *hearing* the child coughing in the next room, insists they be moved. This seems ridiculous to a reader unfamiliar with the medical theories I've cited, but Mann's readers of the period surely did not find it so.

21. This is what Dr. Simon and other physicians called the predominance of *la vie spinale* over *la vie cérébrale*, an idea that was echoed by Gustave Le Bon.

22. My notion differs from the philosophical idea developed in von Kleist's "Uber das Marionetten Theatre," a text that has, however, been profitably brought to bear on German Expressionist film. On the other hand, my idea of the puppet/marionette is very similar to the one that Anne-Marie Quévrain and Marie-Georges Charconnet-Méliès presented at the first Cerisy colloquium on Méliès. Anne-Marie Quévrain's great-grandfather was involved in Shadow-Theater as well as in magic shows (see Chapters 3 and 5). The writers, one of them a psychologist, raise the question of the "obscure double who can be the distant Other, whose differences the explorer-colonist inventories . . . or the part of ourselves . . . our shadow who decides to lead its own life, or who makes itself into a machine subjugated by the suggestion of the thaumaturge. . . . Shadow-play exhibitors, hypnotizers, and alienists of this period would be agent-witnesses of a sort of social 'return of the repressed' facilitated by certain forms of popular spectacle" (Quévrain and Charconnet-Méliès 228). Regretfully, the authors never followed up their insight (so close to my own) with subsequent work on the subject.

23. Stage productions included *Biltry*, a burlesque; *Drilby*, a "poetic parody" (both in 1895); and *Thrilby*, a "dramatic parody."

24. From the February 1900 *Bookman* cited in "Trilby and Trilby-Mania: The Beginning of the Bestseller System,," by Edward Purcell (*Journal of Popular Culture*, vol. XI [summer 1977]) 75.

25. See Lombroso for strict parallels between genius and epilepsy.

26. Elaine Showalter cites the passage on Trilby's "impressionable nature" and points out some of the elements in Trilby's hysterical makeup that I analyze

here. In addition, she tells us that Du Maurier himself studied and experimented with hypnosis in the 1850s, and explains that artists' models were ideal hypnotic subjects since they were "already practising self-hypnosis in long poses," staring into space with limbs rigid (preface to *Trilby* xxi). Also see Marie Lathers' extremely interesting essay on the model in nineteenth-century France: "The Social Construction and Deconstruction of the Model in 19th-Century France," in *Mosaic* 29 (June 1996).

27. As Maria Tatar points out in *Spellbound*, the notion of sympathy has a very different resonance in the nineteenth century, thanks to its link to magnetism and electricity.

28. Music is likely to transmit hysteria. "When one thinks of the powerful psychological effects of music, one wonders if a single great composer in the world exists who isn't hysterical" (Galopin 127). "Music . . . can determine [in certain individuals] extremely grave hysterical phenomena" (129). It is first the creator who is hysterical, and who then transmits his hysteria to the audience.

29. Du Maurier's medical savoir should surprise no one: the point of putting the explanation in Gecko's mouth underlines just how very widely disseminated these facts were. Mark Micale is quite right to speak of a "culture of hysteria." I too have used this term in several papers given between 1985 and 1995, as well as in my 1989 article, "Le Caf'conc'." Science, in the last half of the nineteenth century, provides more sensational phenomena than any other source (see my "Le Merveilleux scientifique"). Doctors read novels and novelists read medical texts (see, for example, Beizer on this).

CHAPTER THREE

1. The term *beuglant* first appeared in 1860. "What used to be called a beuglant no longer exists. Nearly everywhere, one has replaced this ruminating appelation by that of 'music-hall' which comes to us from beyond the English Channel (the verb beugler means to moo or to bellow)" (from *La Soirée parisienne*, November 1902, in Caradec and Weill 182–83). There is much overlap in the shift from the term café-concert to music-hall, but one can say that the presentation of truly grand revues typified it, since smaller revues appeared on the caf'conc' programs at the turn of the century, as well as acrobats, pantomimes, trained animals, and clowns. The Folies-Bergère was a music-hall from 1886 on, the Ba-Ta-Clan from 1890, and the Olympia was baptized a music-hall at its inception.

2. A half-century earlier, Théophile Gautier complained that curiosities like Tom Pouff (also from England) "are at best worthy of exhibit in the amphitheater and the School of Medicine. There is something revolting in seeing the infirmity of a puny" creature (81). Little Tich, Polaire, Mistinguett, and other performers discussed here can be seen in the video of Pierre Philippe's extraordinary docu-

mentary, "Le Roman du Music-Hall," made for the French and German public television channel, ARTE, in 1993. It was produced by La Sept Video and Cameras Continentales/Gaumont. It can be purchased from La Sept Video, 66 rue Sebastien Mercier, Paris 75015.

3. The Incoherents, many of whom were central figures in artistic cabarets like the Chat Noir, were accused of being anarchists: Jules Levy denied the label, stating that they were "a new force" (in Crafton 34). In fact, the cofounder of the Chat Noir, Jules Jouy, was an anarchist, as were several other personalities, such as Félix Fénéon, involved in the artistic life of the cabaret.

4. Antoine's Théâtre Libre, purveyor of Naturalism, staged documentary *rosse* (crass, low) plays built around thieves, apaches, prostitutes, sexual deviance, and cruelty to women and children. *Rosse* plays were also frequently included on the Grand Guignol program. The *rosse* genre already existed in the cabaret, powerfully exploited by Aristide Bruant.

5. Tics often accompanied hysteria and were studied by psychiatrists such as Charcot, Janet, Richet, and, of course, Gilles de la Tourette. Tourette supposedly died prematurely of the syndrome that he studied—an eloquent testimony to the danger of contagion in pathologies of hysteria.

6. *Ubu* was re-created at the Festival of Avignon in 1991 and at the Théâtre du Palais Royal in spring 1993 by Nada Theater with Babette Masson and Guilhem Pellegrin as Mère and Père Ubu. All of the other characters were played by vegetables (not actors *dressed* as vegetables but rather vegetables as marionettes, manipulated by Mlle Masson). This enabled the actors, themselves reveling in furiously hyperbolic gestures, to literally tear apart, burn, devour, and urinate on their adversaries. The leeks, as nobles whom Ubu condemns to *passer à la trappe* (here, a huge iron bucket), lent themselves particularly well to this function. The expressiveness of bodily contortions and dislocations was implicitly stated by Jarry in an article for *La Revue Blanche*: "What superiority over actors these great artist-acrobats have" (67).

7. Observations of hysterics with hemiplegia and other forms of asymmetry showed that "hysterical disorders had a marked tendency to manifest themselves on the left side of the body" (Harrington 81). Moreover, some psychologists, anthropologists, and criminologists maintained that brain asymmetry was indicative of intellectually inferior groups (e.g., women and "savages"). "It is perfectly well established that 'superior degenerates' are sometimes asymmetrical in the cranium or face" (Grellety, *Névrosés* 17). See Anne Harrington's fine study of the double brain for the development of like notions in the context of hysteria, as well as for the complex mind/body debate in nineteenth-century psychology and neurology. Harrington is an excellent source for readers who want to familiarize themselves further with the broad medical context for mid- to late-nineteenth-century culture.

8. Many of the songs mentioned in this study can be found in *Paris Qui Chante*, as well as in Meusy, Rivière, and Xanrof.

9. Degas's lithograph (1877–1878), composed of three subjects, is entitled "Mlle Bécat aux Ambassadeurs." It shows the singer very clearly reproducing an hysterical contracture of both hands.

10. The rare individual today who has heard of the tradition of epileptic singers also situates the genre at the end of the nineteenth century. However, Huysmans's art criticism alerts one to the existence of the genre twenty-five years earlier. Obviously, the writer's choice of adjective may at first seem more personal than factual, and scanty evidence indeed upon which to base a new date of origin. In addition, the performance style itself may easily have predated the naming and launching of the genre by the media. Despite these reflections, my conviction nonetheless remains that there was a correlation between the emergence of this tradition and the rise in cases of hysteria. The reading of Paulus's memoirs confirmed the fact that Huysmans's choice of adjective was not idiosyncratic.

11. See Joseph Roach's brilliant study on performance, doubling, detachment, and mimesis, *The Player's Passion*, for a sustained reflection on the relation of performance to bodily response in the actor.

12. Willy wrote this novel with Armory, who claimed that the title character was based on Jane Avril. In it, a hyperexcitable caf'conc' dancer and gigolette named Picrate, Henri Maugis—a neurasthenic man-about-town—, and his Breton protégé, Yves de Kerkrist, spend the entire second half of the novel in an insane asylum as guests of Maugis's friend, who is a resident doctor there. (Jane Avril, on the other hand, was an involuntary resident at the Salpêtrière.)

Gigolettes, the feminine form of gigolos, often became *gommeuses* with the purpose of attracting a larger clientele. Offstage, the cabaret and *caf'conc'* were frequented by clandestine prostitutes, and the fear of syphilis as well as the protection of public morals made these places the target of many attacks. The poster for the Folies Bergère's big summer revue, "Sans culotte, Mesdames!" (Knickers Off, Ladies!), displayed a bare-breasted woman lifting her skirts in back to the admiring gaze of a row of distinguished gentlemen. Other posters for the Ba-Ta-Clan, La Cigale, and Aux Ambassadeurs called out to passers-by: "Nude Cocotte," "Paris tout nu," or "A nu les Femmes!"

13. Certainly the mechanical movements of the doll Coppelia reproduce these characteristics in Léo Delibes's very popular ballet (libretto by Nuittier and Saint-Léon) based on E. T. A. Hoffmann's novella, *The Sandman*. Note that the genre of dance given for *Coppelia* is the Ballet-Pantomime, a genre popularized in France at the beginning of the twentieth century by Mazurier. As for the depiction of madness in French ballet, one immediately thinks of Adolphe Adam's ballet *Giselle*, libretto by Gautier. It has been admirably analyzed in relation to

pathology by Felicia McCarren. See her *Dance Pathologies* for an exploration of the relation between sickness and performance.

14. Tom Gunning, discussing American vaudeville in relation to the cinema of attractions, also comments on the disparate components of vaudeville programs and quotes the Russell Sage survey of popular entertainments, which compared a night at the variety to "a ride on a streetcar or an active day in a crowded city" ("Cinema of Attraction[s]" 68).

15. Dr. Galopin always overstates his case, but his work is a good example of the sort of vulgarization of medical research that the general public was apt to read in newspaper columns.

16. There is constant emphasis on "modernity" in the cabaret. Rodolphe Salis referred to his Chat Noir cabaret of the Boulevard Rochechouart as the "temple de la Modernité" and ordered those who entered to remove their hats: "On t'a prié d'être moderne!" (We've asked you to be modern!). "On veut du nouveau [des chansons bizarres]—et on en a" (We want something new—and we've got it) (in Richard 253).

17. The name was inspired by a Viennese waltz, the "Hydropathen-Valse." Spas specialized in cures of hydrotherapy, but so did psychiatric hospitals, and cold showers were among the most often prescribed treatments for neurasthenia and hysterical ailments. Goudeau, though, took the meaning of the name for its contrary meaning, that is, a phobia of water (among those who could, thus, only tolerate alcohol). In the "Hydropathe Song," when one "drinks too much wine, everything moves. / So let's drink the funny wine / . . . White in the morning, red in the dark (we suffer from water)" (Cros and Corbière 394).

18. The performance date is given as 1908 in Mel Gordon's *The Grand Guignol: Théâtre des peurs de la Belle Epoque*, but the date on the microfilm at the Bibliothèque Nationale is 1905.

19. Méténier was the co-founder of the Théâtre Libre in 1887, and founder ten years later of the Grand Guignol. He sold the latter a year later to Max Maurey, who succeeded in his ambition to tap into the Parisian public's "fascination with the morbid [evidenced by their] devouring pulp novels [and] tabloid exposés, flock[ing] to freak shows and wax museums" (M. Gordon 17).

20. The history of gesture in the cabaret is also a political one. Already in the 1850s, gesture had acquired a special status in the cabaret. After June 1848, gestures were substituted for words that had been declared taboo by the government censors. That led to the censorship of certain gestures. But this new repression was unsuccessful; it inspired singers to create a more elaborate system of gestures, one whose code was nonetheless easy to decipher: for the censored gesture, the artist substituted its opposite (the hand on the rear-end became the hand over the abdomen). I would like to thank Concetta Condemi for this information (see her *Les Cafés-Concerts*).

21. The "little cat" is "very small, cool, and round, all velvety like a peach. . . . If you want to uncover what its modesty was hiding, you have to give up trying to guess" (*donner votre langue au chat* = literally, "give your tongue to the cat").

22. Georges Méliès created silhouettes for the Théâtre d'ombres at the Chat Noir in 1890, and his first films made with artificial light (in early 1897) were of Paulus's act at the Ba-Ta-Clan. He also filmed the singers Fragson, Polaire, Polin, and Paul Delmet. The milieu of the cabaret, like his background in the magic theater, contributed to a vision of the world that placed considerable emphasis on illusionism.

23. Writers in the period, too, often present the supernatural and hysteria as interchangeable, as in Jean Lorrain's description of Swinburne's villa with its "luxurious furnishings and bizarre wall decorations, luxury of sorcery or at the very least of pure hysteria" (*Sensations* 12).

24. Between 1883, when it was published, and 1903, the year of Rollinat's death, three editions of this volume of poetry were published and more than 7,000 copies were sold.

25. I thank Bernard Gendron for this reference.

26. Mark S. Micale has produced some of the best work on male hysteria; see his "Hysteria Male/Hysteria Female."

27. An excerpt of the "5 o'clock" *phono-scène*, juxtaposed to the gait of an hysterical patient at the Salpêtrière, is presented as an illustration of my research in the video documentary *Le Roman du Music-Hall*.

28. I saw these films, "Report on the Salpêtrière in the archives of the 13th arrondissement (series 20)" and "Document of the Salpêtrière: 'Maladies nerveuses,' January 1912," in July 1992 in the archives of the Gaumont Cinémathèque. The latter film includes three of the seven patients seen in the former: (1) the woman with a limp and contracture of the left hand, whose right arm rotates from the elbow as she tries to catch her hand, (2) the woman with hair clipped short, talking to herself emotionally and looking at the camera as she grimaces, and (3) the last (male) patient who executes the "dance" steps. I would like to thank Béatrice Valbin, film editor at the time at Gaumont, for making me aware of the existence of these films and for her enthusiastic interest in this project. I am also grateful to the documentarian, writer, and former archivist at Gaumont, Pierre Philippe, for his interest in my work.

CHAPTER FOUR

1. Storey writes that "the taste for violence and cruelty in the fin-de-siècle Pierrot . . . awaits further discussion to be fully accounted for" (*Pierrot* 126). I believe that the artistic expression of violence and pain is tied to the trope of hysteria as cultural ethos.

2. The anarchist antics of Raymond Queneau's adolescent, Zazie, also seemed to call for the zigzags in her name, and the very French expression for the act of creating chaos also contains them: "*semer la zizanie.*"

3. Huysmans was also a founding member of the Cercle.

4. In the 1960s, the letter "Z" was chosen by the Revolutionary youth movement (after the assassination of Georgos Lambrakis) to symbolize the destructive lightning of revenge.

5. Jean Delabroy's penetrating analysis of Huysmans's style in the *Croquis parisiens* in relation to the structure of the writer's piece on "Les Folies-Bergère in 1879" is exceptional in its focus.

6. Examples of the composition in zigzag appearing in the *Chat Noir*: Steinlen's "Le Corbeau et le chat" and "Histoire d'un chat, chien, et pie"; Fernand Fau's "Cortège solonnel du Chat Noir"; and Willette's "Pierrot a gagné le gros lot."

CHAPTER FIVE

1. The 1935 film was directed by Henry Hathaway and the title role played by Gary Cooper; it immediately became one of the favorite films of the Surrealists. The modern scientific element referred to in the book review is thought transmission, and the occult element is the ability of the two lovers to meet each night in a shared dream.

2. In *L'Image-mouvement*, Gilles Deleuze makes a distinction between an excess of light in German Expressionist film and an excess of movement in early French cinema. In Expressionism, the presence of somnambulists emphasizes the intensity of light, whereas in the French school, excess of movement is emphasized by robots, puppets, and automatons (73–76). This appreciation contains a great deal of truth but needs to be amended to take into account the films discussed in the present chapter.

3. My focus is historically specific in relation to this dynamic, and my aim is therefore different from Raymond Bellour's in his work on hypnotism. Bellour is interested in hypnotism's role in the power of enunciation, and hence, in the organization of the narrative. His analysis rests primarily on a connection between, on the one hand, the film state and hypnosis and, on the other, the Freudian psychoanalytic notion of the ego ideal (as developed in *Group Psychology and the Analysis of the Ego*). "This allows us to understand more clearly how the cinema produces a deep identification, both subjective and social, which explains the very great fascination it exercises." The invention of the cinematograph (by its creation of a *dispositif*) and the invention of psychoanalysis (by its creation of a stage, as in "*l'autre scène*") radicalized the very powerful image-making tendency that began in the nineteenth century. Both inventions "inherited . . . all of the elements that were crystallizing during those years around

hypnosis" (Bellour, in Bergstrom 100–102). Reassembling the elements surrounding hypnosis and seeing how they became a part of cinema is my aim as well; Bellour's analysis of this inheritance leaves aside the very set of notions I discuss here: theories dating from the 1880s of imitation and of the automatisms of the corporeal unconscious.

4. See, for example, Dheur.

5. See my "Pathologies" for a further elucidation of theories such as this one.

6. In a somewhat different register, Thierry Lefebvre brings to light a frequent ("thousands of victims") visual disturbance caused by early film and that was called *cinématophtalmie* in the period. At least until 1913, this new spectacle was reputed to "hurt the eyes." Flickering was caused by a long phase of obturation and a problem in the superimposition of images caused by worn-out perforations in the film that produced a "trembling, indeed a jiggling (*trépidation*), on the screen" (Lefebvre 133). Dr. Etienne Ginestous, oculist at the Bordeaux children's hospital, delivered a paper on *cinématophtalmie* in 1909, which was later published in *La Gazette hebdomadaire des sciences médicales.*

7. See Rosalind Williams's discussion of Haugmard in *Dream Worlds.*

8. Henri Bergson had already done so in *L'Evolution créatrice*, but not in the same detail as Munsterberg would a decade later.

9. A half-century later, Christian Metz, too, drew an analogy between somnambulism and film spectatorship: his "exhuberant" or "childlike" spectator has "something in common with somnambulism" because the motor behavior "is triggered by sleep" (*Le Signifiant imaginaire* 125).

10. Similarly, Frank Woods remarked in 1910 that when the sense of reality is destroyed, it is "as if a hypnotist were to snap his finger in the face of his subject" (in Hansen 83).

11. Burch thinks that by 1922 spectators recognized that Mabuse wasn't looking at them, but "at an *other*, within or through him. . . . They were prepared to identify with Mabuse's victims in the same way that they surrendered to the powers of the director, i.e. surrendering but 'not for real'" (*In and Out of Synch* 215). My take here is different: I believe the film's self-reflexivity inscribes the spectator's *other*, held in thrall by the director of the film, embodied by the hypnotist *in* the film, and that this other is the corporeal unconscious which truly *belongs* to the real spectator and is actively called upon, acted upon, and mise en scène by the gaze.

12. It is not my intent to discuss the related topic of dream and film in this chapter, but Jean Epstein's extraordinarily acute remarks on dream should at least be alluded to here. For example: the "strict similarity between the ways that the values of a 'cinegramme' and of an oneiric image signify," not only because they are both symbolic representations of feeling, but because the close-

up in cinema is the equivalent of the way a dream magnifies and isolates signifying details, and because they both possess their own unique temporality. "Both constitute visual discourses, from which one might conclude that the cinema should become the instrument appropriated for the description of this profound mental life of which dream memory gives us a rather good example" (*Le Cinéma du Diable* 70–71). Film's nature is to "translate imagistic poetry which is the metaphysics of feeling and instinct" (72). It is a "culture reputed dangerous for reason and morals . . . since it reaches into the study of the affective and irrational self" (73).

13. Drs Toulouse and Mourgue presented their study to the Congress of the Association for the Advancement of Science in 1920. Psycho-physiological studies of the spectator were not confined to France: in America, the pulse rate of female spectators watching a kissing scene in a Rudolf Valentino film was monitored, as Miriam Hansen reports (262). The crucial element of Valentino's "sex appeal" or direct entry to the spectator's libido is not his torso but his "Svengali glare," as Dick Dorgan, the writer of the epigraph to this chapter recognized (in Hansen 258).

14. The reader is asked to recall the citation from Dr. Henri Ey in Chapter 1, which shows that vision, in late-nineteenth-century psychophysiology, always includes a motor component. Contemporary commentary on the cabaret cited in Chapter 3, as well as commentary on film in Chapter 6 offer further confirmation of the spectator's "need" for these stimuli.

15. My idea of identification with the representations on screen differs from Christian Metz's "primary" and "secondary" identification (identification with the "look"—the spectator being the condition of perception—or with the person). Richard Allen argues that the spectator's experience of a film often involves "projective illusion," a sense that one is watching not a reproduction of reality, but a fully realized world of experience. Projective illusion is an illusion of the senses and not of reason: *seeing* something that isn't there is not synonymous with *believing* it is there. To my thinking, for the spectators of 1900, the uncertainty as to the source of their perception of a bizarre but real world could also imply a pathology of the perceptual apparatus. Allen offers a psychoanalytical interpretation of what is taking place here, namely, the psychic force of iconic imagination to evoke a previously lived event. I propose instead that the hypnotic state encouraged by film creates the optimum situation for incorporation of the cinematic image.

16. In 1920, when Toulouse and Mourgue presented their study to the Association for the Advancement of Science, they had only measured one sensation with precision: anxiety. Had they studied comedies as well, would they have verified that anxiety was also present during images of corporeal pathologies?

17. The camera moves too; "il trépide" (Cendrars, *ABC* 23); note the use of the same verb as in Montorgueil's description of Charcot/cabaret.

18. Vlada Petric discusses what he terms "oneiric cinema" in a similar vein: Like "the most powerful dreams [and] hallucinations . . . characterized by a strong sensation of movement through space, truly oneiric films produce a powerful sensory-motor impact on the viewer." In addition, the "multi-directional optical motion on the screen stimulates the viewer's motoric centers" (9).

19. In *Le Cinéma du Diable*, Epstein refers to moralists who loudly proclaim that the cinema is a "school for stupidity, vice, and crime" (12). These critics are clearly fearful of the influence that film exercises through imitation.

20. Lionel Landry observed that "enthusiasm [for *Caligari*] is intense. M. Vuillermoz speaks about *Caligari* the way Théophile Gautier did about *Hernani*, and the most talked-about filmmakers demonstrate their approval by imitating it" (in Abel, *Film Theory* 268–69). Blaise Cendrars, on the other hand, detested the film because it was "hybrid, hysterical, and pernicious" (271).

21. The settings were, as Kracauer saw, a "perfect transformation of material objects into emotional ornaments." The reviewer (whom Kracauer cites, but with whom Kracauer disagrees) stated that "the notions of sick brains [were rendered] through expressionist pictures" in this film; I believe that he was right on the mark.

22. In her important book, *Screening the Body*, Lisa Cartwright, discussing the film in the context of Watson's work as a radiologist, sees the interior space of the house as a figure for the interior space of the body (138).

23. The years 1898 and 1889 also produced the films *Chez le magnétiseur* (Gaumont) and Méliès's *Le Magnétiseur*.

24. The first of Trilby's performances differs from the one in the novel: here the entire orchestra is composed of Gypsies ("Svengali et son orchestre tzigane," reads the poster), a nod to the vogue for Gypsy music in Parisian restaurants of the thirties and into the seventies. The intensified presence of this marginal group, the object of Bourgeois fantasies, is comparable to the co-presence of apaches, cabaret, and hypnotism (all in the paradigm of the lower faculties) in *Les Vampires*.

25. His reviews were published in the journal *Le Courrier cinématographique* beginning in 1911.

26. Emile Cohl, the inventor of European film animation, was a caricaturist and a member of the literary-artistic group Les Incohérents (following his participation in the club of Hydropathes) before becoming a filmmaker. As Donald Crafton points out, more than any other caricaturist, he drew on the puppet stage for inspiration. Cohl's films are analyzed in relation to hysterical gesture in the following chapter.

27. Antonio Costa discusses the notion of mind screen in "Pour une interprétation iconologique du cinéma de Méliès," in Malthête and Marie.

28. The notion of doubling, judging from its frequent use in films of the early twentieth century, seems to have been as fascinating to spectators then as it had been in the previous century. Its association with somnambulism is present even later in the century. In Marcel Carné's 1937 *Drôle de drame*, Scotland Yard has in its employ a somnambulist who spends his time sleeping on the couch where the "crime" was committed. At the pivotal moment, with all the characters present at the film's end, he springs to his feet from a supine position, arms rigid and extended, crying, "I know where the body is hidden!" The presence of a somnambulist is not at all odd in a film that is constructed around *the double life* led by the hero, played by Michel Simon: Molyneux is a respectable, bourgeois writer of books on carnivorous plants; under a pseudonym, Félix Chapel, he writes sensationalist murder novels.

29. Billy Bitzer was the cameraman on this film, before he worked with Griffith. A lost 1908 Méliès film of the same name exists, but the scenario bears little resemblance to the Edison film discussed here.

30. This urge to dance is the subject of many early film comedies. In Alice Guy's *Le Piano irrésistible* (Gaumont, 1907), first moving-men, then a family, then artisans, and finally a policeman are affected by the rhythm and begin dancing like automatons. When the pianist collapses from fatigue, they force him to continue.

31. A quintessential figure of anarchy in the period, the *apache*, was associated with dance movements, sexuality, and violence. The fascination in cinema with the apache ran through melodrama to comedy. In the comic Bébé series, "Bébé apache" (Feuillade), the child star disguises himself as an apache in order to capture the band who beat up his father, a policeman. The film opens with a scene of imitation. Two policemen enter the frame; one has been beaten up, and the other mimes the movements of his aggressor—so convincingly that it makes the first cop suffer the pains a second time. A nice illustration of the impact of movement on the viewer!

32. Several Méliès films stage the involuntary movements of spectators in imitation of the show they're watching. In *Le Conseil de Pipelet ou un tour à la foire* (1908), the arm and leg movements of the spectators mime those of the wrestlers at a fair; in *The Woes of Roller Skates* (see the next chapter), it is first a can-can number, then an exhibition of roller skating, that are mimed. In both films, the spectators become participants.

33. Hypnosis is a recurring them in Feuillade's films. At the center of his 1918 serial *Tih-Minh* are two rival hypnotists, La Marquise Dolores da Santa Fe and Dr Clauzel.

34. I quote from the English translation, which was published in the *Annual Reprints of the Smithsonian*.

35. Anne-Marie Quévrain and Marie-Georges Charconnet-Méliès noted the overlap between doctors, sorcerers, and hypnotists in "Méliès et Freud."

36. All the following scenario citations are from this volume. A current, complete filmography, along with all surviving original scenarios, can be found in appendix 1 in Malthête's *Méliès: Images et illusions*, as well as in the published proceedings of the Cerisy Colloquium, *Georges Méliès: l'illusioniste fin-de-siècle?*, edited by Malthête and Marie.

CHAPTER SIX

1. Zecca's *Grimace Contest* was made a decade after Gaumont's *Horrible Grimaces* (1898). Tom Gunning has written a wonderful essay, "In Your Face: The Gnostic Mission of Early Facial Photography and Film," read after this book was completed. In it, he considers the grimace film in relation to the *Iconographie photographique de la Salpêtrière*, at one point engaging with my article "Le Caf'conc' et l'hystérie."

2. Noël Burch was perhaps the first critic to insist on the aesthetic connections between early cinema and "vaudeville," as well as melodrama and Grand Guignol. See his "Primitivism and the Avant-gardes."

3. Emile Reynaud's 1877 invention, the praxinoscope, allowed him to animate delicately painted *saynetes* (little stories) turning in a drum and reflected by mirrors in the center of the cylinder; he later modified the invention, joining the images on a continuous strip, which he projected onto the back of a screen. His "Théâtre Optique" was presented at the Musée Grévin from 1892 to 1900. Destitute and ill in 1917, Reynaud threw his work into the Seine. His machines and surviving work can be seen at the crozatier museum of Le Puy-en-Velay.

4. Monsieur Hulot's very gait is the sign that he is literally out of step with society's carefully ordered, indeed regimented and acceptable ways of moving. Without being pathological, his mechanical manner of walking (as though he's in danger of pitching forward on his face), spinning around, or serving the ball in a tennis match all highlight the dominance and anarchical unpredictability of the body.

5. "From 1895 on, the railroad occupies an important place in the vocabulary, thematic repertoire, and representative strategies of filmmaking. . . . [Early] filmgoers were treated to numberless views of trains arriving and departing" (Kirby 113). Kirby's analogy between the railroad and film is multifaceted, but the thrust of her essay has to do with the shock to perception in both. Her thinking here is similar to my own: "If shock was by this time a programmed unit of mass consumption, and a principle of modern perception, it could clearly turn back in on itself and frighten—or thrill—with the force of trauma" (121). She notes the same reaction to film that I have underlined here: the shock and anxiety contained in film spectatorship (or in railway travel, in Kirby's essay) can be called hysterical. "The assaulted spectator is the hysterical spectator" (71). Working

with a different corpus of films, Kirby identifies this crucial aspect of spectatorship with the paradigm of the railroad, whereas I have identified it with the spectator's bodily perception of the hysterical movement on screen.

6. This insight came out of a 1990 conversation with Helen Tartar. Even in 1913, one was struck by the "continuous trembling [that] vibrates [and] jiggles" (Doumic 920).

7. Jenkins also draws from James Sully's essay on laughter, which warns that if laughter becomes the normal state, "one could literally laugh oneself to death or into insanity" (42). In chapter 2 of his book, Jenkins interprets theories of laughter, stressing the underlying importance of evolution theory and social Darwinism in mass entertainment, as I've done here.

8. *Photogénie* is a complex and not always stable concept in Delluc and Epstein. For Epstein it has movement at its very basis, whether the movement be accelerated, slowed down, or in close-up. Rhythm is the essence of cinematic form, and rhythm is composed of movement (see the beginning of Epstein's essay "Magnification").

9. In a similar vein, Gilles Deleuze ascribes the "reality of the film image becom[ing] more than real" to the automatic and material nature of the machine which acts directly on the unconscious mechanisms of the psyche: "le mouvement automatique fait lever en nous un automate spirituel qui réagit à son tour sur lui" (*L'Image-temps* 203).

10. My thanks to Pierre Courtet-Cohl for bringing this text to my attention.

11. See Linda Williams's "Film Body" for a psychoanalytic reading of dismemberment and integration in Méliès, which focuses on phallic objects and sexual difference in the "unprecedented illusion of presence of film body." "Méliès complicates and refines this mastery over the threat of castration through the drama of dismemberment and reintegration performed on all bodies, and through the celebration of the fetish function of the cinematic apparatus" (532). See also Lucy Fischer's "The Lady Vanishes" for an examination of the dismemberment of the female body.

12. This citation from Cocteau's 1935 *Portraits-Souvenir: 1900–1914* appears in a wonderful article, "Fetishes and Motorcars," by Bernard Gendron, who notes its allusions to dismemberment and to mechanical violence and modernity. Gendron states that it is the city and the machine that is being evoked here, not the jungle or the fetish (or the primordial, which he mentions earlier). In fact, as I hope to show once again in my analysis of Lang's *Metropolis* in the Epilogue, the modernity of things mechanical often belongs to both the paradigm of the city *and* to the corporeal unconscious, thanks to the notion of the automatism. I'd like to thank Bernie Gendron here for directing me to René Meizeroy's book, *Masques*, for my research on the cabaret.

13. Méliès's use of spirits and other supernatural phenomena hearkens back

to Robertson's phantasmagoria, as Sadoul has pointed out. In the 1899 "religious and fantastic" *Diable au couvent*, the devil, resisting attempts at exorcism by the priests, nuns, and choir nearly succeeds in conquering a convent, but is finally made to disappear by Saint George. Possession by the devil was, of course, an extremely frequent event in hysterical symptomology, and led psychiatrists to see that possession and sorcery in past centuries had in fact been cases of hysteria.

14. Note that the humor in these "crazy and mystifying scenes" (250) is poised between insanity and magic. What better evidence can be found to show that the filmmaker's idea of how the spectator perceived these clownesque movements, as well as his awareness of their *effect* on the spectator, correspond to the double vision of hysterical and supernatural *energumène* I've been proposing?

15. See Lisa Cartwright's *Screening the Body* for the relationship between X-rays and film. The genre of scientific cinema, from the study of insects and plants to the filming of surgery and of epileptic fits, comprised a sizable corpus in film's first two decades. Film, heralded as an educational tool, expanded and deepened the medical gaze and the general public's curiosity surrounding the body.

16. The scenario of the Bosetti film was lifted from Méliès's *La Cardeuse de matelas*. (This theme is not new: in an 1847 pantomime, "Pierrot pendu," at the Funambules, Pierrot disguises himself as a mattress.) In Bosetti's *The Tic*, a visit to Paris by a newlywed couple is constantly interrupted by men following the young woman when her tic causes her to twitch her head in their direction and wink. The automatism of the tic reveals the "erotomania" of the female hysteric.

17. Madeleine Malthête-Méliès commented that this film made her "very ill at ease."

18. The two films containing the most stop-action camera work are *Le Mélomane* and *Le Diable noir*.

19. These canvasses were in fact exhibited at the Salon des Incohérents, and some of them could be seen at the Musée d'Orsay's 1992 show on the milieu of the fin-de-siècle cabaret.

20. One test for making a positive diagnosis of spasmophilia is Chvosteck's sign: tapping the cheek with an instrument to test nervous reflex causes an involuntary contracture of the upper lip.

EPILOGUE

1. Comolli notes Lewis's borrowing of gags from Mack Sennett and from Chaplin, but—probably because the films were not available in the 1960s—neglects their resemblance to the films of Emile Cohl or to André Deed's "Boireau" series ("Petit lexicon").

2. Bukatman also perceives Lewis's persona as a "malfunctioning automaton" (195) and notes the "hysterical male psyche" of his characters, but situates these symptoms in the context of Freudian psychoanalysis.

3. There are others, Segundo de Chomon, for example, who have not entered into our discussion.

4. The Fontainebleu manager's office is totally destroyed by the vibrations produced by the plane flying overhead piloted by the bellboy. The chaos-effect of the Lewisien character is represented in *The Errand Boy* by Willard's simple knock on the door of a house that has been dynamited by Bugsy. At this tap on the door, the house crumbles to the ground.

APPENDIX

1. This Appendix, composed of screening notes, is not intended to be a detailed analysis of German Expressionist or comic film, but rather an indication of convergences with the themes evoked here in the context of French culture. Other national cinemas, naturally, have their own context for the production of films and for spectatorship. On a personal note, my love of German silent film dates from 1966–1969, when I was fortunate enough to see nearly all of Murnau's and Lang's Expressionist oeuvre at the Cinémathèque Française. I saw Lubitsch's films during the same period.

2. Like Méliès in France, Walter R. Booth in England had also been a professional magician before becoming one of the pioneers of film animation.

3. In an essay on the actress, Ross Chambers writes that she appears either as an artificial doll or as "a messenger of the unknown." Nineteenth-century science and the occult are intertwined here as elsewhere (15).

4. Other elements in *Die Puppe* recall nineteenth-century hysteria. Hilarius is a somnambulist. During the wedding night he walks along the foot of his bed to the window and then out onto the roof. In the monastery, before the final scene, Ossi begins dancing in almost exactly the same manner as the *gommeuses* of the café-concerts. As she dances, the monks *imitate* her steps, until they're chased away by their superior. But he, too, is irresistibly compelled to imitate her dance steps.

5. I am referring here not only to suggestion, but to the ill effects of the voluntary production of optical illusions and of hallucinations at the end of the nineteenth century. See, for example, Dr. Paul Dheur's *Les Hallucinations volontaires*, James Sully's *Les Illusions des sens et de l'esprit* (anonymously translated by Henri Bergson), or my "Le Merveilleux scientifique," where I begin to analyze the importance of this phenomenon.

WORKS CITED

Abel, Richard. "The 'Blank Screen of Reception' in Early French Cinema." *Iris* 11 (summer 1990).

———. *The Ciné Goes to Town: French Cinema, 1896–1914*. Berkeley and Los Angeles: University of California Press, 1994.

———, ed. *French Film Theory and Criticism: A History/Anthology, 1907–1939*. Vol. 1. Princeton, N.J.: Princeton University Press, 1988.

Allen, Richard. *Projecting Illusion: Film Spectatorship and the Impression of Reality*. Cambridge: Cambridge University Press, 1995.

Allendy, Dr. "La Valeur psychologique de l'image." Reprinted in Marcel L'Herbier, *L'Intelligence du cinématographe* (Paris: Corréa, 1946).

Aragon, Louis, and André Breton. "Le Cinquantenaire de l'Hystérie, 1878–1928." In *La Révolution surréaliste: Collection Complète*. Paris: Jean-Michel Place, 1991.

Arnoux, Alexandre. *Du muet au parlant: Souvenirs d'un témoin*. Paris: La Nouvelle Edition, 1946.

Artaud, Antonin. "Cinema and Reality." In *French Film Theory and Citicism: A History/Anthology, 1907–1939*, vol. 1., edited by Richard Abel. Princeton, N.J.: Princeton University Press, 1988. First published in *Nouvelle Revue française*, 1 November 1927.

———. *Oeuvres complètes*. Vol. 4. Paris: Gallimard, 1964.

Azam, Eugène. *Hypnotisme et double conscience: Origine de leur étude et divers travaux sur des sujets analogues*. Paris: Baillière, 1893.

Ballet, Gilbert. *Rapports de l'Hystérie et de la Folie*. Clermont-Ferrand: Imprimerie de G. Mont-Louis, 1894.

Banquart, M.-C. *Maupassant, conteur fantastique*. Paris: Minard, 1976.

Barbey d'Aurevilly, Jules. "Maurice Rollinat: Un Poète moderne." *Le Chat Noir*, 1 June 1882.

———. "Maurice Rollinat: Un Poète moderne." *Le Constitutionnel* (Paris), 1 June 1882.

Bardèche, Maurice, and Robert Brasillach. *Histoire du cinéma*. Paris: Denoël and Steele, 1935.
Barna, Yon. *Eisenstein*. Bloomington: Indiana University Press, 1973.
Baroncelli, Jacques de. "Pantomime, Music, Cinema." In *French Film Theory and Criticism: A History/Anthology, 1907–1939*, vol. 1., edited by Richard Abel. Princeton, N.J.: Princeton University Press, 1988. First published as "Pantomime, musique, cinéma," *Ciné-Journal*, 4 December 1915.
Barrès, Maurice. "La Folie de Baudelaire." *Les Taches d'encre* 2 (5 December 1884).
Baudelaire, Charles. *Curiosités esthétiques: L'Art romantique*. Paris: Garnier, 1962.
Béhar, Henri. *Le Monstre et la marionnette*. Paris: Larousse, 1973.
Beizer, Janet. *Ventriloquized Bodies: Narratives of Hysteria in Nineteenth-Century France*. Ithaca, N.Y.: Cornell University Press, 1994.
Bellour, Raymond. *L'Analyse du film*. Paris: Albatros, 1980.
Benayoun, Robert. *Bonjour Monsieur Lewis*. Paris: E. Losfeld, 1972.
Benjamin, Walter. *Illuminations*. Edited by Hannah Arendt, translated by Harry Zohn. New York: Schocken Books, 1969.
Bergson, Henri. *L'Evolution créatrice*. Paris: F. Alcan, 1908.
———. *L'Enérgie spirituelle*. Paris: Presses Universitaires de France, 1960.
———. *Le Rire*. Paris: Presses Universitaires de France, 1964.
———. *Essai sur les données immédiates de la conscience*. 1888. Reprint, Paris: Presses Universitaires de France, "Quadrige" collection, 1988.
Bergstrom, Janet. "Alternation, Segmentation, Hypnosis: Interview with Raymond Bellour." *Camera Obscura* 3–4 (1979): 100–102.
Bernheim, Hippolyte. *De la suggestion*. Paris: Doin, 1884.
———. *Recueil de faits cliniques, 1883–86*. Paris, 1890.
Bersaucourt, Albert de. *Au Temps des Parnassiens*. Paris: La Renaissance du livre, 1921.
Bertrand, Alexandre. *Du magnétisme animal en France et des jugements qu'en ont portés les sociétés savantes*. Paris: Baillière, 1826.
Binet, Alfred. *Alterations of Personality*. Translated by Helen G. Baldwell. New York: D. Appelton and Co., 1896. Originally published as *Les Altérations de la personnalité* (Paris, 1892).
———. "The Hysterical Eye," *On Double Consciousness*, in *Significant Contributions to the History of Psychology, 1750–1920*. Series C. Medical Psychology, edited and with prefaces by Daniel N. Robinson. Washington, D.C.: University Publications of America.
———. "The Psychology of Prestidigitation." In *Annual Reprints of the Smithsonian*. Washington, D.C.: Government Printing Office, 1896. First published as "La Psychologie de la prestidigitation," *Revue des Deux-Mondes*, 15 August 1894.

———. "Reflections on the Paradox of Diderot." *L'Année Psychologique* (1896).
———. *La Suggestibilité.* Paris: Reinwald, 1900.
Binet, Alfred, and Charles Féré. *Le Magnétisme animal.* Paris: Alcan, 1887.
———. "Recherches expérimentales sur la physiologie des mouvements chez les hystériques." In *Archives de Physiologie normale et pathologique.* Paris: Masson, 1887.
Bizet, René. *L'Epoque de Music Hall.* Paris: Pamphlets de Capitole, 1927.
Boleslavsky, Richard. *Acting: The First Six Lessons.* New York: Theater Arts Books, 1969.
Bonnassies, Jules. *Le Théâtre et le peuple: Esquisse d'une organisation théâtrale.* Paris: Le Chevalier, 1872.
Bourneville, Désiré-Magloire, and Paul Regnard. "Observation IV: Hystéro-Epilepsie; Exstases." In vol. 1 of *Iconographie photographique de la Salpêtrière,* edited by Désiré-Magloire Bourneville and Paul Regnard. Paris: Delahaye et Lecrosnier, 1877.
Bousquet, Henri, and Riccardo Redi, eds. *Pathé frères: Les Films de la Production Pathé (1896–1914).* Special issue of *Quaderni di Cinema,* no. 37 (January–March 1988).
Breton, André. "Comme dans un bois." *L'Age du cinéma,* nos. 4–5. (August–November 1951).
Briquet, Pierre. *Traité clinique et thérapeutique de l'hystérie.* Paris: Bailliere, 1859.
Brissaud, Ernest. *Leçons sur les maladies nerveuses.* Edited by Henri Meige. Paris: Masson, 1895.
Broch, Hermann. *Les Somnambules.* Vol. 1, *1888—Pasenow ou le Romantisme.* 1931. Reprint, Paris: Gallimard, 1956.
Bruant, Aristide. *Dans la rue, chansons et monologues.* Paris: A. Bruant, 1889.
Brunius, Jacques. *En Marge du cinéma.* Paris: Arcanes, 1954.
Bukatman, Scott. "Paralysis in Motion: Jerry Lewis' Life as a Man." In *Comedy / Cinema / Theory,* edited by Andrew Horton. Berkeley and Los Angeles: University of California Press, 1991.
Burch, Noël. "Un Mode de représentation primitif." *Iris* 2, no. 1 (1984).
———. "Primitivism and the Avant-gardes." In *Narrative, Apparatus, Ideology,* edited by Philip Rosen. New York: Columbia University Press, 1986.
———. *In and Out of Synch: The Awakening of a Ciné-Dreamer.* Translated by Ben Brewster. Aldershot, U.K.: Scolar Press, 1991.
Cahiers du Cinéma, no. 198 (February 1968) [special issue on Ernst Lubitsch and Vera Chytilova].
Canudo, Ricciotto. "The Birth of a Sixth Art." In *French Film Theory and Criticism: A History/Anthology, 1907–1939,* vol. 1., edited by Richard Abel. Princeton, N.J.: Princeton University Press, 1988. First published as "Naissance d'un sixième art," *Les Entretiens idéalistes,* 25 October 1911.

Caradec, François. *Feu Willy*. Paris: J.-J. Pauvert, 1984.
Caradec, François, and Alain Weill. *Le Café-concert*. Paris: Atelier Hachette/ Massin, 1980.
Carroy, Jacqueline. "Hystérie, Théâtre, et Littérature au XIXe siècle." *La Psychanalyse à l'université* 7, no. 26 (1982).
Cartwright, Lisa. *Screening the Body: Tracing Medicine's Visual Culture*. Minneapolis: University of Minnesota Press, 1995.
Cendrars, Blaise. *ABC du cinéma*. Paris: Editions Réunies, 1926.
———. "The Modern: A New Art, the Cinema." In *French Film Theory and Citicism: A History/Anthology, 1907–1939*, vol. 1., edited by Richard Abel. Princeton, N.J.: Princeton University Press, 1988. First published as "Modernités—Un nouveau art: le cinema," *La Rose Rouge*, 12 June 1919.
Chadourne, Andre. *Les Cafés-concerts*. Paris: Dentu, 1889.
Chambers, Ross. *L'Ange et l'automate*. Paris: Minard, 1971.
Champfleury. *Souvenirs des Funambules*. Paris: Michel Lévy, 1859.
Champsaur, Félicien. *Nuit de fête*. Paris: Offenstadt, 1902.
———. *Paris le massacre*. Paris: Dentu, 1885.
Charcot, J.-M. *Leçons sur les maladies du système nerveux faites à la Salpêtrière*. vol. 1. Paris: Delahaye, 1872.
———. *Leçons du mardi à la Salpêtrière, polyclinique*. In *Oeuvres complètes*. Paris: Publications du Progrès Médical, Lecrosnier et Babé, 1889.
———. Preface to *Hypnotisme et double conscience*, by Eugène Azam. Paris: Baillière, 1893.
Charney, Leo, and Vanessa Schwartz. *Cinema and the Invention of Modern Life*. Berkeley and Los Angeles: University of California Press, 1995.
Chertok, León, and Raymond de Saussure. *Naissance du psychanalyste: De Mesmer à Freud*. Paris: Payot, 1973.
Chessex, Robert. "Mes Mémoires de cinéma." Manuscript. 1969. Cohl Archives, Bourg-la-Reine, France.
Clark, T. J. *The Painting of Modern Life: Paris in the Art of Manet and His Followers*. Princeton, N.J.: Princeton University Press, 1984.
Coates, Paul. *The Gorgon's Gaze: German Cinema and Expressionism*. London: Cambridge University Press, 1991.
Cocteau, Jean. *Portraits-souvenir: 1900–1914*. Paris: Bernard Grasset, 1935.
———. *The Art of Cinema*. London, New York: Marian Boyars, 1994.
Coissac, G.-Michel. *Histoire du cinématographe: De ses origines à nos jours*. Paris: Cinéopse, 1925.
Colette. *My Apprenticeships and Music Hall Highlights*. London: Secker and Warburg, 1957.
Comolli, Jean-Louis. "Chacun son soi." *Cahiers du Cinéma*, no. 197 (December 1967) [special issue on Jerry Lewis].

———. "Petit lexique des termes lewisiens." *Cahiers du Cinéma*, no. 197 (December 1967) [special issue on Jerry Lewis].
Condemi, Concetta. *Les Cafés-concerts, histoire d'un divertissement*. Paris: Quai Voltaire, 1992.
Coquelin, Constant, and Ernest Coquelin (dit ainé et cadet). *L'Art de dire le monologue*. Paris: Ollendorff, 1884.
Coquelin, Ernest. *Le Monologue moderne*. Paris: Ollendorff, 1881.
———. *Le Rire*. Paris: Ollendorff, 1883.
———. *La Vie humoristique*. Paris: Ollendorff, 1883.
Coquiot, Gustave. *Les Cafés-Concerts*. Paris: Librairie de l'art, 1896.
Corbin, Alain. *Les Filles de noce: Misère, sexualité et prostitution 19e et 20e siècles*. Paris: Aubier-Montaigne, 1978.
Cosandey, Roland, André Gaudreault, and Tom Gunning, eds. *Une Invention du diable? Cinéma des premiers temps et religion*. Sainte-Foy et Lausanne: Presses de l'Université. Laval et Editions Payot, 1992.
Crafton, Donald. "Audienceship in Early Cinema." *Iris* 11 (summer 1990).
———. *Emile Cohl, Caricature, Film*. Princeton, N.J.: Princeton University Press, 1990.
Crary, Jonathan. *Techniques of the Observer: Vision and Modernity in the Nineteenth Century*. Cambridge, Mass.: MIT Press, 1992.
Cros, Charles, and Tristan Corbière. *Oeuvres complètes*, Introduction, edited by Louis Forestier and Pierre-Olivier Walzer. Paris: Gallimard, 1970.
Dagonet, Henri. *Nouveau traité élémentaire des maladies mentales*. Paris: Baillière, 1894.
Delabroy, Jean. "La Représentation tête-bêche." *La Revue des Sciences Humaines* 170–71, nos. 2–3 (1978).
Delay, Jean. *Etudes de psychologie médicale*. Paris: Presses Universitaires de France, 1953.
Delboeuf, Joseph-Rémi-Léopold. *Magnétiseurs et médecins*. Paris: Alcan, 1890.
Deleuze, Gilles. *L'Image-mouvement*. Paris: Le Seuil, 1983.
———. *L'Image-temps*. Paris: Le Seuil, 1985.
Delluc, Louis. "Photogénie." In *Ecrits cinématographiques*, vol. 1. Paris: Cinémathèque Française, 1985.
Desnos, Robert. *Cinéma*. Paris: Gallimard, 1966.
Dheur, Dr. Paul. *Les Hallucinations volontaires*. Paris: Société des Editions Scientifiques, 1899.
Diamond, Elin. "Realism and Hysteria: Toward a Feminist Mimesis." *Discourse* 13 (fall–winter 1990–1991).
Diderot, Denis. *Paradoxe sur le comédien*. Paris: Plon, 1830.
Didi-Huberman, Georges. *L'Invention de l'hystérie*. Paris: Macula, 1982.

Domarchi, Jean. "Commentaires sur les films d'E. Lubitsch." *Cahiers du Cinéma*, no. 198 (February 1968) [special issue on Ernst Lubitsch].
Doumic, René. "Revue dramatique: L'Age du cinéma." *Revue des Deux-Mondes*, 15 August 1913.
D'Udine, Jean [Albert Cozanet]. *L'Art et le geste*. Paris: Alcan, 1910.
Dugas, Ludovic. *Psychologie du rire*. Paris: Alcan, 1902.
Du Maurier, George. *Trilby*. New York: Harper and Brothers, 1895.
"E.A.D." *Les Cafés-Concerts en 1866*. Drawings by Carlo Gripp and Louis Housset. Paris: Ergot, 1866.
Eisenstein, Sergei. *The Film Sense*. New York: Harcourt, Brace & World, 1947.
———. *Notes of a Film Director*. New York: Dover, 1970.
———. *Cinématisme, peinture et cinéma: Textes inédits*. Translated by Anne Zouboff. Brussels: Editions Complexes, 1980.
Eluard, Paul. Foreword to *Images du cinéma français*, by Nicole Vedrès. Paris: Editions du Chêne, 1945.
Epstein, Jean. *L'Intelligence d'une machine*. Paris: J. Melot, 1946.
———. *Le Cinéma du Diable*. Paris: J. Melot, 1947.
———. "Magnification." In *French Film Theory and Criticism: A History/ Anthology, 1907–1939*, vol. 1, edited by Richard Abel. Princeton, N.J.: Princeton University Press, 1988.
Ey, Henri. *Traité des Hallucinations*. 2 vols. Paris: Masson, 1973.
Fechner, Gustav. *Ästhetik*. Leipzig: Breitkopfund Härtel, 1876.
———. *Religion of a Scientist*, edited by Walter Lowry. New York: Pantheon, 1946.
———. *Elements of Psychophysics*, edited by D. H. Howes and E. G. Boring. New York: Holt, Rinehart, Winston, 1966.
Féré, Charles. *Sensation et mouvement*. Paris: Alcan, 1887.
———. "Yawning in an Epileptic." In *Nouvelle iconographie de la Salpêtrière*, vol. 1. Paris: Lecrosnier et Babé, 1888.
Feschotte, Jacques. *Histoire du Music-Hall*. Paris: Presses Universitaires de France, 1965.
Fischer, Lucy. "The Lady Vanishes: Women, Magic, and the Movies." In *Film Before Griffith*, edited by John Fell. Berkeley and Los Angeles: University of California Press, 1983.
Forestier, Louis. Introduction to "Monologues." In Charles Cros, Tristan Corbière, *Oeuvres Complètes*. Paris: Gallimard, 1970.
Fourrier, Eugène. *Gil Blas Illustré*, 25 September 1892.
Galopin, Augustin. *Les Hystériques des couvents, des églises, des temples, des théâtres, des synagogues, et de l'amour*. Paris: Dentu, 1886.
Gauchet, Marcel. *L'Inconscient cérébral*. Paris: Le Seuil, 1992.

Gaudreault, André, ed. *Ce que je vois de mon ciné*. Paris: Meridiens-Klincksieck; Quebec: Nuit Blanche, 1988.

Gautier, Théophile. "A propos des exhibitions de monstres et de phénomènes." In *Histoire de l'Art dramatique en France depuis 25 ans*. Vol. 1. Leipzig: Hetzel, 1859.

Gendron, Bernard. "Fetishes and Motorcars: Negrophilia in French Modernism." *Cultural Studies* 4, no. 2 (1990).

Ghali, Nourredine. *L'Avant-garde cinématographe en France dans les années vingt*. Paris: Editions Paris Experimental, 1995.

Gilman, Sander L. *Disease and Representation: Images of Illness from Madness to Aids*. Ithaca, N.Y.: Cornell University Press, 1988.

Gohier, Urbain. "Notre peinture." *Le Journal*, 10 October 1911.

Goldstein, Jan. "The Hysteria Diagnosis and the Politics of Anticlericalism in Late 19th-Century France." *Journal of Modern History* 54, no. 2 (June 1982).

Goncourt, Edmond de. *Les Frères Zemganno*. Paris: Flammarion / Fasquelle, 1924.

Goncourt, Edmond de, and Jules de Goncourt. *Manette Salomon*. Paris: Charpentier, 1876.

———. *Journal: Mémoires de la vie littéraire, 1864–1867*. Vol. 7. Monaco: Editions de l'Imprimerie Nationale de Monaco, 1957.

Gordon, Mel. *The Grand Guignol: Théâtre des peurs de la Belle Epoque*. Annotated and with a preface by Agnès Pierron. Paris: Laffont, 1975.

Gordon, Rae Beth. "Le Merveilleux scientifique and the Fantastic." *L'Esprit Créâteur* 28, no. 3 (fall 1988).

———. "Le Caf'conc' et l'hystérie." *Romantisme* 64 (1989).

———. *Ornament, Fantasy, and Desire in Nineteenth-Century France*. Princeton, N.J.: Princeton University Press, 1992.

———. Laughing Hysterically: Gesture, Movement, and Spectatorship in Early French Cinema." In *Moving Forward, Holding Fast: The Dynamics of Nineteenth-Century French Culture*, edited by Barbara Cooper and Mary Donaldson-Evans. Amsterdam: Rodopi, 1997.

———. "Pathologies de la vue et du mouvement dans les films de Georges Méliès." In *Georges Méliès: Illusioniste fin de siècle?*, edited by Jacques Malthête and Michel Marie. Paris: Presses de la Sorbonne-Nouvelle, 1997.

Gorki, Maxime. *Nijegorodskilistok*, 4 July 1896. In *New Theater and Film 1934–1937: An Anthology*, edited by Herbert Kline. New York: Harcourt, Brace, Jovanovitch, 1985.

Goudeau, Emile. *Dix ans de Bohème*. Paris: Librairie Illustrée, 1888.

Goudet, Stéphane. "Naissance d'une génération." In *Les Princes du rire*, under the direction of Nicolas Schmerkin. [Brochure of the Fatty Arbuckle / Buster Keaton film series programmed by the Musée d'Orsay and the magazine *Repérages*, 22 October–15 November 1998.]

Grellety, Lucien. *Souvenirs de Rollinat: Étude médico-psychologique*. Macon: Protat Printers, 1907.

———. *Névrosés et décadents*. Macon: Protat Printers, 1913.

Grojnowski, Daniel, and Bernard Sarrazin. *L'Esprit fumiste: Le Rire fin-de-siècle, anthologie*. Paris: Corti, 1990.

Guiches, Gustave. *Au Banquet de la vie*. Paris: Editions. SPES, 1925.

Guilbert, Yvette. *La Chanson de ma vie*. Paris: Grasset, 1927.

———. *L'Art de chanter une chanson*. Paris: Grasset, 1928.

Gunning, Tom. "An Unseen Energy Swallows Space: The Space in Early Film and Its Relation to American Avant-Garde Film." In *Film Before Griffith*, edited by John Fell. Berkeley and Los Angeles: University of California Press, 1983.

———. "The Cinema of Attraction[s]: Early Film, Its Spectator, and the Avant-Garde." *Wide Angle* 8, nos. 3–4 (1986).

———. "An Aesthetic of Astonishment: Early Film and the (In)Credulous Spectator." *Art and Text* 34 (spring 1989).

———. "Primitive Cinema—A Frame-up? or The Trick's on Us." *Cinema Journal* 28, no. 2 (winter 1989).

———. "Now You See It, Now You Don't: The Temporality of the Cinema of Attractions." *The Velvet Light Trap* 32 (fall 1993).

———. "In Your Face: The Gnostic Mission of Early Facial Photography and Film." *Modernism / modernity* 4 (January 1997).

Hansen, Miriam. *Babel and Babylon: Spectatorship in American Silent Film*. Cambridge, MA.: Harvard University Press, 1991.

Harrington, Anne. *Medicine, Mind, and the Double Brain: A Study in 19th Century Thought*. Princeton, N.J.: Princeton University Press, 1987.

Haugmard, Louis. "L'Esthétique du cinématographe." *Le Correspondant* (Paris), 25 May 1913.

Hayes, Francis. "Gesture: A Working Bibliography." *Southern Folklore Quarterly* 21 (December 1957): 218–317.

Henry, Charles. *Introduction à une esthétique scientifique*. Paris: Hermann, 1885.

———. *Sensation et énérgie*. Paris: Hermann, 1911.

Huysmans, Joris-Karl. "Autour des fortifications" [in *Drageoir aux épices*]. In *A rebours / Drageoir aux épices*. Paris: Union Générale des Editions, 1975.

———. "L'Exposition des Indépendants en 1881." In *L'Art moderne / Certains*. Paris: Union Générale des Editions, 1975.

———. *En rade*. With a preface by Jean Borie. Paris: Gallimard, 1984.

Iconographie photographique de la Salpêtrière. Edited by Désiré-Magloire Bourneville and Paul Regnard. 3 vols. Paris: Delahaye et Lecrosnier, 1877–1880.

Jacques-Charles. *100 ans de Music-Hall*. Geneva and Paris: Jeheber, 1966.

———. *Le Caf'conc'*. Paris: Flammarion, 1966.

James, William. *The Principles of Psychology*. Vol. 1. New York: Dover Publications, 1950.

Janet, Pierre. *L'Automatisme psychologique: Essai de psychologie expérimentale sur les formes inférieures de l'activité humaine*. Paris: Alcan, 1889.

———. *Les Obsessions et la psychasthénie*. Paris: Alcan, 1903.

Janin, Jules. *Deburau: Histoire du théâtre à quatre sous*. Paris: Librairies des Bibliophiles, 1881.

Jarry, Alfred. "Gestes." *La Revue Blanche* 9 (January 1902). Reprinted in vol. 27, Slatkine Reprints (Geneva, 1969).

Jeanne, René. *Cinema 1900*. Paris: Flammarion, 1965.

Jeanne, René, and Charles Ford. *Histoire encyclopédique du cinéma*. Vol. 1, *Le Cinéma français, 1895–1929*. Paris: Lafont, 1947.

Jenkins, Henry. *What Made Pistachio Nuts: Early Sound Comedy and the Vaudeville Aesthetic*. New York: Columbia University Press, 1994.

Jost, François. "Métaphysique de l'apparition." In *Une Invention du Diable? Cinéma des premiers temps et religion*, edited by Roland Cosandey, André Gandreault, and Tom Gunning. Sainte-Foy et Lausanne: Presses de L'Université Laval et Editions Payo, 1992.

———. *Le Temps d'un regard: Du spectateur aux images*. Paris: Méridiens Klincksieck; Québec: Nuit Blanche, 1998.

Keil, Charles. "Spectatorship and the Apparatus in Early Cinema." *Iris* 11 (summer 1990).

Kirby, Lynne. "Male Hysteria and Early Cinema." *Camera Obscura* 17 (May 1988).

Kittler, Friedrich. *Discourse Networks 1800/1900*. Translated by Michael Metteer, with Chris Cullens. Stanford, Calif.: Stanford University Press, 1990.

Kovacs, Katherine Singer. "Georges Méliès and the *Féerie*." In *Film before Griffith*, edited by John L. Fell. Berkeley and Los Angeles: University of California Press, 1983.

Kracauer, Siegfried. *From Caligari to Hitler: A Psychological History of the Germans*. Princeton, N.J.: Princeton University Press, 1970.

Kuenzli, Rudolf. *Dada and Surrealist Film*. New York: Willis, Locker, and Owens, 1987.

Labarthe, André. "Lewis au pays de Carroll." *Cahiers du Cinéma*, no. 132 (June 1962).

Lacan, Jacques. *Le Séminaire*. Vol. 3, "*Les Psychoses.*" Paris: Le Seuil, 1981.
Lahor, Jean [Henri Cazalis]. *L'Art nouveau: Son histoire, l'art nouveau étranger à l'Exposition, l'art nouveau au point de vue social*. Paris: Lemerre, 1901.
L'Herbier, Marcel. "Hermes and Silence." In *French Film Theory and Criticism: A History/Anthology, 1907–1939*, vol. 1., edited by Richard Abel. Princeton, N.J.: Princeton University Press, 1988. First published as "Hermès et le silence," *Le Film*, 29 April 1918.
La Ville de Rigné, Raymond. *Les Rôles de l'âme et du cerveau dans le sommeil magnétique*. Vichy: Imprimerie Wallon Frères, 1907.
Lebensztejn, Jean-Claude. *Chahut*. Paris: Hazan, 1989.
Le Bon, Gustave. *La Psychologie des foules*. Paris: Alcan, 1937.
Lefebvre, Thierry. "Une 'maladie' au tournant du siècle: La Cinématophtalmie." In *Théorème 4: Cinéma du premier temps, Nouvelles contributions françaises*, edited by Thierry Lefebvre and Laurent Mannoni. Paris: Presses de la Sorbonne-Nouvelle, 1996.
Le Forestier, Laurent. "Le Cinéma des premiers temps, comique par essence?" In *Cinéma: Le Genre comique* (*Proceedings of the Montpellier Colloquium*), edited by François Ramirez and Christian Rolet. Montpellier: Centre d'Etudes du XXe siècle, Université Paul Valéry, 1997.
Legrand du Saulle, Henri. *Les Hystériques: Etat physique et état mental*. Paris: Baillière, 1883.
Lepelletier, Edmond. "A l'Elysée-Montmartre." *Le Chat Noir*, 16 February 1884.
[Lesclide]. *Mémoires et pantomimes des Frères Hanlon-Lees*. With a preface by Théodore de Banville. Paris: Reverchon et Vollet, [1880?].
Leutrat, J.-L. *Vie de fantomes: Le fantastique au cinéma*. Paris: Editions de l'Etoile/Cahiers du Cinéma, 1995.
Levy, Shawn. *The King of Comedy*. New York: St. Martin's Press, 1996.
Lombroso, Cesare. *L'Homme de génie*. Paris: Alcan, 1889.
Lorrain, Jean. *La Ville empoisonnée: Pall-Mall Paris*. Paris, Jean Crès, 1936.
———. *Sensations et souvenirs*. Paris Bibliothèque Charpentier, 1895.
Mac-Nab. *Poèmes mobiles et poèmes incongrus*. Preface by Coquelin Cadet. Paris: Vanier, 1886.
———. *Chansons du Chat Noir: Musique nouvelle ou harmonisée avec Camille Baron*. Paris: Au Ménestrel, n.d.
Malthête, Jacques. *Essai de reconstitution du catalogue français de la Star-Film*. Bois d'Arcy: Service des Archives du Film, 1981.
———. *Analyse descriptive des films de Georges Méliès rassemblés entre 1981 et 1996 par la Cinémathèque Méliès*. Paris: Cinémathèques Méliès—Association Les Amis de Georges Méliès, 1996.
———. *Méliès: Images et illusions*. Paris: Exporégie, 1996.

Malthête, Jacques, and Michel Marie, eds. *Georges Méliès: l'illusioniste fin de siècle?* Proceedings of the Cerisy Colloquium. Paris: Presses de la Sorbonne-Nouvelle, 1997.

Malthête, Jacques, et al. *158 Scénarios de films disparus de Georges Méliès*. Paris: Association des Amis de G. M., 1986.

Malthête-Méliès, Madeleine. *Méliès l'enchanteur*. Paris: Hachette, 1973.

———, ed. *Méliès et la naissance du spectacle cinématographique*. Colloque de Cerisy. Paris: Klincksieck, 1984.

Mander, Jerry. *Four Arguments for the Elimination of Television*. Brighton: Harvester, 1980.

Mann, Thomas. "Mario the Magician." In *Eleven Modern Short Stories*, edited by Leo Hamalian and Edmond Volpe. New York: Putnam's, 1970.

Mannoni, Laurent. *Le Grand Art de la lumière et de l'ombre*. Paris: Nathan, 1994.

Margueritte, Paul. *Printemps tourmenté*. Paris: Flammarion, 1925.

Marquezy, Robert. "L'Homme hystérique." *Bulletin Medical* 67 (29 August 1888).

Marshall, Henry Rutgers. *Pain, Pleasure, and Aesthetics*. London: Macmillan, 1894.

Mawer, Irene. *The Art of Mime*. London: Methuen, 1932.

McCarren, Felicia. "The 'Symptomatic Act' Circa 1900: Hysteria, Hypnosis, Electricity, Dance." *Critical Inquiry* 21 (summer 1995).

———. *Dance Pathologies: Performance, Poetics, Medicine*. Stanford, Calif.: Stanford University Press, 1998.

Meizeroy, René. *Masques*. Paris: Havard, 1887.

Méliès, Georges. "Les Vues cinématographiques." In *Annuaire générale et internationale de la photographie*. Paris: Plon, 1907.

Metz, Christian. "A propos de l'impression de réalité au cinéma." *Cahiers du Cinéma*, nos. 166–67 (May–June 1965): 75–82.

———. *Le Signficant imaginaire: Psychanalyse et cinéma*. Paris: Union Générale des Editions, 1977.

Meusy, Victor. *Chansons d'hier et d'aujuourd'hui*. Paris: Ferreyrol, 1889.

Miannay, Regis. *Rollinat: Poète et musicien du fantastique*. Paris: Bibliothèque Introuvable, 1981.

Micale, Mark S. "Charcot and the Idea of Hysteria in the Male Gender: Medical Science and Medical Diagnosis in Late 19th-Century France." *Medical History* 34 (October 1990).

———. "Hysteria Male / Hysteria Female." In *Science and Sensibility*, edited by Marina Benjamin. London: Basil Blackwell, 1991.

———. *Approaching Hysteria: Disease and Its Interpretations*. Princeton, N.J.: Princeton University Press, 1995.

Michaïlowski, Dimitri. "Etude Clinique sur l'Athétose double." In *Nouvelle Iconographie de la Salpêtrière*, vol. 5. Paris: L. Bataille et Cie, 1892.
Michiels, Alfred. *Le Monde du comique*. Paris: Calmann Lévy, 1886.
Mistinguett. *Toute ma vie*. Paris: Julliard, 1954.
Mitry, Jean. *Esthétique et psychologie du cinéma*. Paris: Editions Universitaires, 1965.
Montorgueil, Georges, Georges d'Esparbès, André Ibels, and Maurice Lefèvre. *Les Demi-Cabots: Le Café-Concert, le Cirque, les Forains*. Paris: Fasquelle and Charpentier, 1896.
Moussinac, Léon. *Naissance du cinéma*. Paris: Editions d'Aujourd' hui, 1983.
Munsterberg, Hugo. *The Photoplay: A Psychological Study*. New York: D. Appleton and Co., 1916.
Neibaur, James, and Ted Okuda. *The Jerry Lewis Films: An Analytic Filmography of the Innovative Comic*. Jefferson, N.C., and London: McFarland, Inc., 1995.
Niver, Kemp R. *Early Motion Pictures: The Paper Print Collection in the Library of Congress*. Washington, D.C.: Library of Congress, 1985.
Nohain, Jean, and Françis Caradec. *Le Pétomane, 1857–1945: Sa vie—son oeuvre*. Los Angeles: Sherbourne Press, 1967.
Nordau, Max. *Psychophysiologie du génie et du talent*. Paris: Alcan, 1902.
———. *Degeneration*. Translated by George Mosse. New York: H. Fertig, 1968.
Nouvelle iconographie de la Salpêtrière. Paris: Lecrosnier et Babé, 1888–1890; L. Bataille et Cie, 1892–1895.
Nye, Robert. *Crime, Madness, and Politics in Modern France: The Medical Concept of National Decline*. Princeton, N.J.: Princeton University Press, 1984.
Ollier, Claude, et al. "Commentaires sur les films de E. Lubitsch." *Cahiers du Cinema* no. 198 (February 1968).
Oughourlian, Jean-Michel. *Un Mime nommé desir*. Paris: Grasset, 1982.
Ouvrard. *La Vie au café-concert*. Paris: Imprimerie Paul Schmidt, 1894.
Paraf, Pierre. *Les Métiers du théâtre*. Paris: Octave Doin, 1923.
Paris Qui Chante. Edited by Polin. Vols. 1–4 (1903–1906).
Paul, William. *Ernst Lubitsch's American Comedies*. New York: Columbia University Press, 1983.
Paulus [Paul Habans]. *Trente ans de café-concert: Souvenirs recueillis par Octave Pradels*. Paris: Société d'Editions et de publications, 1908.
Pearson, Roberta. *Eloquent Gestures: The Transformation of Performance Style in the Griffith Biograph Films*. Berkeley and Los Angeles: University of California Press, 1992.
Péricaud, Louis. *Le Théâtre des Funambules*. Paris: L. Sapin, 1897.
Petric, Vlada. "Oneiric Cinema: The Isomorphism of Film and Dreams." Unpublished manuscript.

Polan, Dana. "Being and Nuttiness: Jerry Lewis and the French." *Journal of Popular Film and Television* 12, no. 1 (1984).
Ponnau, Gwenhaël. *La Folie dans la littérature fantastique*. Paris: CNRS, 1990.
Pradels, Octave. "Les Premiers Café-Concerts des Champs-Elysées," in dossier "Café-Concerts," Bibliothèque de l'Arsenal, Paris.
Purcell, Edward L. "Trilby and Trilby-Mania: The Beginning of the Best Seller System." In *Journal of Popular Culture* vol. XI (Summer 1977).
Quévrain, Anne-Marie, and Marie-Georges Charconnet-Méliès. "Méliès et Freud: Un Avenir pour les marchands d'illusions." In *Méliès et la naissance du spectacle cinématographique*, edited by Madelaine Malthête-Méliès. Paris: Klincksieck, 1984.
Racamier, P.-C. "Hystérie et théâtre." *L'Evolution psychiatrique* 12 (April–June 1952).
Ramirez, François, and Christian Rolet, eds. *Cinéma: Le Genre comique (Proceedings of the Montpellier Colloquium)*. Montpellier: Centre d'Etudes du XXe siècle, Université Paul Valéry, 1997.
Rearick, Charles. *Pleasures of the Belle Epoque: Entertainment and Festivity in Turn-of-the-Century France*. New Haven, Conn.: Yale University Press, 1985.
Regnard, Paul. *Les Maladies épidémiques de l'esprit: Sorcellerie, magnétisme, morphinisme, délire des grandeurs*. Paris: Plon-Nourrit, 1887.
Renault, Georges, and Gustave Le Rouge. *Le Quartier Latin*. Paris: Flammarion, 1899.
Ribot, Théodule. Review of *On Illusions, a Psychological Study* by James Sully (1881). *La Revue Philosophique de la France et de l'étranger* 12 (October 1881).
———. "Les Conditions organiques de la personnalité." *Revue Philosophique de la France et de l'étranger* 16 (December 1883).
———. *Les Maladies de la volonté*. Paris: Baillière, 1883.
———. "Review of the October 1889 issue of the journal *Mind*." *Revue Philosophique de la France et de l'étranger* 29, no. 1 (January 1890): 109–10.
———. *Diseases of Personality*. Chicago: Open Court Publishing Co., 1895.
———. *Essai sur l'Imagination créatrice*. Paris: Alcan, 1900.
Richard, Lionel. *Cabaret, Cabarets*. Paris: Plon, 1990.
Richepin, Jean. *Braves gens: Roman parisien*. Paris: Dentu, 1886.
———. "La Gloire du geste." In *Théâtre chimérique: Vingt-sept actes de pantomime*. Paris: Fasquelle, 1896.
Richer, Paul. *Etudes Cliniques et thérapeutiques sur l'hystéro-épilepsie our la Grande hystérie*. Paris: Delayaye and Lecrosnier, 1881.
———. *La Marche et la station chez l'homme sain et chez les malades myopathiques*. Paris: Revue Scientifique, 1894.
———. *L'Art et la médecine*. Paris: Gaultier, 1901.

Richet, Charles. *L'Homme et l'intelligence*. Paris: Alcan, 1884.
———. *Recherches expérimentales et cliniques sur la sensibilité*. Paris: Masson, 1877.
———. "Les Démoniaques d'aujourd'hui: Etude de psychologie pathologique." *Revue des Deux Mondes*, 1 and 15 February 1880.
———. "La Personnalité et la mémoire dans le somnambulisme." *Revue Philosophique de la France et de l'étranger* 15 (March 1883).
Rivière, Henri. *L'Album du Chat Noir*. Paris: G. Ondet, 1886.
Roach, Joseph R. *The Player's Passion: Studies in the Science of Acting*. Newark: University of Delaware Press; London and Toronto: Associated University Presses, 1985.
Robinson, David. "Rise and Fall of the Clowns." *Sight and Sound* 56, no. 3 (summer 1987).
Roche, J. M. de. *Le Succès dans la vie ou l'influence sur ses semblables par le magnetisme, l'hypnose, et les Rayons N*. 3d ed. Paris: L'Union psychique, 1909.
Rollinat, Maurice. *Les Névroses*. Paris: Charpentier, 1883.
———. *L'Abîme*. Paris: Charpentier, 1892.
Romains, Jules. *Puissances de Paris*. Paris: Figuière, 1911.
Romi. *La Petite histoire des café-concerts parisiens*. Paris: Jean Chitry, 1950.
Roubinovitch, Dr. Jacques. "L'Hystérie male." Diss., Ecole de Médecine, Paris, 1899.
———. "La Pathologie mentale à la fin du 19e siècle." Lecture given at the Saltpêtrière Hospital, 21 January 1900. In *Bulletin médical* (Paris: Imprimerie Gainch, 1900).
Sadoul, Georges. *Histoire générale du cinéma*. Vol. 1, *L'Invention du cinéma (1832–1897)*. Paris: Denoël, 1946.
———. *Histoire générale du cinéma*. Vol. 2, *Les Pionniers du cinéma 1897–1909*. Paris: Denoël, 1947.
———. *Méliès*. Paris: Seghers, 1961.
Scarry, Elaine. *The Body in Pain*. Oxford: Oxford University Press, 1985.
Schiller, Friedrich von. "On the Contemporary German Theater." In *Schillers Sämmtliche Werke: Vollständig neudurchgesehene Ausgabe in einem Bände*. Stuttgart: J. C. Cotta, 1874.
Schwartz, Hillel. *The Culture of the Copy*. Cambridge, Mass.: Zone Books, 1996.
Schwartz, Vanessa. "Cinematic Spectatorship before the Apparatus." In *Cinema and the Invention of Modern Life*, edited by Leo Charney and Vanessa Schwartz. Berkeley and Los Angeles: University of California Press, 1995.
Séat-Cohen, Gilbert. *Problèmes du cinéma et de l'information visuelle*. Paris: Presses Universitaires de France, 1961.

Shaviro, Steven. *The Cinematic Body*. Theory out of Bounds. Minneapolis: University of Minnesota Press, 1993.
Showalter, Elaine. Preface to *Trilby*, by George du Maurier. Oxford: Oxford University Press, 1995.
———. *Hystories: Hysterical Epidemics and Modern Culture*. New York: Columbia University Press, 1997.
Silverman, Debora. *Art Nouveau in Fin-de-Siècle France: Politics, Psychology, and Style*. Berkeley and Los Angeles: University of California Press, 1989.
Singer, Ben. "Modernity, Hyperstimulus, and Popular Sensationalism." In *Cinema and the Invention of Modern Life*, edited by Leo Charney and Vanessa Schwartz. Berkeley and Los Angeles: University of California Press, 1995.
Simon, Pierre-Max. *Sur l'hallucination visuelle (preuve physiologique de la nature de cette hallucination*. Paris: Baillière, 1880.
———. *L'Hygiène de l'esprit au point de vue pratique de la préservation des maladies mentales et nerveuses*. Paris: Baillière, 1881.
Sollier, Paul, and A. Souques. "Un cas de mélancolie cataleptiforme." In *Nouvelle Iconographie de la Salpêtrière*, vol. 3. Paris, Lecrosnier et Babé, 1890.
Souriau, Paul. *L'Esthétique du mouvement*. Paris: Alcan, 1889.
———. *La Suggestion dans l'art*. Paris: Alcan, 1893.
St.-Jean, Célestin. *Guide du magnétiseur spirite*. Paris: Librairie Spirite, 1912.
Stebbins, Genevieve. *Delsarte System of Expression*. New York: E. S. Werner, 1887.
Storey, Robert. *Pierrot: A Critical History of a Mask*. Princeton, N.J.: Princeton University Press, 1978.
———. *Pierrots on the Stage of Desire*. Princeton, N.J.: Princeton University Press, 1990.
———. *Mimesis and the Human Animal: On the Biogenetic Foundations of Literary Representation*. Evanston, Ill.: Northwestern University Press, 1996.
Sully, James. *Les Illusions des sens et de l'esprit*, anonymously translated by Henri Bergson. Paris: Baillière, 1883.
Talmeyr, Maurice. "Cafés-concerts et music-halls." *Revue des Deux-Mondes*, 1 February 1902.
Tarde, Gabriel de. *Les Lois de l'imitation*. 1890. Reprint, Paris: Kimé, 1993.
Tatar, Maris. *Spellbound: Studies on Mesmerism and Literature*. Princeton, N.J.: Princteon University Press, 1978.
Thérésa. *Mémoires de Thérésa*. Paris: Dentu, 1865.
Thornton, E. M. *Hypnosis, Hysteria, and Epilepsy*. London: Wm. Heinemann, 1976.

Toulet, Emmanuelle. *Le Spectacle cinématographique à Paris de 1895 à 1914*. Thesis, Ecole des Chartes, 1982.

———. *Le Cinématographe, invention du siècle*. Paris: Gallimard, 1992.

Toulouse, Edouard, and Raoul Mourgue. "Réactions respiratoires au cours des projections cinématographiques." In *Naissance du Cinéma*, edited by Léon Moussinac. Paris: J. Povolozky, 1925.

Tzara, Tristan. "Alfred Jarry." *Europe*, nos. 555–56 (July–August 1975).

Valbel, Horace. *Les Chansonniers et les cabarets artistiques*. Paris: Dentu, 1885.

Vedrès, Nicole. *Images du cinéma français*. Paris: Editions du Chêne, 1945.

Veith, Ilza. *Hysteria: The History of a Disease*. Chicago: University of Chicago Press, 1965.

Veuillot, Louis. *Odeurs de Paris*. Paris: Palme, 1867.

Vuillermoz, Emile. "Before the Screen: *Les Frères corses*." In *French Film Theory and Criticism: A History/Anthology, 1907–1939*, vol. 1., edited by Richard Abel. Princeton, N.J.: Princeton University Press, 1988. First published as "Devant l'écran: *Les Frères corses*," *Le Temps*, 7 February 1917.

Weill, Alain. *Le Café-Concert: Affiches de la bibliothèque du Musée des Arts Décoratifs*. Paris: Imprimeries du lion, 1977.

Weinberg, Herman G. *Ernst Lubitsch: The Lubitsch Touch*. Translated by Gretchen P. Berg. Paris: Editions Ramsay, 1994.

Williams, Alan. *Republic of Images: A History of French Filmmaking*. Cambridge, Mass.: Harvard University Press, 1992.

Williams, Linda. "Film Body: An Implantation of Perversions." In *Narrative, Apparatus, Ideology*, edited by Philip Rosen. New York: Columbia University Press, 1986.

———, ed. *Viewing Positions: Ways of Seeing Film*. New Brunswick, N.J.: Rutgers University Press, 1994.

Williams, Rosalind. *Dream Worlds: Mass Consumption in Late Ninteenth-Century France*. Berkeley and Los Angeles: University of California Press, 1982.

Willy. *La Môme Picrate*. Paris: Albin Michel, 1904.

Winter, Marian Hannah. *Le Théâtre du merveilleux*. Paris: Oliver Perrin, 1962.

Wolff, Alfred. "Courrier de Paris." *Le Figaro*, 9 November 1882.

Xanrof, Léon. *Chansons sans-gêne*. Paris: G. Ondet, 1892.

Yhcam. "Cinematography." In *French Film Theory and Criticism: A History/Anthology, 1907–1939*, vol. 1., edited by Richard Abel. Princeton, N.J.: Princeton University Press, 1988. First published as "Cinématographie," *Ciné-Journal*, 1912.

ARCHIVES

Bibliothèque nationale de France, Departement des Arts du Spectacle. Collection Rondel, RO Vol. 6: *Chansons, Music-Hall.*

Dossiers on Cabaret and Cafés-Concerts: Alcazar d'été, Ambassadeurs, Ba-Ta-Clan, Café-Concerts, Café Morel, Casino de Paris, Eden, Eldorado, Parisiana, Scala, Zenith, Zig-Zag

Dossiers on Performers: Blondinette D'Alaza, Dranem, Eugénie Fougère, Libert, Lidia, Mistinguett, Naja, Ouvrard, Polaire

INDEX

In this index an "f" after a number indicates a separate reference on the next page and "ff" indicates separate references on the next two pages. A continuous discussion over two or more pages is indicated by a span of page numbers. *Passim* is used for a cluster of references in close but not consecutive sequence.